JOURNAL FOR THE STUDY OF THE OLD TESTAMENT
SUPPLEMENT SERIES
52

Editors
David J A Clines
Philip R Davies

JSOT Press
Sheffield

The Conflict of
Faith and Experience
in the Psalms

A Form-Critical
and Theological Study

Craig C. Broyles

Journal for the Study of the Old Testament
Supplement Series 52

To my Mother and Father,
whom to honor is a joy

Copyright © 1989 Sheffield Academic Press

Published by JSOT Press
JSOT Press is an imprint of
Sheffield Academic Press Ltd
The University of Sheffield
343 Fulwood Road
Sheffield S10 3BP
England

Printed in Great Britain
by Billing & Sons Ltd
Worcester

British Library Cataloguing in Publication Data

Broyles, Craig C.
    The conflict of faith and experience in the
    Psalms.
    1. Bible. O.T. Psalms-Critical studies
    I. Title   II. Series
    223.'206

ISSN 0309-0787
ISBN 1-85075-052-1

CONTENTS

PREFACE

This book is a revision of my dissertation accepted by the University of Sheffield in 1984 for the Ph.D. I wish to thank my supervisor, Professor David J.A. Clines, who provided the kind of direction that gave me freedom to explore but also kept me from fruitless paths.

I have made the effort to keep footnotes to a minimum. References to scholarly works follow the abbreviations of *Old Testament Abstracts* and *Journal of Biblical Literature*. The major commentaries on the Psalms are denoted simply by the author's name which appears in capital letters.

For encouragement and suggestions I would like to thank the faculty in the Department of Biblical Studies at the University of Sheffield and friends and colleagues at Tyndale House in Cambridge. I wish to express gratitude to the editorial committee of Sheffield Academic Press for accepting this work for the JSOT Supplement series. For financial support during my Ph.D. studies my thanks go to Tyndale House for their grant and especially to my parents. Their generous financial contribution has been but a token of all that they have given me. It is to them I dedicate this work. Finally, I thank my dear wife, Karelle, who has helped this specialist in lament to see new horizons of praise.

Chapter 1

THE SEARCH FOR THE BEST VIEW:
A PROPOSAL FOR PSALMS INTERPRETATION

A. INTRODUCTION

The importance of the Psalter as a testimony of the faith of ancient Israel needs little argument. While J. Wellhausen and others had regarded the Psalms as the private poetry of the pious few, most scholars now consider them to be the central, cultic repository of the communal faith, much as the hymnbook serves today in modern worship. Suffice it to say in the words of G. von Rad that the Psalter

> shows us how these acts [namely the exodus and Yahweh's choice of David and Zion] affected Israel, and how Israel on her side accepted and understood this existence in immediacy with Jahweh and in proximity to him, that is, the steps which, in this proximity to Jahweh, she took to justify or to be ashamed of herself, in her own eyes and before Jahweh.... The way in which she saw herself before God, and pictured herself before him, is worth the highest attention theologically.[1]

How then can we open a way into this corpus of ancient poetry, which is so significant for an understanding of Israel's faith? Anyone who hopes for the final answer to this question would do well to heed the principle voiced by T.S. Eliot with regard to Shakespeare: 'About anyone so great, it is probable, that we can never be right; and if we are never right, it is better from time to time we should change our way of being wrong.'[2]

The diversity of paths pioneered by past interpreters of the Psalms bears witness to this confession. Until the past century most of the Psalms were understood to be authored by David, and so the process of interpretation began with the attempt to fit each psalm into a specific historical moment of David's life. A psalm was viewed as a personal expression that brought to light David's subjective response to events narrated in the books of Samuel. Later when Davidic authorship was disclaimed, the Psalms were placed largely in a Maccabean milieu. The method of interpretation, however, remained much the same: determination of their historical setting was still the initial aim. Along with this historical-biographical interpretation there developed a more devotional approach which endeavored to typify the subjective experience of these historical authors, thus establishing the subjective norms that the godly should strive to emulate (as distinct from the more objective ethical injunctions of the Pentateuch). This has been practiced as long as Ps. 1 has been viewed as an introduction to the Psalter.[3] In the Christian Church this approach was particularized into a christological interpretation, where the Psalms, above all, typify Christ and his godly life, especially since David was seen to prefigure the Messiah.

The methods of psalm interpretation did not undergo a radical change until H. Gunkel introduced form-critical study into Psalms research. Here the interpreter sought to develop a sensitivity to the typical nature of psalmic language. While Gunkel argued that the literary forms emerged from typical occasions within the cult, he believed that most of the psalms preserved in the Psalter were not cultic liturgies, but more personal poems based on cultic prototypes.

From this approach there arose the 'cultic method'. S. Mowinckel sought to rid biblical scholarship of its 'cult-prejudice' that personal feelings could not be expressed through what is formal, conventional, and structured. In his view, '... a cultic interpretation—and a real understanding—of the psalms means setting each one of them in relation to the definite cultic act—or cultic acts—to which it belonged'.[4] By 'cult' most scholars meant 'festival cult'.[5] More specifically, Mowinckel located most psalms in the autumn 'Enthronement Festival'. A. Weiser believed that the autumn festival focused more on covenant renewal and that many of the extant psalms reflect different features of this festival. Other scholars, such as H. Birkeland, A.R. Johnson, and J. Eaton, saw the king as the principal speaker of the psalms and thus concentrated on the royal cult.

In stark contrast to the two approaches just mentioned, Stylistic Criticism returned to reading each psalm as a unique text. A psalm's individuality, however, does not stem from the particular experience of David's life out of which it grew but from the uniqueness that each psalm possesses as a poetic text in its own right. Genre or *Gattung* study may not be entirely ignored, but such literary forms are viewed simply as a part of the materials at the disposal of the poet.

This sampling of the variety of approaches to the Psalms is not meant to suggest that they are contradictory, nor that they are mutually exclusive. It does make clear, however, that those texts that they endeavor to interpret are multidimensional. One may analyze a lament psalm in this way. A lament psalm relates an experience, so it conveys a narrative. It presents this within a metrical structure, so it is poetry. It asks for something from God, so it is prayer. It pleads a case, so it is argument. It expresses a faith, so it is theology. This list is but the beginning. The experience itself that a lament psalm describes has its own set of dimensions. It may be historical, it may be cultic, but it is certainly psychological and social.

This discussion helps to give a balanced perspective on the nature of our task. It makes clear that before discussing methods of psalm interpretation we must first give more attention to what a psalm is and all that it represents. I say 'represents' because a psalm signifies more than first appears. It represents a process, which will now be sketched out briefly.

The principal form-critical components or 'motifs'[6] of lament psalms may be labelled as follows, with examples noted from Ps. 13, an individual lament, and Ps. 80, a corporate lament:[7]

1. Address and introductory petition (13.2a; 80.2-4)
     [Reference to earlier saving deeds (—; 80.2, 9-12)]
2. Lament
     a. I (13.3a; —)
     b. Thou/God (13.2; 80.5-7a, 13)
     c. They/foe (13.3b; 80.7b, 14, 17)
     [Protest of innocence (17.3-5)]
     [Plea for forgiveness (51.3-4, 9, 12-14, 16)]
3. Confession of trust (13.6a; —)
4. Petition
     a. to be favorable ('Hear!') (13.4a; 80.15a)
     b. to intervene ('Save!'/'Punish') (13.4b; 80.15b ,18)
     [Motifs to motivate God to intervene (13.5; 80.16)]
5. Assurance of being heard ('He has heard') (6.9-11)
6. Vow of Praise (13.6b; 80.19)
7. Narrative praise (13.6b; —)

A brief 'exegesis' of the above pattern reveals the following. A lament psalm is not lamentation. It does more than simply bemoan current hardship. It seeks change. As H. Gunkel notes, 'The aim of the lament is to attain something from Yahweh'.[8] The petitions contained in these psalms indicate this purpose most clearly. Even in psalms where petitions play a minor role or are lacking altogether, other motifs, such as the lament itself, appear to take up the same function (e.g., see the interpretations of Pss. 77 and 89 in Chapter 6).[9] It would exaggerate, however, the significance of this motif and its imperatival form to label these poems as 'psalms of petition'. The lament, the actual description of the hardship, usually forms the largest portion of these psalms. They contain not merely a cry for help but also a statement of the wrongs suffered. Moreover, the lament functions not simply to report an incident to Yahweh or to achieve catharsis for the psalmist, but to motivate Yahweh to act on the psalmist's behalf, usually by making the description evocative and provocative.[10] Thus, it joins with the petition to establish an appeal. A lament psalm is primarily an *appeal.* Interpretation of lament psalms must therefore explore how these psalms form an appeal.

As just noted, the lament describes a hardship and the petition to which it is adjoined seeks to obtain release from this hardship. A lament psalm thus points outside of itself to a *distress*, to which it forms a verbal response. The meaning that a psalm bears cannot be isolated from experience. By its very nature it refers to an event, which may be tangible or simply psychological.

There is a secondary aspect of a psalm's situational context, but the allusions to it are not so direct, because it would have been assumed. I speak here of the social context in and for which the psalm was composed. Recent scholarship has identified the cult (whether official or domestic) as the probable setting. Aside from incidental clues that allude to cultic acts, personnel, and places,[11] the stylized language of these poems directs us toward such a public setting wherein social conventions played an influential role. Interpretation of lament psalms must therefore probe these psalms for clues regarding the distresses that occasioned them and the social contexts in and for which they were composed.

The descriptions of the hardships contained in the lament sections proper exceed what could be called bare phenomenal description. The reports of distress include an interpretation of that distress. They say not only 'I am afflicted' but often 'You have afflicted me'. Attributing events to God cannot simply be traced to a particular religious world view since the lament psalms themselves distinguish between human and divine causation (see Chapter 5). For these descriptions to evoke pity from Yahweh or to provoke him to anger effectively, they must have credibility before the addressees, principally Yahweh but also the community of worshippers. This suggests that there must have been mutually agreeable criteria for the *interpretation* of life's distresses. As noted by E. Gerstenberger, 'In the cultic life of Israel they had formed for themselves over generations and thus decided which language was possible before God, which goals were worthy of pursuit before Yahweh'.[12] In other words, if a psalmist were to blame his affliction on God without sufficient grounds, his appeal would be misdirected from the start. Interpretation of lament psalms must therefore examine and compare psalms in order to uncover on what bases psalmists interpreted life's distresses.

The above analysis results in laying forth the logical stages of development of lament psalms. A psalmist encounters distress. He interprets that distress. He formulates an appeal appropriate to that interpretation.

The process of exegesis I propose will thus try to trace each lament psalm through its stages of composition: from the distress to the interpretation of the distress to the appeal. This approach aims to take the exegete step by step through the whole process of experience that a lament psalm represents. It seeks to understand not only the appeal in its final form but also the rationale of that appeal. Why did the psalmist formulate the appeal the way he did? What factors, concrete and conceptual, shaped this appeal?

Although the first two stages must be inferred from the final appeal, they are inevitable prerequisites for the composition of a lament psalm. If any interpretation aims at unfolding a psalm in all of its dimensions, it must endeavor to sound them out, no matter how speculative the enterprise may first appear. The quest for the meaning of texts demands not just 'What?' but also 'Why?' Whether the extant poems yield such information can be known only after rigorous exegesis. The procedure outlined below will discuss how the conventional tools contribute at each stage, particularly by delimiting their proper use.

Finally, a word must be said about the psalmist. A psalm represents a communication process from a speaker to an addressee. Although one cannot appeal to the 'author's intention' as though it could be apprehended apart from the psalm itself, one cannot ignore the psalmist for he is an element of the psalm's context, just as much as God the addressee is and as the social context is. There is, however, an ambiguity in this term. 'Psalmist' can signify either the composer of the psalm or the worshipper using the psalm. By and large I will be referring to the composer. Although recent scholarship has for good reasons been hesitant in talking about individual 'authors' of biblical texts, no community— no matter how common their unity—wrote the lament psalms. The conventional language of these psalms certainly shows a strong social influence, but their intricate structure (see further below) and deliberate movement—in most cases—betray the work of a single mind.[13]

The distinction between composer and worshipper, however, may in practice not be so important. In the pre-exilic cult the Psalms were viewed as inspired poetry,[14] and certainly as part of the sacred worship they were considered sacred words. In postexilic times they were seen to be part of 'the law of Yahweh' (Ps. 1) and therefore profitable for meditation. Worshippers thus received these psalms as models through which they might properly articulate their faith and experiences. If a worshipper encountered a distress and then took up an appropriate psalm, the psalm would have guided him in the interpretation of his distress and in the expression of his appeal.[15] Meanwhile, his own personal experience would have given specific tones to the more generalized psalmic language. And even if a worshipper came to a psalm with no immediate experience of distress, the psalm would have evoked in his imagination the sense of that distress. In worship the Psalms not only follow religious experience; they lead it. As inspired poetry they summon worshippers into their movement. Psalms are thus both expressive and evocative.[16] In effect, the psalmist, whether composer or worshipper, would have passed through each phase that a lament psalm represents: a distress, and interpretation of it, and an appeal from it.

B. SITUATION

A psalm is not an autonomous entity, a verbal art form abstracted from the world. Some of the proponents of the 'New Criticism' in general literary studies while trying to avoid both the 'intentional' (the meaning of a text is to be identified with the author's intention) and 'affective fallacies' (the meaning of a text is to be identified with the reader's response) have in effect tried to speak strictly within the confines of the poem. But, as W.K. Wimsatt notes, 'if anything about poetry is clear at all it is that a poem is not really a thing, like a horse or a house, but only *analogically* so'.[17] Words, images, and descriptions of a poem obtain meaning—in part—by referring to things and events outside of the poem itself. It is this act of referring that ties poems—in varying forms and degrees—to the world of experience.

In current research when one thinks of the situational context, or *Sitz im Leben*, to which a psalm refers, one normally thinks of the institutional or cultic context. While this interest is legitimate and has contributed to our understanding, it has overshadowed a more direct reference of the lament psalms themselves, namely the distresses from which the psalmists seek release. By the 'distress' of a psalm I simply mean that particular hardship which a lament psalm laments, or one may say, that particular hardship for which this psalm could be used as an appropriate appeal.

H.-J. Kraus, though using another term, also seeks to direct scholarly attention in this direction. In the latest edition of his commentary he re-introduces the concept of 'theme' into biblical studies, which M. Noth had used in his study of the Pentateuch.[18] He considers that 'such cooperation and correlation of form criticism and theme orientation is indispensable, if Psalm research is not to sink into "formula criticism" and formalism'. He uses this notion of theme, along with form criticism, to group the psalms. His examples of psalmic groupings are 'prayer of the sick', 'prayer of the accused', and ' prayer of the sinner'. The thematic aspect of these labels, however, points to what I would call the particular distresses underlying the psalms.

This discussion raises two questions. First, are the descriptions of distress concrete or metaphoric? Thus far scholarship has reached no consensus on the matter. One may contrast, for example, the recent works of W. Beyerlin and K. Seybold on the one hand and O. Keel on the other.[19] Beyerlin and Seybold seek to determine the specific institution and rituals associated with certain groups of lament psalms. Keel sees much of the imagery applied to 'enemies' in the laments as psychological 'projections', not as real descriptions. For the most part, scholars appear to identify literal and metaphoric portions according to the social setting that they have postulated. While Davidic authorship was maintained, the military imagery took center stage; now the cultic and/or legal language has become the focus of attention. The difference between the historical-biographical and cultic approaches described above is not that the former is more literalistic; the difference lies in which allusions one takes literally and which one takes figuratively.[20] Since a comprehensive answer to this question would require a detailed study of the history of the genre beginning with Sumero-Akkadian prayers, no general answer will be attempted here. Rather, the probabilities for each psalm will be weighed individually.

Second, were laments composed for a singular or a recurring occasion? For the laments of the individual the general nature of the language would seem to indicate the latter. Such a conclusion, however, might be hasty. The language of the corporate laments is just as general, but most commentators try to locate them in a particular moment of Israel's history. This effort can be justified on the grounds that most of these communal laments depict national catastrophes, and the narrative books of the OT record many comparable disasters. Thus, individual laments, though their language is very open-ended, may have been occasioned by a specific, concrete distress. On the other hand, even if some communal laments did emerge from particular incidents, they appear to have been reapplied to new situations.[21] Thus, even if the individual laments had also originated out of singular occasions, after being entrusted to the public cult they were adapted to similar, repeatable occasions.

The social context in and for which lament psalms were composed is the second aspect of their situational context. The cultic approach to psalms interpretation has contributed significantly to our understanding of these poems before us:

> As in the case of all the literature of Israel, we must think of the Psalms as primarily not written literature at all. We must put away all thoughts of paper and ink and look on the Psalms as having their source in the life of the people. They played a part there before they took literary form at all. The most important fact in this connection is that the singing of Psalms was originally a part of worship.[22]

In other words, it would be improper to understand the psalms as governed simply by literary factors. A sudden change of address, for example, may not have been included for literary effect but because it suited the psalm's use in worship.

The actual circumstances in which the psalms were sung, at least for the laments of the individual, remain in debate. Most scholars would agree that the setting for the laments of the community was the public fast, specially summoned because of a sudden national disaster.[23] To use the laments of the individual, scholars suppose the worshipper either went to the temple where the official priesthood oversaw the ceremony,[24] or he remained at home where a 'ritual expert' led in their use.[25] The trend in recent scholarship seems to lean toward the latter.

Some cautions need to be expressed regarding a cultic approach to the Psalms. In some instances, the search for the institutional setting has blurred the principal object of study: the locus of meaning has become the situation of the psalm rather than the psalm itself.[26] The texts became simply a means by which one could discern social rites and institutions. In its most extreme form, 'text' became equated with social context. The frame of reference used in sociological studies was imposed on the psalms themselves, in effect reducing their meaning to their 'horizontal' dimensions and excluding the theological dimension.[27] This preoccupation with how social factors caused certain forms of literature to appear was part of a wider movement prevailing in literary studies outside the Bible. R. Wellek and A. Warren in *Theory of Literature* note that this interest in social causes was an attempt of literary critics 'to emulate the methods of the natural sciences'.[28]

We have been rightly directed to see the psalms as oral literature, but we must beware of the assumption that it is somehow more 'alive' than written literature (e.g., as one scholar put it, 'Gunkel sought to liberate the literary forms from the written page'[29]). It would be a mistake to infer from the designation *Sitz im Leben* that the real 'life' of literature is not contained in the literature itself but in the social situation which it reflects. Though oral performance certainly presents certain qualities that the written page lacks, as a generalization it is misleading. A written work, in fact, invites a closer reading which brings to light the many subtleties and depth of texts.

C. INTERPRETATION

Both D.A. Knight and R. Knierim argue that, by and large, the concept of *Sitz im Leben* has been used too narrowly to refer strictly to the institutional setting of a text. They propose that other important facets to the setting of passages include epochal/historical, ideological/theological, literary, and linguistic (i.e., preconceptual) aspects.[30] The framework according to which psalmists interpreted their distresses would be a part of the ideological or theological setting. They would have interpreted their hardships according to the traditions maintained by the social and religious context in and for which they composed their psalms.

To my knowledge, however, this aspect of the context of lament psalms has not been pursued. Within some commentaries one can find some interest in how psalmists interpreted their distresses, but even if such comments are present they are usually made in passing.[31] It would be helpful to consider not only individual psalms but also how they vary among themselves.

The primary question is that of causation: Is the responsibility for the distress to be traced to a human or divine agent? Whenever conflict occurs on a strictly 'horizontal' level in the lament psalms, two distinct forms of characterization appear: the psalmist versus his enemies and the righteous versus the wicked.[32] Whenever God is considered to be the agent of the distress, his action in some cases may appear reasonable (e.g., as judgment on sin) but in other cases it is not so, thus giving rise to complaint.

This problem of the agent causing the distress can be stated most clearly with respect to the lament section proper and its grammatical subjects, of which there are three alternatives. The statements, 'I am afflicted', 'you have afflicted me', and 'my foes have afflicted me', are all equivalent aside from their subjects. Why then is God or the psalmist or the adversary chosen as the subject of the lament?

To understand these models of interpretation we must endeavor to note for what reasons a particular form of interpretation was attached to any given distress. This demands that we search for correlations between the kinds of distresses, the agents of the distresses, and any other relevant factors found among the lament psalms. Thus, we shall elucidate not only the end product of interpretation, namely the appeal, but also some of the criteria according to which the psalmists interpreted life's distresses. More particularly, we shall gain insights into how they ascertained the action of God in their experience.[33]

To explain the nature of this second stage in the process of interpreting psalms, it may be helpful to contrast it with the third stage of interpreting the psalm's appeal. Studying the final appeal of a psalm means studying that psalm as it lies before us. Studying the psalm in its interpretive or compositional stages means examining each of its expressions as a choice of several alternatives and asking why each expression is phrased as it is. This stage thus concerns the selectivity of the psalmist. It is not superfluous to the study of the meaning of these psalms, for the meaning of an expression is in part contingent on what that expression does not mean.

D. APPEAL

In this process of interpreting lament psalms the bulk of the discussion must be found here because, quite simply, we have more to work with. The first two stages are presupposed by the text and so must be inferred from the clues available, but the whole of the appeal is before us.

The dominant approach for interpreting the components of psalms and how they form an appeal has been 'form criticism'. Indeed, form criticism as a tool of OT studies appears to be most at home in the Psalter.

We must begin by considering the term 'genre'. R. Knierim in his article, 'Old Testament Form Criticism Reconsidered', observed: 'One of the facts is that we are no longer so clear as to what exactly a genre is. More pointedly: It is doubtful whether this has ever been clear.'[34]

Defining 'genre' is difficult because it is not a feature of texts that immediately strikes the reader like a theme or a historical reference. Earlier classification schemes for the Psalms, in fact, were based on these more obvious features (e.g., psalms of creation, psalms of the exile).

An essential premise of form criticism is that recurring social occasions give rise to recurring patterns of speech. For each activity of society where words are important, the language which best suits that activity would be shaped as a matter of social habit. In other words, by recurring use literary conventions would develop. Moreover, as familiarity would grow, these conventions could signal this particular use without the intention of the speech or text being stated explicitly.

The thinking underlying form criticism accords well with what scholars have determined about the study of words, or semantics. A word should be defined, they say, on the basis of its *use*, not its etymology.[35] The study of the meaning of a text should begin with its use, not with the sources from which it drew. Generic studies focus on texts in action, how they work. A genre thus describes a class of texts exhibiting the same use or function.

This implies that the modern interpreter should approach 'genre' from two angles. We can begin with the immediate data, namely the written texts, and in our case the 150 psalms. Or we can begin with the religious and social causes that occasioned these texts. The former approach was emphasized by Gunkel. He saw that certain psalms shared common features that point to a common social context. The latter approach was emphasized by Mowinckel. He began with what must have been the social context of psalms, in this case the public cult, and extrapolated from it what must have been the speech needs of that social context. He then classified psalms according to the speech needs of the cult.[36] Both approaches need to be done, and their findings need to be correlated. We cannot merely do a literary analysis, because as already noted a psalm is not a literary text merely—it is a product of, and therefore shaped by, the cult and its requirements. Nor can we merely do a sociological analysis, because we simply do not know enough about the sociology of ancient Israel, especially the sociology of its worship. Indeed, our principal source of information about ancient Israelite worship is the Psalms themselves.[37] Moreover, we must be aware of two cautions. We cannot assume that the social occasion dictates precisely the form of the speech, as though once we can spell out the social context, we can predict precisely what the speech would sound like. Secondly, we must heed Knierim's cautions about the assumption that each genre must have a specific social setting.[38]

To understand what genre is and how it functions we must make clear that it is not a heuristic tool for use only by scholars who wish to classify the Psalms (genre is not to be equated with 'genus') and reconstruct Israel's ancient liturgies. Genre is, in fact, a tool used by everybody, whether consciously or unconsciously.[39] While reading a newspaper, for example, one quickly discerns and adjusts to a multitude of genres. Reading a text of any one genre triggers off in readers' minds a set of associative qualities that enable them to understand it correctly. (Editorials are not read with the same hermeneutic as straight reportage.)

We will first look at genre as used by the psalmist and then look at it as used by the listeners/readers. For psalmists the various genres presented them with the traditional pattern for composing a psalm, for example how to request something of God. This statement is of course oversimplified. We must not make a sharp dichotomy between form and content, as though psalmists had their well-formed ideas, which they simply poured into a pre-set form. The pre-existing genre pattern obviously shaped the psalmists' initial ideas.

In this light, the three stages of psalm composition outlined above are also oversimplified. The psalmist encounters a distress and he wants to make an effective and therefore acceptable appeal, so he employs a conventional genre. But we must also be reminded that the psalmist is aware that there exists the possibility of making an appeal to God—in the first place—from the pre-existing genre. It is therefore impossible to say which came first, the idea of crying to God for help or the genre of lament. Both contribute simultaneously to the composition of a lament psalm.

The listeners/readers of the Psalms must be considered in three categories. The principal listener for the psalmist was, of course, God. The psalmist, by using a traditional pattern of speaking to God, could be assured that his prayer would be presented in form acceptable to God. A second category of listeners/readers of psalms was those who heard the psalm performed in its original setting. From certain signals within the psalm text itself and from the context of its actual performance, the congregation would have been directed to the proper aim and understanding of the psalm. The third category of listeners/readers is those who have at hand only the text itself; no explicit instructions regarding its proper use are extant. For us we must correlate the psalms themselves with what information we can glean elsewhere of the Israelite cult.

Genre thus serves as a shared pattern of communication by which speakers can make themselves understood to listeners. In many respects it functions no differently from any element of grammar that may indicate the mood, voice, etc., of a sentence. K. Koch suggests that genre criticism may be viewed as a 'higher grammar', that is, a grammar beyond the sentence. In the words of Gunkel, 'The ancients were as familiar from infancy with the laws of literary forms as they were with the rules of Hebrew grammar'.[40] According to M.J. Buss, a genre is used as 'a pattern of expectation within a culture regarding what can or will be said'; it is thus a 'virtual class which describes a possibility'.[41] I would specify it further as *a virtual composite of conventions*, where 'convention' is used in both its objective and subjective senses: a convention may describe a 'social habit' or 'custom' and it may describe an 'agreement'. Thus, certain *social habits* of speech signal an assumed *agreement* between speaker and listener. On the part of the speaker the agreement signifies an intention; on the part of the hearer (and thus interpreter), an understanding of how the utterance is to be understood, or one may even say, it indicates a mode of interpretation.[42]

In the same way a genre may also be described as a '*design*'. A design can signify both a 'sketch' and a 'purpose': certain outlining marks of a text (as in a *sketch*) indicate the *purpose* of the text. As a design may exist as a sketch drawn out on paper or as a mental scheme, so a genre may exist both in its concrete manifestation and as a 'virtual class'.

The signals of a genre need not take the form of a structure since that limits arbitrarily the possibilities of how one can formulate a genre.[43] These signals or clues may also consist of formulae or a complex of motifs.

In view of the above, 'genre' may be defined as a shared pattern of communication, usually shaped in a particular social context, that signals certain expectations on how a text/speech is to be understood.[44]

Three values of genre criticism deserve mention. First, it provides the most suitable classification of the Psalms thus far.[45] As S. Mowinckel remarks, 'All scientific research demands a proper arrangement of material, a classifying and a grouping, so that the things which belong together may be seen in their mutual connexions and illuminate one another.'[46] Form criticism succeeds not only in establishing the general categories but also in analyzing the typical elements or motifs that constitute each category (e.g., laments against foes, petitions for intervention). We thus begin to see how the parts of a psalm work together to form a whole. The helpfulness of such analysis for the sake of further comparisons will be evident from the results of Chapter 2.

Second, form criticism is more than a heuristic device serviceable for scholars. Since its classification is based on the use of psalms, its chief contribution is that it directs the interpreter toward the principal aim or use of a type of psalm. Other classification systems for the Psalms (e.g., according to historical period or author) do not direct the interpreter to the essence of a psalm, but simply to a feature of a psalm. For example, Mowinckel notes (in one of the best, brief apologetics of form criticism I have seen) that Pss. 90 and 139 are often read today as meditations on the eternity and omnipresence of God. But form criticism rightly directs us to the reason these motifs take a place in these psalms, namely to move Yahweh to act on the worshipper's behalf.[47] Since the definition of a thing is best determined by its use, form criticism thus keeps the exegete focused on what a psalm really is because he sees what it does.

Third, form criticism aids the exegesis of particular psalms. One may at first question the value of discovering that certain forms of language are typical or conventional. But such discovery need not suggest, as some have supposed, that this language is bland or impersonal, particularly in the case of the Psalms.[48] On the contrary, conventional language enables a poet to compact meanings into a form of 'shorthand'.[49] By the mere use of a word or phrase he can allude to an entire tradition. Form criticism has helped bring to light the associations and overtones that certain motifs inject into a poem. More particularly, it can elucidate the meaning of a phrase that is unclear within the confines of a single psalm. If one can identify it as a motif common to other similar psalms, then one may be able to understand how this phrase is meant to contribute to this psalm. Form criticism may also help in certain cases where the principal significance of a psalm may not be what the psalm appears to say in isolation, but how it uses conventions in unconventional ways. Thus, one must often consider whether the conventional or the move away from the conventional is what is most significant for the meaning of a psalm.[50]

Many discussions of the lament category, while commenting on the motifs found among these psalms, overlook some important distinctions and nuances. As valuable as the works of Gunkel, Mowinckel and Westermann indeed are, when reading them one may get the impression that the lament psalms form a fairly uniform category, that is, that the motifs discussed are represented in evenly among the psalms.[51] For example, one may assume while reading Westermann's *Praise and Lament in the Psalms* that the motif 'the reference to God's earlier saving deeds' appears in even distribution through the category. In the next chapter we will see that this is not the case. One must note not simply the occurrence of a motif but also how it is distributed throughout the genre. In so doing one may, in fact, discover that the lament category itself has its own subcategories and its own spectrum of 'colors'. In addition, some scholars have used the labels 'lament psalms' and 'complaint psalms' interchangeably. But Chapter 2, by noting which motifs occur in which psalms, will show that the label 'complaint' is appropriate only for a subcategory of lament psalms.

Another shortcoming of these form-critical studies is that once a particular motif is identified, it is often assumed that this motif has the same function in each psalm of that category. Rather, one should note the consistency and variation in the function of each motif among the psalms. For example, Chapter 2 will also show that though the praise of God appears in many lament psalms, it connotes different things in different psalms. In some cases, it appears to be unqualified praise; in others, it is a reminder to God of what he has promised.

One must be cautious in one's use of form criticism. The genres and their motifs should not be thought of as rigid models. The typical must not be allowed to overshadow the unique. R.J. Clifford notes that,

> A particularly unhappy consequence of the dominance of form is the determination of the poetic unit primarily by considerations of form. The unit length becomes coequal with the extent of the form that is used. The poet thereby loses his license to write long poems or to recast old conventions to new uses. Oversensitivity to the conventions of the genre the poet is judged to be employing can easily set up expectations in the critic's mind about the length and purpose of a unit and the presence of secondary material.[52]

Finally, analysis must always culminate in synthesis. While many commentaries have able analyzed psalms—discussing words, phrases, verses, and form-critical motifs—they often do not give concerted attention to how the parts compose a whole. The reader of the commentary is often left with the job of figuring out how the psalmist uses this language within his own poetic structure. One might say that Psalms commentaries need to go beyond explaining the 'public meaning' of psalmic language (*la langue*, 'language' or 'the whole stock of words, idioms and syntax available, the potential, the common property of all users') to explaining the 'user's meaning' (*la parole*, 'speech' or 'any particular and actual use of language by a speaker or writer').[53] The exegete must elucidate how these individual motifs function and contribute toward a psalm's total meaning. Form-criticism is a handy tool for analyzing the 'anatomy' of a psalm, but its helpfulness in determining the 'physiology' of a psalm has not found as widespread use.

Hebrew poetry is largely paratactical, which means it is often up to the interpreter to infer the logical connections within the poem.[54] Particularly because of the elliptical nature of Hebrew verse, our task may be described as elucidating the *train of thought*. This means spelling out the logical progression from one verse to another.

While studying a lament psalm, we must keep in mind where its 'train of thought' is headed. As noted above, the aim of lament psalms is to obtain something from God. How then did psalmists endeavor to achieve this? How did they argue their case before God? What arguments were considered valid in ancient Israel?

To answer these questions one should apply rhetorical analysis in the purest sense of the term, as the study of argumentation. One must, however, guard against the study becoming more an investigation of stylistic devices and structures than of meaning (which has been a tendency of some rhetorical analyses). One must describe how the psalmist does it while keeping focused on what he is trying to do. If we simply note the structures inherent in a poem without asking 'So what?', we go no farther than describing the public meaning of these forms. As with words and phrases, we must also consider the *function* of these structures and techniques. The interpretation of a psalm's appeal thus entails the unfolding of how the psalm proceeds to argue its case.

While applying rhetorical criticism, the interpreter must bear in mind that the psalms originated primarily as liturgical compositions and were thus shaped—in part at least—by cultic exigencies. The movement of a psalm is thus determined not only by what may be logically necessary but also by ritual requirements. Even so, liturgical language is not without its own logic, especially when it comes to trying to obtain God's favorable intervention. Liturgical laments, being language that was hammered out and preserved through the generations, are appeals that were believed to be compelling to the Most High.

The methods of biblical criticism touched on thus far are impressive, but there is the temptation to be so impressed with them as a 'scientific' tools that one forgets that one is reading poetry. To understand the Psalms properly we must understand the nature of poetry. Poetry is especially the language of emotion,[55] imagination, and the transcendent. Poetry is a way of transcending the limitations of referential language to speak of the mysteries of human experience and of God. Metaphor helps to illustrate this. While it is not the exclusive property of poetry, it most frequently appears there. This figure of speech, which uses a 'vehicle' to speak of a 'tenor', is particularly suited for describing the transcendent in terms of the concrete.

The inadequacy of language to communicate even the simplest of experiences is felt by everyone, whether poet or not. For example, W. Nowottny, an English literary critic at the University of London, notes the inevitable failure of discursive or analytical language to describe all that may occur in the experience of viewing a flower in a jug inside a room ('a wallflower, dark red, darker at the centre, wilting at the edges, lit by the morning sun, spraying out of its jug, reflected in a mirror').[56] Discursive language could not recreate 'the simultaneous interpenetration of each attribute or quality by every other, the mutual modifications operating over the whole network of relationships inhabited by a thing'. Thus, if referential language fails to capture the visual experience of a flower in a jug, how much less can it express 'a moment in the mind, or a mood, a vision, or an attitude'? This problem of communicating the 'wholeness' of human experience is one that poetry labors to overcome.

To try to achieve this, poetry uses words differently and it places those words into unique structures. While in discourse words embrace meaning, in poetry they explode meaning (as in metaphor). They do not merely convey a referent; they also evoke an associative context. Thus, a tree may not simply be a tall structure with bark and leaves but life, strength, shelter, etc. Moreover, these words in poetry are not assembled as in a linear equation where they serve as building blocks that contribute additively toward the whole. They are woven into a network of interrelationships—a poetic structure—where the whole becomes more than the sum of the parts.

The peculiar properties of poetry, especially as it relates to time, may be illustrated further by contrasting it with narrative. Poetry can differ from narrative in relation to time. In narrative, time is normally sequential; in poetry it is often punctiliar. Poetry seeks to express all that is experienced intuitively at a moment of time. While a poem takes time to read, all of its parts are to be felt simultaneously. Thus, in the reading of a poem the most accurate interpretation may occur at the intuitive level where this 'event' is re-experienced as a whole, not at the cognitive level where it can only be expressed in its parts with discursive language. Since poetry usually presents a synthetic picture of an experience, it is imperative that interpretation of the Psalms include both analysis and synthesis.

The intricate structures of psalms, already mentioned, seem to verify this.[57] One cannot assume that when a psalmist composed the first verse of a psalm, he had no thought of what might follow. The very nature of some structures, such as a chiasmus, shows that each part of a psalm corresponds to other parts and that each is to be read in light of the other. What is said toward the end of the psalm may qualify what was said at the beginning. The exegete must also recall that the Psalms are properly 'heard' or 'sung' poetry as opposed to 'read' poetry. When poetry is heard one tends to grasp it more intuitively as a whole, than if one read it simply as a printed specimen for analytical investigation.

The possibility that a psalm articulates the experience of a moment can be illustrated with Ps. 13. A common way of reading the movement in this psalm is represented in A. Weiser's commentary. Regarding the final verse (vv. 5-6 in EVV), he says,

> What the poet has asked for is granted to him: his eyes have been opened. The fear which by its violent fluctuations made his impatient heart tremble has subsided, and the prayer ends on the serene note of a firm and confident assurance. Just as the lamentation and the prayer have done, so the affirmation of trust, too, starts at the cardinal point—with God. But now the worshipper is assured of the grace of God for which he had yearned and prayed, and, trusting in that grace, he has reached a firm position which enables him by God's help to disregard all his present suffering and look into a bright future.[58]

Weiser's interpretation is possible, but it assumes that the psalmist 'drops' each line as he leaves it for another. Rather, in light of the 'wholeness' of poetry, it seems more likely that he holds on to each line until he has gathered the whole.[59] All the lines of the poem would be voiced, as it were, in a single breath. Each part of the psalm would be experienced simultaneously.

This illustration with Ps. 13 helps to bring to light two problems when one tries to read psalms as integral units. What if the psalm appears to show a progression in its movement? In Ps. 13, the lament is not permitted to have the last word but must instead yield to confidence and praise. In spite of the psalmist's opening sense of betrayal, he ends on a note of trust. Progression is certainly an element in psalmody, but this need not entail abandonment of what has preceded. While the motifs are picked up in a certain order, they need not replace what preceded—they may simply be assembled into the whole. These lines, which analytically perceived appear to move simply from one to the next, may in psalmic poetry reflect the same 'simultaneous interpenetration' as Nowottny's example, the flower in the jug. A psalm may be a 'progressive whole', but it is still a whole nonetheless.

A second problem concerns inner 'contradictions' or incongruous elements within a single psalm. But, as in the case of Ps. 13, supposing the psalmist had experienced mixed emotions in the midst of distress (both a sense of betrayal and a sense of trust), how else could he express such 'contradiction' except by paradox?

What is true of contradictory emotions may also be true of contradictory meanings or literary forms (e.g., praise and lament) in the same psalm. What we often qualify in discursive language with 'Yes, but ...' may in poetry be represented simply as 'contradictory' statements in parataxis.[60] As Nowottny points out, complex literary devices may interfere with 'our natural tendency to abstract a much simplified "content" from a stream of words .... This "interference" is not an obstacle to understanding but a challenge or an invitation to take a new route to understanding'.[61] What is considered contradiction by the *wissenschaftlich* mind may simply be good poetry. The psalmist may simply be presenting differing (even disjointed) perspectives or features of the same experience without explicitly attempting to resolve the apparent contradiction. Indeed, this conflict may be a key element of the psalm's message.

Because poetry does not convey meaning additively—as a sum of individual items—but globally or integrally—as a network—the interpretive process cannot proceed simply in a linear, step-by-step fashion. Research must be a repeated process of analysis and synthesis, a repeated engagement of wholes and parts. It cannot simply move along a line, but must try to move along an upward spiral, returning and returning to the same facets of a text but each time, after reflection upon the other features, at a higher level of understanding.

Laments, being poetry and therefore literature,[62] place certain strictures on the goals of interpretation, as J. Barr's comments make clear:

> In so far as a work is really literary and not merely informational in its scope and character, it can perhaps be said *to be its own meaning*, or to set forth its own meaning. For a work to be literary in character means that it does not have a detachable meaning which might have been stated in some other way; the way in which it was stated in the work is in fact the 'message' or the 'meaning' of this work. Any comment on such works can therefore aim only at elucidating the work and sending the reader back to the work itself; it cannot hope to encapsulate the meaning in another set of words.[63]

The task of 'ex-egesis' is indeed to 'lead' the meaning 'out' of a text, but if that signifies an extraction of its meaning, a translation of literature into discursive language, then the task is misdirected from the start. Interpretation, since it occurs in discursive language, must always speak in parts and can therefore at best lead us toward the whole, which a poetic structure represents. It can never represent it. Since interpretation is not meant to dispense with the text but to illuminate it, its goal, as L. Alonso Schökel notes, is 'an orienting of the reader to enable him to read and see the image correctly'; or put most simply, interpretation is 'an introduction to reading'.[64] In the words of L.E. Keck and G.M. Tucker, 'the aim of exegesis is to give the text its own voice'.[65]

This task of pointing the reader to those clues of the text that should lead to a proper reading is crucial for understanding ancient texts. The signals that should clue the reader in to certain associations may not be detected by the modern reader. This is particularly the case for the Psalms, which through the centuries have proven themselves to have immense depth. In sum, our aim is to elucidate the psalms and then send the reader back to them.

In view of the above proposal for the interpretation of lament psalms, one must respond, Does it work? That is really two questions. Can the questions set forth be answered? That is part of what the following seven chapters will try to show. Does it provide a comprehensive picture of a psalm? That is a question no single interpreter can answer.

Chapter 2

PSALMS OF PLEA AND PSALMS OF COMPLAINT

A. INTRODUCTION

One of the purposes of biblical interpretation is to give readers a more refined understanding of biblical texts. To have more than simply a vague appreciation of the Psalms one must be able to detect the subtleties of consistency and variation in their language. This chapter aims at elucidating distinctions in lament psalms that are often overlooked. It endeavors to be, as it were, a finer prism which further discerns the subtleties of color. As new shades are exposed, the richness of color is brought to light. Generalizations may be helpful for learning or for classification, but it is often the detail that adds color and interest.

This chapter will pick up the question raised in Chapter 1 about how coherent a category the lament genre is. This and the next three chapters will, in fact, argue that at each of the three stages outlined above (situation of distress, interpretation of the distress, and the appeal to God) a clear sub-genre of lament psalms emerges. This observation, we shall see, has bearing on our understanding of the Psalter as a whole. Since it is advisable to work from the clear to the unclear, we shall begin with the final appeal of the psalm itself and then move to the distress reflected in the psalm (Chapter 4) and to how the psalmist interprets it (Chapter 5). Chapter 3 will take a closer look at the key expressions of complaint.

Even a casual reading of the Psalms reveals that their basic forms of speech may be described most generally as praise and lament, or praise and petition. Whether one's approach to the Psalter is historical, cultic, devotional or literary, there is general agreement that the basic kinds of psalms are praise and lament. There are two basic stances taken in this poetry concerning God: some acclaim the majestic attributes and deeds of Yahweh, while others appeal for his assistance. H. Gunkel posits that 'in the alternation between lament and thanksgiving runs the whole life of the pious'.[1] C. Westermann also lays great emphasis on this point. In the Preface to the fifth edition of his book newly titled *Praise and Lament in the Psalms* (1977), he writes:

> In my years of work on the Old Testament, particularly on the Psalms, it has become increasingly clear to me that the literary categories of Psalms of lament and Psalms of praise are not only two distinct categories among others, but that they are the literary forms which characterize the Psalter as a whole, related as they are as polar opposites.[2]

Westermann therefore considers praise psalms and lament psalms not as mere categories but as the polar opposites of the Psalter that define its range of expression.

Two observations, however, call into question the accuracy of this conclusion that the 'polar opposites' of psalmic expression are adequately described by the categories of praise psalms and lament psalms. Both observations, in fact, come from Westermann himself. As the title to the first four editions of his book, *The Praise of God in the Psalms* (*Das Loben Gottes in den Psalmen*), implies, he goes to great lengths in tracking down expressions of praise throughout the Psalter, in both praise and lament psalms. He even goes so far as to say that 'there is no petition, no pleading from the depths, that did not move at least one step (in looking back to God's earlier saving activity or in confession of confidence) on the road to praise'.[3] Although there are several lament psalms that may be regarded as exceptions to this generalization, the question must be raised: If most lament psalms uphold the praise of God in some form, can they be described as the 'polar opposite' of praise?

A second question stems from another observation of Westermann's, which in my reading of the Psalter appears to be essentially correct. He notes that 'in praise the one being praised is elevated' and that 'the most important verbal mark' of praise is that 'the one being praised is the subject' of the sentence.[4] Therefore, if to praise means to predicate of God elevated attributes and actions, then logically the opposite of praise would be to predicate of God demeaning or unfavorable attributes and actions, which, as we shall see, brings us to what I call a 'God-lament'.

The significance of such sentences where God is the grammatical subject thus becomes evident. Our study will therefore focus upon the lament psalms and the predications of God made in them. The 'God-lament' psalms should interest us particularly since it is this expression that appears logically to be the polar opposite of praise. We will endeavor to study the presence and absence of praise and the presence and absence of its opposite, namely the God-lament, to see if their distribution within the lament category forms a clear pattern. Can we draw a clear line between laments that maintain the praise of God and those that have this God-lament? The praise psalms will be discussed in the conclusion, where they will be compared and contrasted with the psalms of the lament category.

B. THE GOD-LAMENT

The remarks here will simply introduce this motif. Further substantiation and clarification can be found in Chapter 3.

The lament section proper of a lament psalm is composed of any combination of three possible forms, each of which may be identified by the grammatical subject of the sentence. There is the 'I/We-lament', the 'Thou(God)-lament' and the 'They(foe)-lament'. Ps. 13 illustrates each of these forms:

Ps. 13.2   How long, Yahweh? Will *you* forget me forever?
        How long will you hide your face from me?
    3   How long shall *I* take counsel in my soul,
        with grief in my heart all the day;

how long will *my enemy* be exalted over me?

All three grammatical forms lament a hardship that has come upon the psalmist, but the 'Thou-lament' presents the psalmist's perception of God's role in the distress. Some of these God-laments concern Yahweh's disposition toward the psalmist; others focus on the mode of his intervention, or non-intervention, in the affairs of the psalmist. Both of these aspects can be illustrated from Ps. 89:

> Ps. 89.39   But you have rejected and despised;
> you have become furious with your anointed.
> 41   You have broken down all his walls;
> you have made his fortifications a ruin.

Verse 41 ties itself to God's action in the immediate distress. Verse 39 concerns his attitude or posture toward the psalmist. Those God-laments that speak of God's (non-)intervention can be subdivided according to the nature of God's role in the distress: in some he is considered to be passive and in others actively engaged. In other words, God's action may be concessive or causative. Ps. 89.41, quoted above, exemplifies the latter, while Ps. 74.11 illustrates the former:

> 74.11   Why do you withdraw your hand,
> and keep your right hand back in your bosom?

Nuances can be given to the more basic meaning when the God-lament appears in a question form. The interrogative 'Why?' implies reproach (e.g. 22.2).[5] 'How long?' suggests urgency (e.g. 13.2) and the simple finite verb (perfect or imperfect) indicates, as with all rhetorical questions, a more persuasive note (e.g. 85.6).

What purpose do such God-laments serve? Do they do nothing more than describe the psalmist's perception of God's role in the distress, as though he were simply a third actor in the drama? Do they connote complaint? Or could they be regarded as an indirect form of praise for deserved judgment or for beneficial chastisement?

A clue may be found in the kinds of sentences in which most God-laments appear. In contrast to the 'I'- or 'they'-laments, the God-laments often appear in the form of a rhetorical question.[6] As will be established in Chapter 3, these questions imply reproach or complaint.

Another suggestive characteristic of the God-laments is that they are often juxtaposed with expressions that recount the past praise of God. The resulting contrast makes clear that what God is seen to be doing in the present distress is contrary to his past praiseworthy behavior. It is this incongruity with God's traditional conduct that signals the tone of complaint in this lament.

The function of a God-lament expression in any given psalm is generally made clear by either one or both of these distinctives. Two exceptions are Pss. 39 and 102. Although their God-laments (39.6, 12; 102.11, 24) do not convey complaint as strongly as the rest, this sentiment is indicated by the tenor of the God-lament itself (e.g., 'You have lifted me up and cast me down', 102.11) and by other motifs in the psalm (e.g., 'Turn your gaze from me that I may smile', 39.14).

There are certain instances, however, where God's action against the psalmist is described as a just and therefore reasonable action. In Ps. 38 the statement, 'For your arrows have pierced me; and your right hand has descended upon me' (v. 3), substantiates the previous request that Yahweh not allow his wrath to gain the upper hand in his chastisement (v. 2). Its subordination to this petition (כי; no other 'God-lament' begins in this way) shows that it is stated to prevent any intensification in the psalmist's suffering, not to rebuke God for his affliction as such. The following verses make clear that Yahweh's action is just. The parallelism of v. 4 indicates that his anger is due to the psalmist's sin. Verses 5-6 speak of the sin itself as the cause of suffering.

Ps. 51, one of the so-called 'penitential psalms', also attributes the psalmist's affliction to God: 'Let the bones which you have crushed rejoice' (v. 10b). Since this attribution is subordinated to a petition for joy, it does not connote a rebuke against God but an affirmation that he who has the power to break has the power to heal. Moreover, the earlier confession, 'You are righteous when you speak; you stand blameless when you judge' (v. 6b), in face of the psalmist's sin, makes clear that such punishment was considered just.

Ps. 69 is somewhat similar, but this time the attribution of distress to God is subordinated to a foe-lament: 'For they have persecuted the one you have smitten; and they talk of the pain of the one you have wounded' (v. 27). Since the concern throughout vv. 19b-29 is the enemy, it is apparent this lament is focused on the pain the foes have added to Yahweh's affliction of the psalmist. The psalmist's own admission of his previous 'folly' (v. 6) may account for this.

In view of the above, we must distinguish between 'lament'—which includes the I/We- and foe-laments, and those God-laments that do not connote complaint—and 'complaint', namely, most of the God-laments. Lament can be addressed to anyone; complaint must be addressed to the one responsible. A lament focuses on a situation; a complaint focuses on the one responsible. A lament simply bemoans the state of things; a complaint contains a note of blame and rebuke.

In sum, most God-laments are expressions of complaint regarding God's disposition or action, which the psalmists in their distresses interpret as being indifferent or hostile.

Of the approximately 65 lament psalms in the Psalter there are roughly 21 that contain a 'God-lament' that connotes complaint.[7] Further support for reading these expressions as complaints can be found at the close of this chapter and especially in the expositions of individual psalms in Chapters 6 and 7.

In psalms that contain no God-lament, God may be the subject of a sentence in which he appears indifferent to the psalmist, but in each instance it is expressed as a citation from enemies. In Ps. 71.11 the psalmist's foes announce, 'God has forsaken him', but the psalmist counters this with various petitions: 'Do not cast me off ...; do not forsake me', and 'O God, do not be far from me'. In Ps. 94.7 the wicked claim, 'Yahweh does not see; nor does the God of Jacob pay attention'. But the psalmist immediately rebukes such thoughts with teachings from the wisdom tradition (vv. 8-15). Note also the assertions of the adversaries in Pss. 3.3 and 59.8, each of which brings into sharper relief the psalmist's own confessions of trust and praise (3.4-7; 59.9-11).

C. THE CONFESSION OF TRUST

A motif common among the lament psalms is what Gunkel and others after him have labelled the 'confession of trust'.[8] These expressions occur in three grammatical forms:

1. An attribute is predicated of God ('God is/You are ...')
2. An action is predicated of God ('God will/You will ...'; note only the imperfect verb is used)
3. The psalmist declares his own trust ('I trust/hope ...')

Ps. 31 illustrates each of these forms:

> 31.4 For *you are* my rock and my stronghold;
> for your name's sake *you will lead* me and guide
> me.
> 5 *You will release* me from the net
> which they have hid for me,
> for *you are* my refuge.
> 6 Into your hand *I commit* my spirit;
> you have redeemed me, Yahweh God of truth.

(Note also Ps. 59.9-11.)

The forms that should concern us primarily are the first two since they closely resemble the description of the praise of God. Strictly speaking, they are not narrative praise since they do not describe in the Hebrew perfect a deliverance that has just taken place, for the action is considered still future, as the Hebrew imperfect and context imply. Nor are they hymnic since they do not speak of God's acts and attributes in general but refer specifically to the psalmist's own deliverance. Nevertheless, these expressions do indicate that the praise of God—as a predication of elevating qualities and actions—is upheld in some lament psalms.

The choice of the third form of the confession of trust where the psalmist himself is the grammatical subject denotes the affirmation of the psalmist's personal hope, not the upraising of God's praise as such.[9]

In view of the above, it is striking to note that with but a few minor exceptions (Pss. 10.14, 16; and possibly 42.9; 60.12) the God-lament psalms restrict themselves to this third form of expression, where the psalmist simply affirms his own belief (13.6; 39.8; 42.6, 12; 43.5). And even these expressions are comparatively rare. (Ps. 42.6 [= v. 12 = 43.5], a refrain of the psalm, is explicitly not addressed to God but to the psalmist as a form of self-encouragement. Pss. 13.6 and 39.8 state briefly the fact of the psalmist's trust with no mention of the grounds for that trust.) The confession of trust as a predication of God, that is as a form of praise, is thus virtually absent in these God-lament psalms.

D. THE REFERENCE TO GOD'S EARLIER SAVING DEEDS

A motif of the lament psalms that Westermann considers to be connected with the praise of God is 'the reference to God's earlier saving deeds'.[10] If, however, this motif is intended to connote praise, it is curious to note that it appears solely among those psalms that also contain some complaint regarding the divine activity, namely the God-lament psalms. In isolation this motif does recite and uphold God's mighty redemptive acts with God as the grammatical subject, and this is characteristic of OT praise. But in the context of their psalms they are always set in contrast to the God-lament. The resulting implication is that their function in these psalms is not to extol but to draw out the contrast between the glorious past and the woeful present. They show how God's present action or lack thereof contradicts his traditional praiseworthy manner with his people:

> 80.9 You brought a vine out from Egypt;
> you drove out the nations and planted it.
> 10 You cleared the ground before it,
> and it took root and filled the land.
> 11 The mountains were covered with its shade,
> and the massive cedars with its branches.
> 12 It sent out its boughs to the Sea,
> and its shoots to the River.

13   Why have you broken down its walls,
      so that all who pass by pluck its fruit?
14   Boars from the forest strip it,
      and beasts of the field feed on it.

The inclusion of a reference to God's earlier saving deeds may in fact sharpen the cutting edge of a lament. In Ps. 44, for example, some of the lament expressions (vv. 10-17, 20, 23, 25-26) mirror in reverse what was recounted previously in the reference to God's earlier saving deeds (vv. 2-4), thus making apparent Yahweh's about-face. The forefathers knew his 'favor' (v. 4) and so experienced victory, but this generation lives under his 'rejection' (v. 10; cf. v. 24), which spells defeat. Formerly 'the light of his face' (v. 4) led to triumph, but now the 'hiding of his face' (v. 25) yields failure. In the past, Yahweh put the enemy to shame (v. 8), but now the people are subjected to this treatment (vv. 10, 14-17). Instead of 'dispossessing' (vv. 3, 4) the nations, he now 'sells Israel over' (vv. 12-13).

The function of the reference to God's earlier saving deeds, however, is not merely negative, for besides narrating what Yahweh's conduct once was, they also remind him of what his conduct could and should be. Thus, though they present a contrast with the present, they also by implication call for new intervention in the immediate future. The inclusion of this motif in Ps. 74 (vv. 12-17) shows that the deliverance needed at present is certainly no more than one that Yahweh has already performed.

In view of the above, it is difficult to identify the motif of the reference to God's earlier saving deeds as praise, except perhaps very indirectly. Its primary function is clearly persuasive, not laudatory.[11]

The only hint of this motif among the psalms lacking a God-lament appears in Ps. 83. But here it does not form an independent motif. Instead of serving to draw out the contrast of past and present, it simply adds dramatic effect to the petition (vv. 9-12).

E. NARRATIVE AND HYMNIC PRAISE

Following the terminology of Westermann, we may note that 'narrative praise' (or 'declarative praise' or a 'song of thanksgiving') recounts a specific, recent deliverance, while 'hymnic praise' (or 'descriptive praise' or simply a 'hymn') celebrates God's attributes and deeds in general.

Praise sections, both narrative and hymnic, do appear in the God-lament psalms of Pss. 9-10, 89, and 102. But in Pss. 9-10 and 89, this praise is followed by an extended lament that challenges and even seems to negate this traditional language of adoration. Note, for example, from Ps. 9-10 the following contrasts between notes of praise and their corresponding laments:

9.4	When my enemies turn back, they stumble and perish before you.
10.2a	In pride the wicked pursues the afflicted.
9.10	Yahweh will be a stronghold for the oppressed, a stronghold in times of trouble.
10.8a	From hiding places [the wicked one] kills the innocent.
9.16b	In the net which the nations hid, their own foot is caught.
10.9b	The wicked seizes the afflicted when he drags him away in his net.

(Contrast also 9.6-8 and 10.5.) The function of such praise therefore appears to be similar to that of the reference to God's earlier saving deeds, namely to show Yahweh the contradictory nature of his present behavior and to remind him of what his conduct should be. Yahweh's current conduct is seen to fall short of what the faithful have come to expect of him. In fact, it is the recitation of this traditional praise that makes clear the grounds for complaint in the God-lament.

Furthermore, the use of praise instead of a reference to God's earlier saving deeds would make the transition of mood from the glorious past to the lamentable present even more poignant. Alluding to saving deeds of the past may evoke nostalgia, but narrative and hymnic praise should connote celebration, thus making the turn to lament all the more striking. Ps. 102, an individual lament, recounts praise concerning the destiny of the nation. While it may be said that the psalmist upholds the praises belonging to the community, he does so to bring these traditions to bear on his own private concern that Yahweh not take him away in the midst of his days (v. 25a). This praise finds its place in this psalm, not principally to applaud Yahweh's gracious acts toward Zion, but to move Yahweh to apply on a smaller scale this communal praise to the life of one afflicted (note the aim of the psalm as defined in the superscription).

The non-God-lament psalms likewise turn to praise but more frequently.[12] Since their praise sections do not appear with such contradictory expressions as a God-lament, it seems that this is praise in its own right—praise in the midst of distress. For example:

71.19   Your righteousness, O God, reaches to the
           heavens,
         you who have done great things;
         O God, who is like you?

There may be motivational reasons for the inclusion of this praise but they do not appear to be primary, for there are no contradictory expressions in these psalms to suggest any apprehension that Yahweh might deny its realization. This proclamation of praise implies that the psalmists did not allow their manner of expression to be governed solely by their occasion of distress. It also shows that there is a certain continuity between praise psalms and lament psalms, and that no partition between them can be established without significant qualification.

In sum, among the non-God-lament psalms, praise is presented as a motif in its own right, and is therefore to be uttered as praise. Among the God-lament psalms, there is no praise without a God-lament that challenges or even contradicts this tradition. It therefore appears that these praise traditions are recounted in order to make evident the psalmist's grounds for complaint in the God-lament.

F. THE PETITION

The petitions should be included among the predications of God but their significance cannot weigh so heavily since they are not in the indicative mood.

The character of the petitions found in the God-lament psalms can be distinguished along the following lines. (1) Particularly among the communal laments, their petitions often concentrate on simply bidding God to turn with favor toward the psalmist, as distinct from calling God to direct intervention. This betrays a heightened concern over God's disposition, as one might expect in psalms that express complaint over God's treatment of his people. Such petitions occur with greater frequency among the communal God-laments of which there are 10 (10.12; 44.24; 74.18-20, 22-23; 79.8, 11; 80.2, 4, 8, 15, 20; 85.5, 8; 89.51; 90.13, 17) than among the corporate non-God-laments of which there are 7 (83.2; 106.4; 123.3).

(2) There is a greater density of negative petitions among these psalms (i.e., 'Do not ...'). For instance, appeals requesting that God not remain aloof from the psalmist (a petition concerning God's *favor*) occur more frequently among the individual God-lament psalms, of which there are 8 (22.12, 20; 35.22; 39.13; 102.3) than among the individual non-God-lament psalms, of which there are 36 (27.9; 28.1; 38.22; 55.2; 69.18; 71.9, 12, 18; 109.1; 143.7).

(3) The petitions for intervention are often less specific. In the God-lament psalms of 44; 74; 89 the petitions for intervention are comparatively brief and less specific regarding the form of action Yahweh should take (none in Ps. 89; in Ps. 44 only vv. 24, 27). This suggests the call to intervention is made evident by the structure of the lament itself. The petitions of Ps. 74 illustrate all three of these observations:

74.18   Remember this, Yahweh, the enemy has reviled,
         and a foolish people have scorned your name.
    19   Do not give the life of your dove up to the beasts,
         nor forget forever the lives of your afflicted ones.
    20   Look to the covenant,
         because the the dark places of the land
             are full of groans and violence.[13]
    21   Do not let the oppressed retreat and be
             humiliated;
         Let the afflicted and needy praise your name.
    22   Arise, O God, contend your own case;
         remember how fools reproach you all the day.
    23   Do not forget the voice of your adversaries,
         the uproar of your assailants which ascends
             continually.

In the non-God-lament psalms the petitions may extend beyond the immediate distress and even reflect a more spiritual nature:

86.11   Guide me, Yahweh, in your way,
             so that I may walk in your truth;
         grant me an undivided heart to fear your name.

Most of these are requests for guidance in truth, which as Gunkel noted reflects the psalmist's desire to avoid future sins (5.9; 25.4, 5; 27.11; 143.10).[14] Others are prayers for Israel and so display a broader concern (25.22; 28.9). Note also Ps. 56.6, 12, which concerns the glory of God. In the God-lament psalms the focus remains firmly fixed on the current hardship.

The more submissive stance of the non-God-lament psalms can be illustrated from the occurrences of the request 'Have mercy upon me/us' (חנן). It appears 11 times in these psalms but is absent in the God-lament psalms (with the exception of Ps. 6.3).

The petitions in the non-God-lament category are sometimes prefaced with the phrase 'in your righteousness', as seen in Ps. 31:

> 31.2   In you, Yahweh, I take refuge;
>   let me never be ashamed;
>   in your righteousness deliver me.

See also 71.2; 143.1, 11. While in these psalms direct appeal is often made to righteousness (צדק, צדקה, צדיק; 4.2; 5.9; 7.10; 17.1; 31.18 in addition to the texts listed above), this occurs only once in the God-lament psalms (35.24).

G. THE ASSURANCE OF BEING HEARD

A predication of Yahweh very similar to the confession of trust is the assurance of being heard. It occurs at the close of the psalm *after* the lament and petition have been expressed:

> 6.9   Depart from me all you evildoers,
>   because Yahweh has heard my weeping.
> 10   Yahweh has heard my supplication;
>   Yahweh receives my prayer.
> 11   All my enemies shall be ashamed and dismayed;
>   they shall retreat and suddenly be ashamed.

This motif appears four times in the God-lament psalms (Pss. 6; 9-10; 22; 85). In the first three instances the declaration that 'Yahweh has heard' (Hebrew perfect) precedes a description (Hebrew imperfect) of the deliverance Yahweh will soon perform. In Ps. 85 the שמע is a cohortative and it seems likely that the words of blessing that follow are those recited by a cultic prophet in reply to the lament and petition.[15]

The assurance of being heard is undoubtedly an assertion of confidence and praise, but it depicts Yahweh's response to the psalmist's appeal and is therefore not to be counted as a constituent part of that appeal.

H. OTHER MOTIFS

This study has focused upon the predications of God in the lament psalms in order to discern each psalm's stance relative to praising God and complaining to God. Although it would be arbitrary to assume that psalmists could say something about God only in sentences where he is made the grammatical subject, these predications of God are the clearest witnesses for ascertaining the approach to God reflected in each psalm. That the psalmists phrase their praise in this grammatical construction confirms this observation. There are, however, several lament psalms that do not contain predications of God that would help us to infer the stance assumed in the psalm toward God and his praise. Nonetheless, in these instances we can turn to other motifs that indicate where they stand relative to praising God and complaining to God.

Ps. 26, aside from two petitions (vv. 1a, 9), contains no predications of God. The psalmist does not actually express praise to God (i.e., in the form of a predication), but he does declare that he praises (or at least desires to praise; תודה) Yahweh at the temple (vv. 6-8). The opening petition ('Vindicate me [שפטני], Yahweh') and the assertion of the psalmist's innocence (vv. 1-8), in effect, acknowledge that the addressee, Yahweh, continues to maintain a standard of righteousness. Indeed, the standard that the psalmist strives to maintain is explicitly Yahweh's (v. 3 esp.). This interpretation is confirmed when we compare Ps. 26 with other psalms that approach Yahweh as the righteous judge and seek his vindication. Ps. 7 clearly expresses trust and praise (vv. 9a, 11-12) that God upholds his standard of righteousness over against the wicked (cf. 13-17). Ps. 17 with its confessions of trust (vv. 6a, 7) and its opening petition also portrays the psalmist submitting his plea to Yahweh as the righteous judge. In both of these psalms there appears an assertion of the psalmist's innocence (7.4-6; 17.4-6), which credits Yahweh as being the righteous judge. Ps. 9-10, a God-lament psalm, treats this motif in a different manner. While it has no assertion of innocence, it does contain praise to Yahweh as the righteous judge (though it is perhaps a recitation of past praises; 9.4-13, 16-19). But the lengthy description of the current situation (10.2-12), where the wicked violently oppress the afflicted, calls into question the preceding praise. Hence, complaint is expressed that Yahweh is not maintaining his role as righteous judge: 'Why, Yahweh, do you stand at a distance?' (10.1a).

Like Ps. 26, both Pss. 109 and 137 characterize the enemy as רשע. These and other psalms that describe the foe as רשע (see Chapter 5) attribute the distress entirely to the enemies. Pss. 109 and 137, in particular, focus so much on the cruelty of the foes that little is said of God directly (note also Ps. 141). Ps. 109 does, however, contain brief notes of praise (v. 21b, 'your merciful devotion is good', cf. v. 31). In such רשע-psalms it is therefore not surprising to see that the praise of God is not called into question. God is implored simply to administer justice. The only exception is Ps. 9-10, as noted above.

In Ps. 83, a corporate psalm, praise can be heard in v. 19, but it is not praise in its own right. It is here expressed as a wish that this would become the admission of the enemies. The main interest of the psalm is to *warn* Yahweh of a conspiracy against him and his people (vv. 3-6). Thus no distress has yet come upon the people that might be predicated of Yahweh (contrast Pss. 74 and 79, where the enemy is also depicted as Yahweh's). The praise of God, therefore, need not be questioned. Ps. 83 contains traces of a 'reference to God's earlier saving deeds', but in contrast to how it functions in God-lament psalms (i.e, to show Yahweh how his recent action falls short of or contradicts his past saving deeds), it is used to underscore how Yahweh should act in the near future.

Pss. 69 and 143 have several characteristics in common. First, they both contain only brief notes of praise ('Your merciful devotion is good', 69.17,[16] and 'for you are my God', 143.10). The psalmist of Ps. 143, however, may imply praise for God when he appeals to Yahweh's righteousness (vv. 1b, 11b) and acknowledges his own lack of righteousness before the righteous God (v. 2; cf. Ps. 26 above). Second, both closely resemble several God-lament psalms but contain a more tempered appeal to God. Third, and this may explain the tempered appeal, both betray a consciousness of man's sin before God (69.6-7; 143.2). These psalms will be discussed further in Chapters 4 and 5.

I. CONCLUSION

The predications of God in the non-God-lament psalms affirm the praise of God. The few psalms that have no conclusive predications of God do have other motifs that imply that the praise of God has not been called into question.

The predications of God in the God-lament psalms appear as God-laments, as references to God's earlier saving deeds, as narrative and hymnic praises, as assurances of being heard and as petitions. The petitions show a marked concern over God's disposition. To counter his indifference or hostility they do not cry for mercy; they summon God to conduct himself as he ought toward his people. The assurances of being heard are veritable praises (at least proleptically) but they express the psalmist's response to Yahweh's response to the appeal and are not integral to the appeal itself. The references to God's earlier saving deeds and the narrative and hymnic praises are stated not to extol Yahweh but to show the inconsistency of his present behavior with the past. It is therefore remarkable to note the almost total absence of confessions of trust or of any predications whose aim is to praise.

The consistency and coherence of the kinds of predications of God within these God-lament psalms has shown that the God-lament is not merely a third option among the range of possible lament expressions. With the exceptions of Pss. 38.3; 51.10b; 69.27 noted above, it is to be construed as a complaint. It represents not merely a rhetorical flourish but a distinct form of appeal.

This study of the predications of God in the lament psalms has brought to light a distinction within the lament category regarding a psalm's stance toward the praise of God. Among the non-God-lament psalms, the predications of God affirm him as Savior and so establish the plea that he actualize tradition. In the God-lament psalms, the predications of God do not extol God but establish the incongruity of past and present in the form of a complaint, and thus summon him to his prescribed disposition and conduct. One group of psalms thus affirms the praise of God, the other charges him with denying these praise traditions.

One may characterize this distinction further: the one group simply brings the distress to God's attention; the other brings the distress to God's attention as a matter for which he is at least partly responsible. The non-God-lament psalms appear, as it were, to argue with God, while the God-lament psalms argue against God. The former plead with God but the latter express their case in the form of a complaint or protest. While one may speak of the lament psalms generally as psalms of appeal, the label 'psalms of complaint' should be reserved for the God-lament psalms. Within this category of psalms of appeal there are thus two distinct modes of calling on God to save: 'plea' and 'complaint'.

Moving now from the lament category to the Psalter as a whole, we must recall that 'to praise' means to predicate of God elevated qualities and actions. Judged on the criterion of a lament psalm's use of the praise traditions, the 'psalms of plea' can be considered to have more in common with praise than with complaint psalms. While praise is maintained in the psalms of plea, it is challenged in the psalms of complaint. Moreover, the complaint psalms replace the positive affirmations of God (e.g., the confession of trust) with charges of unfaithfulness. Instead of praise one reads God-lament. It is this observation that brings us to the polar opposite of the praise psalms, namely the God-lament or complaint psalms. It therefore appears that the range of expression found in the Psalter is determined by this polarity of praise and protest, not, as Westermann has maintained, by the polarity of praise and supplication.

This new understanding of the polar opposites of the Psalter helps to clarify the extremes of psalmic expression. If one were to consider the polarity of the Psalms as simply that of praise psalms and lament psalms, then this would imply that the essential difference between them is merely the underlying situation. A festival or deliverance would call forth celebration, while a battle defeat or sickness would demand supplication.[17] The relationship of God and the psalmist, nonetheless, need not be essentially different. This paradigm, however, seems to miss the radical nature of the Psalter. For if, on the other hand, one views psalmic expression as ranging from celebration to complaint, then it is evident that the distinction is not only situational but also relational.

In particular, the psalmist's conception of God is altered. In the psalms of praise and plea, God is approached as benevolent, in the psalms of complaint as indifferent or hostile. In the former he is believed to be an ally, but in the latter he is regarded to be either an aloof bystander or an active antagonist. These protest psalms depict how the distress and tradition collide, thus showing that the psalmist's dilemma is not simply his own but one that threatens the integrity of Yahweh's own character.

This refined understanding of the Psalter's range of expression thus enhances our appreciation of the dynamics of Israel's worship and of their relationship with God. Both praise and protest were considered to be integral expressions of and valid aims in OT faith.

Chapter 3

AN ANALYSIS OF THE COMPLAINT
EXPRESSIONS

A. TRANSLATION

Chapter 2 has made evident that the principal form of complaint is
the God-lament. We shall now explore this expression in greater
detail. Those verses of the Psalter that qualify as complaints read as
follows:

6.4	And my soul is disturbed exceedingly,
	but you, Yahweh—how long?
10.1	Why, Yahweh, do you stand afar off;
	why do you hide in times of drought?[1]
13.2	How long, Yahweh? Will you forget me forever?
	How long will you hide your face from me?
22.2	My God, my God, why have you forsaken me?
	Why are you far from my crying,
	the words of my roaring?[2]
3	My God, I cry by day, but you do not answer,
	and by night, but I have no rest.
16b	But you set me in the dust of death.[3]
35.17a	Lord, how long will you look on?
39.6	Behold, you have made my days as
	handbreadths,
	and my lifetime is as nothing before you.
	Surely every man who stands firm is breath![4]

12   With rebukes you chasten a man for iniquity,
         and you dissolve, as a moth, what he desires.
      Surely every man is breath!

42.8 Deep calls to deep at the sound of your
         waterfalls;
      all your breakers and waves have overwhelmed
         me.

10   I will say to God, my rock,
      'Why have you forgotten me?
      Why do I go mourning under enemy
         oppression?'

43.2 For you are my fortressing God,
         why have you rejected me?
      Why do I go about mourning under enemy
         oppression?

44.10 Yet you have rejected and put us to shame,
         and you do not go out with our armies.

11   You cause us to turn back from the adversary,
      so that those who hate us take spoil for
         themselves.

12   You give us as sheep to be eaten,
         and scatter us among the nations.

13   You sell your people with no profit,
         and you do not gain from their sale price.

14   You make us a reproach to our neighbors,
         a derision and a ridicule to those around us.

15   You make us a byword among the nations,
         a laughing-stock among the peoples.[5]

20   But you have crushed us in a place of jackals,
         and you have covered us over with deep
         darkness.[6]

24   Arouse yourself! Why do you sleep, Lord?
      Awake! Do not reject forever!

25   Why do you hide your face?
      Why do you forget our misery and oppression?

60.3 O God, you have rejected and broken us down;
         you have been angry—restore us!

4   You have shaken the land, you have split it open.

	Heal its breaches, for it totters.[7]
5	You have shown your people severity;
	you have given us intoxicating wine to drink.
12	Have not you, O God, rejected us,
	so that you, O God, do not go out with our armies?
74.1	Why, O God, have you rejected us forever?
	Why does your anger smoke against the sheep of your pasture?
11	Why do you withdraw your hand,
	and keep your right hand back in your bosom?[8]
77.8	Will the Lord reject forever,
	and will he never again be favorable?
9	Has merciful devotion ceased forever?
	Has promise come to an end for all generations?
10	Has God forgotten to be gracious,
	or has he in anger shut away his compassion?[9]
79.5	How long, Yahweh? Will you be angry forever?
	Will your jealousy burn like fire?
80.5	Yahweh of hosts,
	how long will you fume against the prayers of your people?[10]
6	You have fed them with the bread of tears,
	and you have given them tears to drink in large measure.
7	You have made us a contention to our neighbors,
	and our enemies mock us.[11]
13	Why have you broken down its walls,
	so that all who pass by pluck it(s fruit)?
85.6	Will you be angry with us forever?
	Will you prolong your anger to all generations?
88.6	My soul is among the dead,
	like the slain who lie down in the grave,
	whom you remember no more,
	so they are cut off from your hand.[12]
7	You have put me in the lowest pit,
	in the dark places, in the depths.
8	Your wrath has weighed upon me,

and you have oppressed me with all your
        breakers.[13]

9   You have removed my friends far from me;
     you have made me an abomination to them;
     I am kept imprisoned and cannot go out.

15   Why, Yahweh, do you reject my soul?
     Why do you hide your face from me?

17   Your burning anger has overwhelmed me;
     your terrors have reduced me to silence.[14]

18   They surround me like water all the day;
     they have altogether encompassed me.

19   You have removed far from me lover and
        neighbor;
     my friends are the dark region.[15]

89.39 But you have rejected and despised;
       you have become furious with your anointed.

40   You have spurned the covenant of your servant;
     you have profaned his crown to the ground.

41   You have broken down all his walls;
     you have made his fortifications a ruin.

43   You have exalted the right hand of his
        adversaries;
     you have given all his enemies cause for
        rejoicing.

44   You even turn back the edge of his sword;
     and you do not cause him to stand in battle.[16]

45   You have put an end to the scepter of his
        splendor,
     and his throne you have hurled to the ground.[17]

46   You have shortened the days of his youth;
     you have covered him with shame.[18]

47   How long, Yahweh? Will you hide yourself
        forever?
     Will your wrath burn like fire?

50   Where are your former acts of merciful devotion,
        O Lord,
     Which you swore to David in your faithfulness?

90.3   You return man to the dust,

and you say, 'Return, O children of man'.
5   You sow them year by year;
     they become like grass which sprouts anew.[19]
8   You have placed our iniquities before you,
     and our secret (sins) in the light of your face.
13a   Return, Yahweh—how long?
102.11 Because of your indignation and wrath,
     for you have lifted me up and cast me away.
24   He has humbled my strength in the midst of my
          life;
     he has cut short my days.[20]
108.12 Have you not, O God, rejected us,
     so that you, O God, do not go out with our
          armies?[21]

B. THE COMPONENTS OF THE ANALYSIS

The analysis of these complaints is facilitated by the observation of several distinctions among their forms of expression. The most obvious criterion is syntactical: some verses are interrogative, others are declarative. This observation raises the questions: Do the texts display a distinction in meaning or force between the former and the latter? Do they aim at different purposes? Since I/We- and foe-laments in the Psalter rarely take the form of a question, it may also be worth considering whether the interrogative form lends a different nuance to the God-lament expressions.

Another distinction can be drawn among these complaints that relates to the semantic field of the verbs: some concern Yahweh's disposition toward the psalmist (e.g. Ps. 89.39); others focus on the mode of his intervention, or non-intervention, in the affairs of the psalmist (e.g. v. 41). This distinction in the God-lament is much like the one C. Westermann draws regarding the petitions of lament psalms: those requesting God to be favorable ('Hear!') and those requesting him to intervene ('Save!').[22] (To my knowledge Westermann does not apply this distinction to the lament section proper.) At times it is difficult to draw the line for this discrimination. For instance: can one distinguish in the verb עזב

(22.2) between the attitude of forsaking and the action of abandonment? Nevertheless, in most cases the distinction is clear and in the end proves to be helpful.

Once recognized this distinction raises such questions as: Do these psalms consistently associate a particular action of God with a particular disposition of God, and vice versa? Do the laments regarding God's disposition appear to be simply inferences from the nature of the psalmist's distress? Are there any God-lament psalms that consist solely of complaints of God's disfavor?

Those God-laments that speak of God's (non-)intervention can be subdivided according to the nature of God's role in the distress: in some he is considered to be passive (e.g. 74.11) and in others actively engaged (e.g. 89.41). This distinction can be easily perceived, though the line between complaints of Yahweh's disfavor and his passivity may not be so marked, as mentioned in connection with עזב. Questions emerging from this observation are: Are the psalmists consistent in the way they depict God's action in any given psalm, or do expressions presenting God as active and as passive appear side by side? Are there particular distresses wherein God is considered to have an active role but in others a passive one?

Having noted these general distinctions, it will be worth investigating any correlations between the syntax of God-laments and their semantic fields.

One could chart this material under the main headings of syntax (interrogative-declarative) or of semantic fields (disposition-intervention). Though the latter criterion is at times less distinct than the former, it is (by its very nature) more fundamental to meaning and so is given priority. The question and statement forms appear to give nuances to the basic meaning.

The charting of this material is simplified by the observation that virtually all language of active intervention occurs in the declarative (except Ps. 80.13, 'Why have you broken down ...?', and perhaps Ps. 6.4, 'How long [will you continue to chasten]?'), and all language of God's passivity appears in the interrogative. Statements, such as 'You do not answer' (22.3) and 'You do not go out with our armies' (44.10), may at first reading suggest God has been passive. These verses, however, merely negate God's positive action on behalf of the psalmist; they do not necessarily deny his hostile action against the psalmist. That the negative does not in itself exclude God's action altogether can be seen in the line that immediately follows Ps. 44.10: 'You cause us to retreat from the adversary'.

On the charts that follow, these abbreviations are used:

LC	a lament of the community
LI	a lament of the individual
pass	passive
ques	question
int	interrogative

C. THE ANALYSIS OF COMPLAINT TERMINOLOGY

1. The Language of God's Disposition

The laments of God's disfavor are much more standardized than those concerning his (non-)intervention. For the most part, the language describing God's disposition falls into four categories (in order of frequency): wrath, rejection, forgetting, and hiding the face. Since Pss. 77.8-10; 89.50; 90.8 contain other expressions peculiar to them, they will be treated in Chapter 6.

a. God's Wrath

The terms that refer to the divine wrath in the complaint psalms are אָנַף, אַף, חֵמָה, חָרוֹן, הַתעבר, זַעַם, קצף, עשׁן and קָנְאָה. כַּעַס appears once in a petition. To my knowledge, the only OT terms of wrath that the Psalms do not employ are זעף and רגז. Regarding the use the OT makes of these terms that compose the Hebrew semantic field for 'anger', B. Wiklander's conclusion seems to be a fair generalization: The various expressions for divine wrath 'can be freely combined and are clearly more or less synonymous, without regard to any "original" meanings'.[23]

Psalm	6	9-10	13	22	35	39	42-43	44	60
Category	LI	LC	LI	LI	LI	LI	LI	LC	LC
Disposition: Question: Interrogative			How long? Will .. forever? How long...?				Why ..? Why ..?	Why ..?	Have not ..?
Disposition: Question: Verb			— forget, hide face				have forgotten have rejected	hide face, forget	have rejected
Disposition: Statement: Verb								have rejected	have rejected have been angry
Intervention: Pass:Ques:Int		Why ..?		Why...?	How long...?			Why ..?	[will not ..?]
Intervention: Pass: Ques: Verb		stand afar off hide		have abandoned, are far	look on			sleep	[not go out]
Intervention: Active: Statement: Verb	(But you— how long) [will chasten]?			[do not answer] set (in dust of death)		have made (as hand-breadths) chasten (with rebukes) dissolve (as a moth)	(breakers & waves) have overwhelmed	put to shame [do not go out] cause to retreat give to be eaten scatter sell (cheaply) make (a reproach) make (a byword) have crushed have covered (w/darkness)	have broken down have shaken (the land) have split (it) open have shown (severity) have given (wine) to drink

Category	LC	LC	LC	LC	LC	II	LC	LC	II
Disposition: Question: Interrogative	Why.. forever?	Will..forever? Will..never? Has..forever? Has..to all generations? Has..? Has..?	How long? Will.. forever?	How long?	Will... forever? Will.. to all genera-tions?	Why...?	How long...? Will..forever? Will..? Where...?	How long?	
Disposition: Question: Verb	have rejected (anger) smoke	reject never be favorable (loyalty) ceased (word) come to an end forgotten to be gracious (in anger) shut away (compassion)	be angry (jealousy) burn (like fire)	fume	be angry prolong (anger)	reject hide face	— hide(yourself) (wrath) burn like fire are (loyalties)		
Disposition: Statement: Verb						remember (no more) [See 'wrath' below]	have rejected despised have become furious have spurned	placed (iniquities before you)	lifted up & cast away
Intervention: Pass:Ques:Int	Why..?								
Intervention: Pass:Ques:Vb	withdraw keep back								
Intervention: Active: Statement: Verb					have fed (w/tears) have given (tears) to drink have made a conten-tion (Why...) broken down?	put (in pit) (wrath) has weighed oppressed (w/waves) removed (friends) made (an abomination) (anger) overwhelmed (terrors) re-duced to silence surround (like water) encompassed removed (friend)	profaned broken down made (a ruin) exalted (foes) gladdened (enemies) turned back (sword) [do not cause to stand] put an end to hurled shortened (days) covered (w/shame)	return (to dust) say 'Return' sow (year by year)	humbled (strength) cut short (days)

אָנַף, with its nominal form אַף, is the word most often used in the OT to refer to anger. It appears to be distributed evenly over the whole OT. In the Psalms Yahweh's אַף is (to be) directed toward his enemies and toward his people in a comparatively equal number of instances. The noun form carries the dual reference of 'nose' and 'anger'. There may be a connection between these meanings in that anger can be detected by intense breathing or by a dilation of the nostrils. אַף is often used in connection with fire (e.g. Ps. 74.1; in 80.5 עשׁן is used by itself to signify Yahweh's anger).[24] All of these images intersect in Ps. 18.8b, 9: 'They trembled because he became angry (חרה). Smoke arose from his nostrils (אַף) and fire from his mouth consumed.'

The term קָנְאָה appears only once in the complaint psalms (79.5), where it is in parallel with אָנַף. In the prophets, the arousal of Yahweh's jealousy is usually connected with Israel's turning to other gods.[25]

חֵמָה is the second most frequent word employed to express 'anger'. As with אַף, it appears in all the major genres of the OT. Most lexicographers agree that this noun derives from יחם, 'to be hot', as corroborated by its frequent association with fire.[26] In its OT usage three distinct meanings appear: 'poison, venom' (six times), 'fiery wine' (four times), 'excitement, anger' (110 times).[27] These senses probably stem from the notion that one is made 'hot' under their influence. Thus חֵמָה probably connotes 'the hot inward excitement accompanying anger'.[28] It is often predicated with verbs that convey a concrete image: חֵמָה 'burns', it 'flares up', and it is 'poured out' like water.[29] In Ps. 88.8 חֵמָה is described as 'resting, weighing' (סמך) upon the psalmist, but the parallel line draws the picture of Yahweh's waves overwhelming him.

חרון is derived from חרה whose original meaning was probably 'to glow, to burn'.[30] The noun always refers to divine anger and in 35 of 41 occurrences appears in construct with אַף. Even when it is used alone the notion of anger is implied, and thus it is best translated 'burning anger'.[31] L.J. Wood's suggestion regarding the semantic distinctiveness of חרה may be correct: 'The meaning of the root differs from such words for "anger" as *'anap, za'am*, and *qatsap*, in that it emphasizes the "kindling" of anger, like the kindling of a fire, or the heat of the anger, once started'.[32]

Since it is uncertain whether הַעֲבֹר and עֶבְרָה were derived from עבר I ('to pass over'), one cannot be sure that they carry the nuance of 'a surpassing measure and/or excess'.[33] S.R. Driver's suggestion that these terms stem from a common root signifying 'the idea of *going beyond* due bounds'[34] is unlikely for it excludes the possibility of righteous anger.[35] J.A. Emerton[36] agrees with G.R. Driver[37] that עֶבְרָה has no connection with עבר I. He translates it simply as 'anger'. Except for two occurrences in the Pentateuch, עֶבְרָה appears only in the Latter Prophets and Writings. Among the complaint psalms it is used only in the communal psalms.

זַעַם is always used in poetic contexts, and aside from Num. 23.7f. is found only in the Latter Prophets and Writings. In the OT the verb seems to denote 'to curse' or 'to be angry' (the emotion behind the curse?).[38] The noun is generally employed to mean 'anger'. B. Wiklander believes the root זעם underwent a shift of meaning. Earlier it meant 'to curse', but its later application to contexts where Yahweh is portrayed as the righteous judge infused it with the meaning 'to be angry'.[39] Note for example Ps. 7, which praises אֵל זֹעֵם (v. 12) as the judge who protects the poor and punishes the oppressor. Among the complaint psalms it appears only in an individual lament of sickness (102.11; cf. 38.4). קֶצֶף, which almost always refers to divine anger, is in the Psalms restricted to the same laments of sickness.

כַּעַס, when referring to God's anger, appears only once in the complaint psalms (85.5). Form critically it is found in a petition, but it refers to the same divine anger that is the object of complaint in the God-lament immediately following, which uses אַנַף and אַף. In the OT the term usually signifies God's response to human conduct that is considered insulting to him, primarily because it violates the first and second commandments.[40] F. Stolz believes the term stems from the influence of Deuteronomistic theology.[41]

We now turn to the semantic field as a whole. When the OT speaks of anger, God is the subject three times as often as man. The name of God that is linked to his wrath is almost always 'Yahweh'.

God's wrath is often expressed by means of two images. When predicated with verbs of burning, it appears as a fire. When predicated with verbs of either pouring out (as a flood?) or drinking (as from a cup), it appears as a fluid.[42] In some instances these images combine (Lam. 2.4; Nah. 1.6; Isa. 42.25; cf. Ezek. 21.36; 22.31). In the complaint psalms God's anger is usually depicted as fire (עשן אף, 74.1; עשן alone, 80.5; כמו־אש חמתך, 89.47; תבער כמו־אש קנאתך 79.5). In Ps. 79 the imagery shifts from that of fire in the God-lament (v. 5) to that of a fluid in the petition immediately following: שפך חמתך. The fluid image may also be suggested in Ps. 88.17 by עלי עברו (cf. 42.8b = Jon. 2.4b; Ps. 124.4, 5).

One should not presume, as is often done, that the OT invariably presents God's wrath as his deliberate response to human sin. It is not always described as morally motivated,[43] nor is it necessarily considered comprehensible.[44] This need not imply that God's wrath was thought to be irrational. When it is encountered, appeal is made to God's revealed will. In the complaint psalms the motivation behind God's anger is, more often than not, unexpressed (Pss. 6; 60; 74; 80; 85; 88; 89; 102; cf. 30).[45] Even in those psalms where sin is acknowledged (79; 90), one detects a note of protest that the expression of wrath is considered excessive (see Chapters 6 and 7). Moreover, in the Psalms God's anger is never associated with beneficial chastisement; in fact, the two seem to be separable (6.2; 38.2).

The emotion of anger, particularly when used of God, usually entails a concrete manifestation (primarily that of punishment). Though these terms for anger in the complaint psalms clearly indicate an emotion, in most contexts the emotion is indistinguishable from its realization (60.3; 74.1; 79.5, 6; 80.5; 85.4-6; 88.8, 17; 89.47; 90.7, 9, 11; 102.11). Only in Pss. 6.2; 77.10; 89.39 (inferred from the Hithpael form) can one distinguish them. Nonetheless, one must not assume that the Hebrew terms for wrath always include the realization of the emotion. That sense may not be borne by the terms themselves but derived from their association with the divine subject. The notion of wrath burning (74.1; 79.5; 80.5; 89.47) probably refers to the fuming within the subject himself, rather than to the hardship experienced by the object.[46]

In the prophets God's expressions of anger against his people are generally considered to be temporary. But in the complaint psalms the question 'How long?' is frequently voiced (79.5; 80.5; 89.47; cf. '... forever?', 85.6). The question of extended duration also appears in 74.1 where לנצח is in the parallel line. (Note also 77.8-10.[47])

Among the complaint psalms, references to God's anger occur more frequently in the communal category (60; 74; 77; 79; 80; 85; 89; 90) than in the individual category (6; 88; 102; cf. 38).

b. God Rejecting

Of the 16 occurrences of זנח (Qal) in the OT, 10 appear in the complaint psalms. The other instances also occur in poetry: Lam. 2.7; 3.17, 31; Hos. 8.3, 5; Zech. 10.6. In Chronicles it appears 3 times in the Hiphil, which BDB regards as a later equivalent of the Qal stem.

The only occasion where it is certain that God is not the subject of the verb is Hos. 8.3: 'Israel has rejected what is good'.[48] Otherwise, the term is reserved for those instances that refer to God rejecting his people.

R. Yaron, noting that זנח appears 6 times without an object, suggests that the intransitive use should be considered as ordinary as the transitive one.[49] But it seems that this supposed intransitive use can be explained more readily by the appearance of this verb in poetic contexts than by the nature of the verb itself. In four of these supposedly intransitive instances other verbs that are normally transitive also lack an explicit accusative (מאס in Ps. 89.39; הוֹנָה, עָנָּה, רִדֵּם in Lam. 3.32-33). In Lam. 3.32 הוֹנָה appears a second time within this כ section of the acrostic and is followed by the object 'sons of man'. In other cases the object appears in a parallel line (44.10, where in several MSS of the Syriac זנח is translated with an explicit object; 74.1; 89.39). In Hebrew poetry an accusative is often stated in only one of the two parallel lines.[50] In Ps. 77.8ff. all the questions are stated absolutely with no mention of the object of God's disfavor. Also in 44.25, which follows a verse containing זנח, the statement 'you hide your face' is used without its frequently attached phrase 'from me/us'. (Note here the object also appears in the parallel line.) Therefore, from the evidence available it seems that זנח is used without an explicit object in poetic contexts, not because the verb itself is intransitive, but to give a peculiarly absolute force to the lament.

Yaron also considers the Akkadian *zenû* 'to be angry' to be a cognate of זנח (which H. Ringgren regards as 'not certain, but likely'[51]) and thus views its meaning as a likely translation of the Hebrew term. He notes that in 3 instances a verb denoting anger parallels זנח (60.3; 74.1; 89.39). It is doubtful, however, that these parallels are sufficient to equate זנח with its supposed Akkadian cognate. Rather, these parallel expressions of anger appear to comprise simply one of the several semantic fields that occur with זנח and that generally indicate a disruption in the divine-human relationship (ceasing to show favor, 77.8; hiding his face, 88.15; מאס, 89.39). 'Anger' is thus a part of the wider semantic field but not necessarily the precise meaning of זנח.

The restricted use of זנח suggests that it gained its meaning from its application in cultic contexts, where people lamented God's bringing disaster upon them. The term could then later be adopted by a prophet such as Zechariah to contrast God's former 'rejection' of his people with their future restoration (10.6). Lamentations, which is regarded by most scholars as a series of cultic laments,[52] uses זנח in the context of God 'rejecting' his sanctuary and handing it over (הסגיר) to the enemy (2.7; cf. 3.17, 31). Within the Psalms it appears only among the complaints since God is the grammatical subject in every case.

Three individual complaints use the term. One laments separation from the temple worship (42-43), another speaks out of lifelong suffering (88), and a third complains of God's withdrawal (77). In Ps. 42-43 זנח appears in the second recital of a lament-'refrain' (43.2), replacing שכח (42.10) which appeared in the first instance. In each case the verb contrasts sharply with the guardian title with which God is addressed: 'God, my rock, why do you forget?' and 'My fortressing God, why do you reject?' With the interrogative 'Why?' repeated in the parallel lines, both refrains imply a connection between God's adverse disposition and the psalmist's mourning of social oppression (a cause-effect relation?). In Ps. 88 the lament of rejection (v. 15) is a response to Yahweh's apparent disregard for the psalmist's prayer (v. 14). The Why? of

God's rejection is echoed in the parallel line by the Why? of God's hidden face. In Ps. 77 זנח begins a series of questions that ponder the unthinkable: 'Will the Lord reject forever?' This is paralleled with the possibility that he may never again show his favor and is followed by other expressions denoting a severance of divine mercy.

In the laments of the people, זנח occurs where Israel appears to have suffered a severe battle defeat (44; 60 [= 108]; 74; 89). In 44.10; 60.12 (= 108.12) זנח is paralleled by ולא תצא בצבאותנו. In both 44.10 and 89.39 it is this term that pivots the poem from praising to lamenting. זנח appears a second time in Ps. 44 in a negative petition with 'forever', paralleled by the lament, 'Why do you sleep?' (v. 24). Another 'Why?' lament complaining of God's hidden face and forgetfulness then follows. While in the first instance (vv. 10ff.) זנח is connected with God's active opposition, here it is associated with his negligence (v. 24-25). In Ps. 60.3 it is used with פרץ ('break down, through'), suggesting active hostility. As mentioned above, זנח is three times paralleled by words denoting God's anger (60.3; 74.1; 89.39).

A second term for 'reject' is מאס. As a rule, מאס with God as its subject is best translated 'reject', because the accusative refers to one whom God had chosen. In some contexts, however, where it is not a matter of the subject choosing between acceptance or rejection, an attitude or an emotion seems to be implied; thus, as BDB suggests, 'to despise' would be a more appropriate translation in these cases. As H. Wildberger notes, מאס should not be regarded as a technical term within a theological system of election.[53] In support of this he observes 17 non-theological uses of the term (though he admits this distinction at times is not a sharp one). Moreover, different contexts suggest different senses of the term and thus demand different translations (as the LXX shows).

מאס is used once with זנח in the complaint psalms (89.39). It may be distinguished in usage from זנח in that it is found in both poetry and narrative, and in the majority of cases man is the subject of the verb (43 of 72 instances in the Qal according to the count of Wildberger[54]).

A third term for 'reject' is נאר whose 'exact meaning', BDB notes, 'is uncertain; probably (from context) *abhor, spurn*'. It occurs only twice in the OT: Ps. 89.40 and Lam. 2.7. In the latter instance נאר occurs with two other verbs, all three with accusatives sharing 'referential identity':[55] זנח and הִסְגִּיר ('to deliver over'). In the complaint psalm it is paralleled by חלל, but the objects of these verbs differ: נאר is followed by ברית, and חלל by נזר ('crown'). In the verse preceding זנח is used along with מאס. Therefore, though the precise nuance of נאר escapes us, its general sense can be discerned from its association with terms of 'rejection'.

The basic meaning of השליך (used once in Ps. 102.11) is 'to throw, cast'. It 'is used in a wide variety of situations ranging from the physical act of throwing an object to the metaphorical use of abandoning or rejecting a person or thing'.[56] Though M. Cogan cites several convincing instances where השליך is best translated 'abandon, expose' (Gen. 21.15; Ps. 71.9; Ezek. 16.5; esp. Jer. 38.6, 9), he overstates his case when he calls it a technical term for exposure.[57] This sense is simply a figurative nuance derived from its basic meaning of 'to cast (away)'.[58]

Its use with God as subject and man as object is frequent, and it usually appears in contexts suggesting personal rejection. השליך מ(על) פנים occurs mainly in what are normally labelled Deuteronomistic passages (2 Kings 13.23; 17.20; 24.20 = Jer. 52.3; Jer. 7.15; 2 Chron. 7.20). In these instances the connection between man's sin and Yahweh's rejection is clear, as it is in Ps. 51.13. But in Ps. 71.9 (where השליך occurs by itself) the only apparent reason for the psalmist's abandonment is his old age. Thus, the interpreter should not presume that behind the language of Ps. 102.11b is the assumption that the psalmist has sinned against Yahweh. With נשא preceding השליך this verse suggests a lifting up and a throwing *down*. This would imply not simply a casting away or rejection, a meaning which is clear from the frequent use of this verb in rejection contexts, but also a casting down, in the sense of violent mistreatment.[59]

c. God Forgetting

Of the 102 times שכח appears in the OT, 33 are in the Psalter, the most occurrences in any OT book. God is the subject of the verb in 17 times in the OT, 9 of which are in the Psalms.[60]

In the lament sections of the lament psalms, שכח always occurs in a question form (19.2; 42.10; 44.25; 77.10; Lam. 5.20). In Ps. 44 the juxtaposition of 'Why ... do you forget?' and 'Why do you sleep?' (v. 24) suggests that God's forgetting is due to his negligence. Unlike most prophetic texts that use שכח, this psalm contrasts the people's not forgetting (vv. 18, 21) with God's forgetting. The accusative of שכח in Ps. 77.10 is not the psalmist but an infinitival phrase: 'to be gracious'. It is the fifth in a series of six questions regarding the absolute cessation of God's mercies.

In the petitions, שכח is preceded by the negative אל־ (Pss. 10.12; 74.19). The intent of these requests appears to be to call Yahweh's attention to his former commitment to the one praying. In Ps. 10 the petition responds to the presumption of the wicked that 'God has forgotten' (v. 11). If Ps. 9-10 is a unity (as will be argued in Chapter 6), this petition summons Yahweh to fulfill the praises sung of him in Ps. 9: Yahweh 'does not forget the cry of the afflicted' (// זכר, 9.13), and 'the miserable will not always be forgotten' (Niphal, 9.19).

In the prophets the possibility of God's forgetting depends on whether the message is one of salvation or judgment. In Isa. 49.14 the prophet apparently cites a lament of the people—'Yahweh has forsaken me (עזב); Yahweh has forgotten me'— but he then answers unequivocally in Yahweh's words, 'I will not forget you'. In this instance the prophet takes up a cultic lament and uses it as a platform from which to give his proclamation of salvation.[61] According to Hos. 4.6 Yahweh responds to the priests who have forgotten his instruction by asserting that he in turn will forget their children. This is the only instance outside of a lament context where the OT states that God forgets his people. Even here the prophet does so with a sense of astonishment: 'even I [will forget]!' This same action-of-man, response-of-Yahweh pattern is seen in the parallel line with מאס. Within this pattern, God's forgetting is clearly deliberate, and שכח should therefore be translated 'ignore'.

Should we suppose that the lament psalmists were always careful to restrict their use of שכח to this sense of 'ignoring', or could the term also include the possibility that the distress has actually passed from God's mind? The latter appears to be more suitable to the lament genre. As noted above in Ps. 44, the question of why God 'forgets' the people's misery is paralleled with the question of why God 'is sleeping' (vv. 24-25). Adjoining this complaint of God 'sleeping' are petitions that he 'arouse' himself and 'awake'. Yet the possibility of God's 'sleeping' is elsewhere explicitly denied by Israel's hymnody (Ps. 121.4). It would thus appear that the lamenter in the midst of his misery may actually question whether or not his distress has actually passed from God's mind, or he may simply wish to evoke a response from God with a rhetorical question.

Lamentations 5 contains probably the least ambiguous use of שכח in a lament context:

Lam. 5.20   Why do you always (לנצח) *forget* us?
              Why do you forsake (עזב) us
                  for such a long time (לארך ימים)?
        21   Turn us, Yahweh, back to yourself,
                  so that we may return;
              renew our days as of old,
        22   unless you have indeed rejected (מאס) us,
              and are exceedingly angry with us.

As the following petition and its subsequent qualification show, שכח in a question form need not imply forgetting in an absolute, complete sense.

Ps. 88.6 expresses the same semantic notion as שכח but instead employs זכר with a negative in a declarative sentence. The belief that God does not remember the dead is paralleled by: 'They are cut off from your hand'. The meaning of זכר is naturally of crucial importance for an understanding of שכח since the latter is a negation of the former. In his study of זכר B.S. Childs notes the inevitable connection between divine thought and divine action:

> God's remembering always implies his movement toward the object of his memory. This action varies in nature, and can be physical or forensic. The objective side of memory is accompanied, in differing degrees, by an internal reaction on God's part. The essence of

God's remembering lies in his acting toward someone because of a previous commitment.[62]

זכר, however, is not simply another word denoting intervention; as Childs himself notes: 'Although the objective side of God's memory is always present with varying emphasis, the importance of the subjective side should not be overlooked.'[63] The indivisible connection between God's thought and its concrete consequence is due to Israel's theology, not to the primary signification of זכר itself.

d. God Hiding His Face

S.E. Balentine in a thorough study of the hiding of the face of God in the OT[64] notes that only סתר, among the other verbs of the semantic category 'to hide', takes פנים as its object. Aside from Exod. 3.6 and Isa. 50.6; 53.3, הסתיר פנים always appears with God as its subject. The phrase is most frequent in poetry. In the Psalms it usually occurs in laments. The cause of the action is normally unspecified, and the protests raised by the psalmists suggest that the action is considered unjustified.[65] The frequent association of the phrase with questions of 'How long?' and '... forever?' conveys the impression that these psalmists did not perceive an imminent end to God's hiding. In the prophets the phrase appears in judgment contexts and less often in proclamations of salvation. The cause of God's hiding is always related to the sin of the people, and its termination is always in view.[66] The lament was almost certainly the original context, the phrase later being adopted by the prophets. The history of the phrase prior to its use in the OT corroborates this conclusion. In the Sumero-Akkadian literature the provenance of the equivalent expression was the lament.[67]

Because of the distinctive use of הסתיר פנים in each of the above contexts, attention will be focused on its appearance in the Psalms. In the lament sections (13.2; 44.25; 88.15), it occurs with an interrogative (twice with 'Why?', once with 'How long?'). It is twice paralleled by שכח once by זנח. In Ps. 13 this God-lament is associated with complaints concerning the psalmist's fruitless reflection and his enemy who has the upper hand (each complaint is prefaced with 'How long?'). The subsequent petitions for God to look and to answer, actions which are associated with the face, may serve as a direct response to this lament about God's hidden face. In Ps. 44.25 the phrase is collocated with 'Why do you sleep?' (v. 24). Since in Ps. 88 'Why do you hide your face from me?' (v. 15) follows 'I call to you, Yahweh, for help; in the morning my prayer comes before you' (v. 14), the phrase suggests that Yahweh has been ignoring the psalmist's petitions. In Ps. 89.47 סתר occurs in the Niphal, presumably with a reflexive meaning. It is paralleled by a reference to God's burning anger.

The phrase הסתיר פנים in the declarative perfect appears in the lament section of Ps. 10 (v. 11) but in the mouth of the wicked. It is this belief which gives them license to continue oppressing the unfortunate. Here it is used in parallel with God 'forgetting' and 'not seeing'. This citation is then followed by a petition for Yahweh to 'arise' and thus to prove this thought of the wicked to be presumptuous.

In the lament psalms the phrase also appears as a petition (27.9; 69.18; 102.3; 143.7), but always in the negative except for Ps. 51.11 ('Hide your face from my sins'). It is usually juxtaposed with an appeal for God to answer (ענה, Pss. 69; 102, also used with 'Turn your ear to me' and 'Hear', v. 2; 143). In Ps. 27 this negative petition is paralleled by other negative petitions relating to abandonment (נטש, עזב, באף, נטה).

The locution is used twice on occasions where it is viewed in retrospect, that is, in 'declarative praise'. In Ps. 30 the poet describes his past distress (sickness?, cf. vv. 3-4, 10) in terms of God hiding his face, his own response being one of dismay (נבהל, v. 8). The parallel line contrasts this with the prior period of Yahweh's favor, though curiously enough the cause of this reversal is not given. Although God's face was hidden, he intervened when the psalmist cried for help (v. 3). This is the only occasion in the Psalms where it is stated matter-of-factly that God hid his face from the psalmist (i.e., all other instances are cries from the depths; here it is viewed in [presumably] tranquil retrospect). Ps. 22 tells a very different story in retrospect. The first half of Ps. 22 laments a distress that is described in a fashion similar to the one of Ps. 30 (both employ language of being near death); and yet the latter half of Ps. 22, which presents itself in the form of declarative praise (see Chapter 7), declares, 'He did *not* hide his face from him' (v. 25)! (Here the phrase is found in parallel with 'he heard' [שמע] and in close connection with 'he did not despise' [בזה] and 'he did not detest' [שקץ].) The assertion is particularly surprising in view of the previous complaint of God's abandonment and remoteness (v. 2), silence (v. 3) and betrayal (v. 16). The diverging retrospective views of distress in Pss. 22 and 30 should caution us when attempting to pin down the precise usage of phrases in Hebrew poetry. It would appear that God's hiddenness is a fitting description of a near-death distress, but it need not however denote an absolute state.

Finally, the phrase appears in the declarative and is stated as an expression of praise of the sovereign Creator (104.29). As in Ps. 30, the response is one of dismay (נבהל). תסתיר פניך is used to signify a complete reversal of the Creator's act of providing (v. 28).

These observations on the use of הסתיר פנים permit the following inferences to be drawn for defining its meaning. The phrase expresses a disposition of the subject, or stated more concretely, it depicts a gesture of unwillingness to perceive or respond, thus conveying a sense of estrangement. The notion of estrangement can be seen by the phrase's frequent association with terms such as שכח, זנח, נטש, עזב, נטה, בזה, שקץ; the gesture of unwillingness to perceive or respond can be seen by the phrase's connection with references to the divine 'senses' and response. This is most evident in the imperatival use of the phrase where it is paralleled by other petitions for God to 'hear', 'turn his ear' and 'answer' (with an oracle?). In addition, in Ps. 13 the request for God to 'look' and 'answer' appears to counter the lament about God's hidden face. This nuance is also represented in thanksgiving, where it is said that God 'hears' the psalmist's cry (22.25), and in conspiracies of the wicked, who assert that God does 'not see' (10.11). In sharp contrast to the use of the phrase in the prophets, the psalmists consider this estrangement to be inexplicable, as is evident from the occurrence of the phrase in the form of a question.

Strictly speaking, הסתיר פנים signifies a disposition of estrangement or the gesture reflecting that disposition.

Nonetheless, because it has to do with God, it can also imply the inevitable consequences. God's hiding is always intertwined with the psalmist's personal and social distress (cf. esp. Ps. 13.2-3). It means that the psalmist is left alone without the possibility of God's help (e.g. 44.25; 88.14-15). The phrase by itself may suffice as a description of dire distress (30.8). The consequences of God's hidden face are spelled out most clearly in the two instances where the application of the phrase extends beyond a specific individual or people—it becomes a universal condition. In Ps. 10.11 the 'wicked' assert their belief that 'he has hidden his face; he will never see it' (cf. v. 13). Their statement, especially since it is not addressed to God or the cultic community, would not have been colored by any attempts to integrate it into a 'theology'—their interests are strictly ultilitarian. (Note that אל is used.) Since it is believed that God does not perceive the actions of men (cf. v. 13), the helpless are at the mercy of those who would oppress them. In Ps. 104.29 God's hiddenness entails nothing less than the cessation of what is needed to sustain life.

2. The Language of God's (Non-) Intervention

This language is much less standardized than the terminology concerning God's disposition. The verbs are peculiar to the particular distress they are describing.

a. God Active

The laments of God's active intervention in the affairs of the psalmist occur, with only two exceptions (Pss. 6.4; 80.13), in the declarative. The complaints of the individual, by and large, concern the imminence of death. Ps. 88 is certainly the most descriptive of this form of distress. The psalmist portrays Yahweh's affliction of him by means of four images that interweave with each other. The first two images of drowning and of darkness are combined in the term בּוֹר, into which God has placed the psalmist (v. 7). It of course bears associations with Sheol (vv. 4-5; cf. 30.4, // שׁאול; 28.1; 143.7). This metaphor is described further as 'the deepest' cistern, the 'dark places', and the 'depths'. The notion of drowning is developed in v. 8 (cf. 2 Sam. 22.5, the משברים of death), v. 17 (on עבר as being overwhelmed by a flood see Ps. 42.8, discussed below), and v. 18. The image of darkness is mentioned again at the psalm's close where it is said to have become the psalmist's only friend. The third image used to described God's affliction of the psalmist is that of social ostracism (vv. 9, 19), which has gone to the extent that he describes himself as an 'abomination' to them. The final image is that of Yahweh's wrath, which is depicted as an active force—not simply as a mode of his disposition—that 'weighs' or 'leans upon' (סמך על) the psalmist (v. 8). In vv. 17-18 his anger is presented as a burning flood.

Ps. 22.16 complains of Yahweh setting the psalmist 'in the ashes of death', which continues the image of dryness in the verse. The poet of Ps. 42.8, with his threefold use of the possessive pronoun, emphasizes that it is Yahweh who has overwhelmed or drowned him as with a flood. (Cf. Jon. 2.3-4 which with almost identical language draws an explicit connection between the waves sweeping over him and the 'depths of Sheol', v. 3.) In Ps. 102.24 the psalmist laments that Yahweh has humbled his strength and cut short (קצר, as in a harvest?) his life. Two complaint psalms express perplexity at the futility of human existence. Ps. 39 bemoans the brevity that Yahweh has given to life ('as handbreadths', v. 6), and laments that even what beauty does exist in one's life Yahweh consumes as a moth (v. 12). No attempts are made to interpret this as divine discipline (as in Ps. 94.12; Job 5.17; Prov. 3.11-12; Deut. 8.5). Ps. 90, a communal psalm, laments the barrenness of life: each generation lasts but a few fleeting moments (vv. 3-6) and even they are colored with fear (נבהל, vv. 7-8, 11), toil (v. 10), and decay (v. 9).

The laments of God's active intervention in the corporate psalms primarily reflect occasions of a battle defeat. Ps. 44 appears to speak from the viewpoint of the defeated army. The lament moves from Yahweh's causing Israel to retreat to his handing the army over to the adversaries, and then to his making a laughingstock of them. This narrative lament climaxes in v. 20 with 'but you have crushed us ...'[68] Ps. 60 mentions the hardships Yahweh has inflicted on the people, and speaks of their staggering effects in the image of Yahweh's making his people drunk (v. 5). In Ps. 89

Yahweh's action is presented as a direct violation of the Davidic covenant. To do this the psalmist employs highly expressive language. Yahweh 'profanes' the royal covenant (v. 40), which is an act that conflicts with his express statement contained in the preceding hymnic portion of the psalm (v. 35). Instead of exalting the Davidic king (vv. 18, 20), he exalts their enemies (v. 43). In this psalm, Yahweh breaks the covenant, destroys their defenses, exalts their enemies (an assertion that goes beyond what is said of the enemies in Ps. 44) and debases the king's splendor. Ps. 80 does not mention a battle defeat specifically, but certainly marauding bands had free play (vv. 13-14). This narrative lament focuses on the sorrow Yahweh has given the people. Verse 13, being the only explicit instance where God's active intervention is made into a question, may underline the psalmist's perplexity as to why God should 'break down' (פרץ, cf. Pss. 60.3; 89.41) their defenses and so give free access to foreigners. In each of these psalms, except Ps. 60, Yahweh is said to have deliberately put his people to shame before their neighbors (44.14-15; 80.7; 89.43).

b. God Passive

As already noted, at times the distinction between complaints regarding God's disposition and those regarding his inactivity is difficult to make. Hence some of the terms discussed here may also touch on the nature of Yahweh's disposition.

The psalmists use רחוק twice (10.1; 22.2) to express the notion that God seems to be remote. In Ps. 10.1 God 'stands' (עמד) at a 'distance' (ברחוק). This verb suggests the complaint is aimed at Yahweh's inactivity rather than at the nature of his disposition. In 22.2-3 Yahweh's remoteness from the psalmist's cry for help (reading משועתי) is described further by the statement that Yahweh has 'not answered' the psalmist by giving him 'rest' from his distress. Most often רחוק appears in the petition to God that he 'be not far off', that is, that he be near to 'help' (22.12, 20; 38.22-23; 71.12; cf. 35.22). Since the antonym, 'to help', is an action, it is probable that God's being at a distance points to his inactivity, not to his disposition.

Parallel to this complaint about Yahweh's 'standing at a distance' in Ps. 10.1 is one concerning Yahweh's 'hiding' (עלם

Hiphal). This term is semantically related to סתר, but they differ in two respects. First, סתר is always collocated with terms that refer to Yahweh's disposition toward the psalmist: forgetting, rejecting, and being angry. Second, the direct objects and the relational contexts of these verbs differ. To 'hide the face' means to sever incoming and outgoing communication with someone with whom there has been a personal relationship. But the object of העלים is most often the eyes of the subject. This idiom means to disregard a matter with the result that justice is not executed (Lev. 20.4; Deut. 22.1ff.; 1 Sam. 12.3; Isa. 58.7; Ezek. 22.26; Prov. 28.27). In none of these of these instances is a prior relationship with the person concerned presupposed. Hence, in two places where it is used of God's disregarding the people's words and actions of prayer (Isa. 1.15; Lam. 3.56), it probably does not connote the personal overtones that 'hiding the face' would.

In view of the above, the question of reproach in Ps. 10.1 may carry a particular sting. In Ps. 9 the psalmist recites the praises of Yahweh as the righteous judge who acts justly by delivering the oppressed, but then in Ps. 10 he describes rampant oppression, which thus calls into question these praises. Thus this question of why Yahweh hides in times of trouble may, by the use of this idiom, suggest that the Judge has hid his eyes from his own justice.[69]

The complaint of Ps. 35 consists of two words: כַּמָּה תִּרְאֶה (v. 17a; cf. v. 22). In this complaint the psalmist acknowledges that Yahweh 'looks on' but the rhetorical question implies that he should do more than merely observe. The action that the psalmist desires is described in the preceding verses. After noting that his praise would consist of celebrating Yahweh as the one who rescues the afflicted (v. 10), the psalmist describes how malicious witnesses afflict him (vv. 11-16). That Yahweh sees oppression and should then intervene is a fundamental of Israel's faith (Exod. 3.7f.; cf. Ps. 106.44ff.).

The image of God 'sleeping' in the Psalms is unique to Ps. 44.24. In Ps. 121.4 it is said expressly that God does not sleep. Ps 78.65 uses the image of Yahweh awaking 'as from sleep'. This should not be taken to imply that Yahweh sleeps; the parallel expression depicts a warrior drunk from wine. The point of comparison is the dramatic turn from no action to action. (See further the discussion of Ps. 44 in Chapter 6.)

In Ps. 74.11 a complaint against Yahweh's withdrawal of his hand follows a lament regarding the foe's continual blasphemy. This implies that the complaint concerns Yahweh's restraint in punishing Israel's and his enemies.

Mention should be made that one cannot infer the psalmist's perception of the nature of God's intervention (whether active or passive) from the language of God's disposition alone. For example, in Ps. 13, where God's active/passive role is not spelled out, the terms 'forget' and 'hide the face' may seem to suggest that Yahweh has simply turned away from the psalmist. But in other laments that do describe the nature of God's activity, mention of God's 'forgetting' (42.10; 44.25) is collocated with descriptions of his active intervention (42.8; 44.11ff.). Mention of God's 'rejecting' (44.10; 88.15; 89.39) also appears with descriptions of his active intervention (44.11ff.; 88.7ff.; 89.41ff.).

D. THE COMPLAINT IN A QUESTION FORM

As noted in Chapter 2 nuances can be given to the more basic meaning of the complaint when it appears as a question.

לָמָּה is the most frequent interrogative, occurring 11 times in 7 psalms. In all but one of these psalms (Ps. 80) it is the sole interrogative of the God-lament. In these lament contexts למה is not simply a request for information. If that were its sole aim then adjoining petitions for change would be out of place. J. Barr, in a thorough study of 'Why?' in biblical Hebrew, notes that 'in the great majority of cases, when Hebrews asked "Why?", they asked it because there was something in the situation, as they saw it, that was deeply wrong'.[70] Concerning the use of למה in the Psalms, he notes that 'the Psalmists characteristically complain that God has neglected them, not that he has been excessively generous—not, at least, within the "Why?" questions'.[71] We shall see in our closer examination of the complaints in Chapters 6 and 7 that sentences introduced with למה imply that the psalmist finds Yahweh's conduct inexplicable.

'How long?' appears 8 times in 7 psalms, either by itself as the only interrogative of the God-lament or else followed by an imperfect verb which introduces a separate question (3 times).[72] Once it is used in conjunction with למה (Ps. 80). 'How long?' is also not simply a request for information, such that if God actually were to answer with a duration of time, the psalmist would be satisfied that his question was answered. It functions rhetorically as an expression of urgency, suggesting, 'This has gone on long enough!' (See further Chapter 4.)

In most cases, the imperfect verbs associated with these interrogatives should probably be translated in the indicative mood, not with a modal verb. For example, Ps. 44.25 should be translated as,

44.25   Why do you hide your face?
         Why do you forget our misery and oppression?

and not as,

25   Why would you hide your face?
      Why would you forget our misery
      and oppression?

Verse 10 similarly laments God's disposition but does so in a declarative form: 'Yet you have rejected'. Both v. 10 and v. 25 concern God's disfavor, but what the former asks the latter simply declares. The psalmist expresses God's disfavor as a real condition. The lament, 'Why do you sleep?' (44.24), is also best translated in the indicative since it is enclosed by commands for Yahweh to awake.

A modal verb may be appropriate in questions such as, 'How long? ... forever?', where the action of the verb is pushed to the extremes of time and of intensity. For example, Ps. 79.5 might best be translated,

79.5   How long, Yahweh? Would you be angry
         forever?
      Would your jealousy burn like fire?

This type of question, by pushing God to the extremes, constrains him to answer with 'No!', and thus to demonstrate the reversal in due course.

The other lament psalm motif that often appears in the form of a question is the so-called 'motivation for Yahweh to intervene', which endeavors to persuade God to act on the psalmist's behalf (e.g. Pss. 6.6; 10.13; 79.10; 88.11ff.; 89.49).[73] The appearance of some God-laments in a question form thus appears to underscore their persuasive tone.

Chapter 4

THE DISTRESSES REFLECTED IN COMPLAINT PSALMS

A. INTRODUCTION

A question that emerges from the results of Chapter 2 is, Why do some psalmists appeal by affirming praise (psalms of plea) and others by charging God with denying the praise traditions (psalms of complaint)? Is there a consistent set of criteria according to which psalmists express plea or complaint? More specifically, since complaint is the more radical form of expression, the one antithetical to praise: On what grounds do psalmists charge God with denying praise traditions?

To answer this we shall first look at the distresses reflected in the laments to see if there are particular forms of affliction that aroused complaint. In the next chapter we shall look at what traditions these distresses call into question, such that a psalmist would feel justified to complain to God. We shall also attempt to discover why God is charged with negligence in some complaints and why he is charged with hostility in others. Our answer to this last question should give us insight into how the psalmists interpreted life's distresses in light of their traditions.

We will now turn to the question, What are the distresses that call the praise traditions into question? Our best hope of answering this would be to compare and contrast the psalms of complaint and the psalms of plea to note which distresses correlate predominantly with the psalms of complaint. This should reveal those distresses that give cause for complaint. We must say 'predominantly' for we cannot assume that the form of distress dictated which form of appeal must appear. Even with conventional language we cannot presume that the appeal would have been predictable solely on the basis of the distress. Such a study should therefore reveal the kinds of distresses in which most psalmists complain. This need not imply that psalmists *must* complain if they encounter these circumstances.

In the analysis that follows we shall see that there appears to be a high correlation between the expression of complaint and two characteristics of the occasions reflected in these psalms. One concerns the intensity of the distress, the other the duration of the distress. Accompanying the God-lament are usually references to a near-death distress (in the individual laments) or a national disaster (in the communal laments), which has persisted for some time.

B. THE INTENSITY OF THE DISTRESS

1. The Laments of the Individual

The psalmist's proximity to death can be expressed in the following forms.

a. Death as Present

22.16b   You set me in the dust of death.
(Cf. v. 21a, 'Rescue my life from the sword',
and other verses that describe extreme physical
suffering, vv. 15-16a, 17b.)

88.4b   My life draws near to Sheol.

5   I am counted with those descending to the pit;
I have become like (כ) a man without strength.

6   My soul is among the dead,
like (כ) the slain who lie down in the grave,
whom you remember no more,
so they are cut off from your hand.

7   You have put me in the lowest pit,
in the dark places, in the depths.

143.3   For the enemy has pursued my life;
   he has crushed my life to the ground;
   he has made me dwell in dark places,
   like (כ) those long dead.

It is difficult to determine whether these psalmists describe themselves as actually being in the sphere of 'death' or merely at death's door. In Ps. 88, for example, does הגיע ל (v. 4b) mean 'to draw near to' or 'to arrive at'? In v. 5 the psalmist simply likens himself (כ) to a dead man and speaks of how others, including God, 'regard' (נחשב) him, but in v. 7 he speaks of being cast into the dark depths, an image pointing to the realm of the dead.[1] How are we to interpret these and other such allusions to 'death'? In the mind of the psalmists, was this realm of death a literary image or a real state of affairs?

This question is addressed by C. Barth in his monograph, *Die Errettung vom Tode in den individuellen Klage- und Dankliedern des Alten Testaments* (1947). He observes that the individual laments generally speak of being near death, not actually in 'death' itself:

> The situation of those in distress is comparable (*vergleichbar*) to that of the dead; but it is not equal (*gleich*) to it.... In each case the experience of the condition of death is only a partial and limited one.... Further it must be remembered that the one in distress never identifies himself directly with a dead person.[2]

The psalmists may compare themselves to the dead, speak of their immediate vicinity to death, or refer to death as a threat, but their petitions to Yahweh indicate that it is not too late for him to act. This, however, is not the case for the dead, whose fate is sealed (Pss. 88.11-13; 6.6; Isa. 38.18-19). Hence Barth acknowledges that these lamenters experience the nearness of death, not death itself.

We would expect the narrative praise psalms, which view the distresses of the lament psalms in retrospect, to describe such near-death distresses in a similar manner. While much of the imagery is similar, the narrative praise psalms sometimes speak of being freed from 'death', not simply from a near-death experience.

30:4   Yahweh, you brought up my soul from Sheol;
        you revived me from those descending to the pit.
116:8   Indeed, you rescued my soul from death,
        my eye from tears,
        my foot from stumbling.

Two lament psalms contain similar expressions, but since these expressions are prefaced with vows of praise, they are to be regarded as praise said in anticipation of deliverance.

56.14   For you have rescued my soul from death
        (Have you not delivered my feet from
        stumbling?),
        that I may walk before God in the light of the
        living.
86.13b You have rescued [or 'will rescue'] my life from
        the depths of Sheol.

These verses signify how the psalmist would describe his distress *after* deliverance took place. Since this is proleptic praise, these expressions should be considered along with those of the narrative praise psalms, not with those of the laments.

Barth agrees that the similarity of allusions to death in the praise and lament psalms suggests that the narrative praise psalms view in retrospect the same distress as the laments: 'The circumstance that the laments also contain hints in this direction thus suffices to show that it is the distress of the lament to which these problematic expressions [of deliverance from death in the praise psalms] refer.'[3]

If both the lament and praise psalms refer to the same form of distress, how are we to make sense of this discrepancy between near-death and in-death descriptions? Barth postulates that underlying these allusions to death is a form of thinking different from our own, which some have called 'primitive mentality':

> In the thinking of the ancient oriental people ... even
> this nearness counts as a real experience of death. Only
> in a limited extent, perhaps only at one point, the one in
> distress comes into contact with the reality of death; but
> just that suffices, for him to experience the entire reality
> of death.[4]

Since the Oriental in his way of thinking sees the whole in the part,
once a man was under the slightest influence of death (e.g.,
sickness) he considered himself 'in death'. If a certain course
appears inevitable, the psalmist sees himself as already at the end of
that course.[5] In support of this supposition, Barth appeals to E.
Cassirer's *Die Begriffsform im mythischen Denken* (1922):

> The similarity is 'never conceived as a "mere"
> relationship, which may perhaps have its origins only in
> our subjective thinking, but is immediately interpreted
> back to a real identity: things cannot appear similar
> without being somehow one in their nature'.[6]

Thus, Barth believes that both the lamenter and the one offering
thanks perceive themselves as actually being in the sphere of
'death'. The reticence of the lamenters to speak explicitly of being
in death may be explained by this 'primitive mentality': they feared
what they regarded to be the inevitable consequences of the spoken
word.

This hypothesis of primitive mentality and some of E. Cassirer's
work in particular comes under review in J.W. Rogerson's
Anthropology and the Old Testament (1978).[7] According to this
theory of primitive mentality,

> ... the yellowness of a book would be perceived as an
> outstanding quality of the object, and if another object,
> not a book, were perceived, which was also yellow,
> mythopoeic thought would presume that there was a
> connection between the two things in virtue of their
> yellowness. In turn, this would affect the practice of
> magic; for by affecting one object, one would also be

affecting the whole class of objects which, for example, had yellowness as a quality.[8]

Thus, a similarity between two objects or states would indicate some ontological connection between them. But Rogerson notes that this theory of primitive mentality is based on conjectures postulated prior to actual anthropological fieldwork. He mentions several studies that show that 'primitives' are much more capable of empirical reasoning than had been recognized previously. Thus, the supposition is unlikely that the ancients were simply unable to perceive the distinction between similarity and identity.

In the case of the allusion to death in the Psalms, we cannot assume that the Israelite poets were unable to distinguish between a psalmist's suffering consequences similar to death and his being identified with the dead. To understand this language referring to 'death', we must begin with the clear statements of the psalmists. It was a given that Yahweh does not intervene for the dead. Thus, the mere fact that these lamenters still petition for Yahweh's help and hope for an answer implies that they distinguish themselves from the dead. Perhaps the most apt interpretation of this language is that the psalmists' distresses have gone to such an extent that they feel themselves already suffering the consequences of death, or at least consequences similar to death. We will see below that the strongest point of comparison between these lamenters and the dead is their inability to praise God.

It therefore seems more likely that the discrepancy between the references to death in the laments and in the narrative praise psalms is not to be explained from the side of the lamenters, namely that they feared the consequences of the spoken word. Rather, the praise psalmists may simply be indicating that the logical end of their distresses would be death. In order to express the highest praise, one might expect them to speak of rescue not simply from the distress as it currently stands but from its ultimate finale. Rather than saying, 'You have rescued me from enemies who plotted my death', or, 'You have rescued me from a distress that would have resulted in death', they assert, for the full force of their praise, 'You have delivered me from death'.

As noted above, the proleptic narrative praise of Pss. 56 and 86 describes the psalmists' deliverance as 'a rescue from death'. It cannot be assumed in each case, however, that the psalmist implies that he is describing his current distress as one of death. It may simply indicate that the logical end of his distress would be death. Noting that both of these psalms also refer to enemies seeking the psalmist's life (56.7; 86.14), the most that can be asserted with certainty regarding the immediate distress is that there exists the threat of death. (See the section below, 'Death Threatened by an Enemy'.)

b. Death as Imminent

39.11   Remove your plague from me;
         I am perishing (כלה) from the blow of your
           hand.

     14   Look away from me, so that I may smile again,
         before I go and am no more.

41.6   My enemies speak evil against me:
         'When will he die and his name perish?'

     9b   And they say, 'He has lain down, never to rise
         again.'

102.12   My days are like an evening shadow,
         and I wither like grass.

     24   He has humbled my strength in the midst of my
         life;
         He has cut short my days.

     25a   I say, 'My God, do not take me away in the
         midst of my days.'
         (Extreme physical suffering is described in
         vv. 4-8.)

In Ps. 102, as distinct from Pss. 22, 88 and 143, the psalmist does not describe himself as already suffering the consequences of death. In v. 12, however, he portrays himself as being in the 'twilight' of his life.

Though one may not presume from 39.11, 14 alone that the psalmist considers death imminent, the opening reflections on the evanescence of life (vv. 6-7a) certainly put the psalmist's own distress in this light.

In Ps. 41.6, 9b we hear of the psalmist's nearness to death from the mouth of his enemies. His illness has made him bedridden. It may be, however, that death is not necessarily an inevitable consequence since his 'enemy does not shout in triumph over' him as yet (v. 12b).

c. Death as a Motive for Yahweh's Intervention

6.6   For there is no remembrance of you in death;
        in Sheol who will give you thanks?
        (Cf. v. 3, '... I am feeble; heal me because my
        bones are terrified'.)

13.4b   Enlighten my eyes, lest I sleep the death.

28.1   To you, Yahweh, I call;
            my rock, do not be deaf to me,
        lest you be silent to me,
            and I be like those descending to the pit.

88.11   Do you perform wonders for the dead?
        Do the 'ghosts' rise to praise you?

12   Is your merciful devotion recounted in the grave,
        your faithfulness in the place of destruction?

13   Are your wonders known in the darkness,
        or your righteousness in the land of
            forgetfulness?

143.7   Answer me quickly, Yahweh;
            my spirit has wasted away.
        Do not hide your face from me,
            or I shall be like those descending to the pit.

Pss. 6.6 and 88.11-13 suggest that if the course of events remains unchanged, God would lose a worshipper. Since God's praise and the psalmist's life are considered to be correlative,[9] the implication is that it is in God's own interest to restore the psalmist to health.

Pss. 13.4, 28.1 and 143.7 state simply that the psalmist would die, if the course of events remained unchanged. It may be inferred from other expressions in these psalms, however, that these motivational clauses lead to the same implication as noted in Pss. 6 and 88. Certain phrases presuppose an established relationship between God and the psalmist (13.4a; 28.1a; 143.1b, 2a, 10a, 11b, 12), wherein the psalmist responds with trust and praise (13.6; 28.6-8; 143.8, 11a).

d. Death in the Image of a Flood

42.8   Deep calls to deep at the sound of your
        waterfalls;
   all your breakers and waves have
        rolled over (עבר) me.

69.2   Save me, O God,
   because waters have come up to my neck.

3   I sink in the muddy depths,
     where there is no foothold;
   I have come into the deep waters,
     and the torrent flows over me.

15   Rescue me from the mud and do not let me sink;
   let me be rescued from those who hate me
     and from the deep waters.

16   Do not let the torrent flow over me,
     nor the deep swallow me up,
   nor the pit shut its mouth over me.
   (Physical pain is suggested by the terms נכה
   [Hi.], 'smitten', v. 27; חלל, 'wounded', v. 27;
   עני וכאב, 'pain and distress', v. 30.)

88.8   Your wrath has weighed upon me,
   and you have oppressed me with all your waves.

17   Your anger has rolled over (עבר) me;
   your terrors have silenced me.

18   They flow around me like water all the day;
   they have engulfed me altogether.
   (See also v. 7b above.)

The realm of death in the Psalms is often portrayed as a flood or as deep waters.[10] In Ps. 88 God's wrath is depicted as waters engulfing the psalmist. At times one is made to think of the waves of the great sea (v. 8b), at times of the depths of a cistern (v. 7b).

The distress has developed to the extent that the psalmist already feels himself overwhelmed (עבר, v. 17) and therefore drowning. (The notion of being reduced to silence in v. 17 also connotes a condition of death.[11]) In Ps. 42 the poet speaks of the torrents from Mt. Hermon (v. 7) as the floods that overwhelm (עבר) him.

In Ps. 69 various images intermingle but the picture of a cistern is dominant ('the pit' and 'the muddy depths'). The 'deep waters' (vv. 3, 15) may include a reference to the primeval chaotic floods, while שבלת indicates a flowing stream. Although Ps. 69 shares with Pss. 42 and 88 in this water imagery, it is less definite regarding the extent to which the psalmist is overwhelmed. In vv. 2-3a the psalmist is up to his neck in water and his feet sink in mire; in v. 3b the torrent flows over him (ושבלת שטפתני). But in v. 16 he prays to avoid this same fate ('Do not let the torrent flow over me', אל־תשטפני שבלת מים) and also to avoid being forever trapped in the cistern.

e. Death as a Shadow over Human Existence

39.6 Behold, you have made my days as
     handbreadths,
     and my lifetime as nothing before you.
     Surely every man who stands firm is breath!

7a   Man moves about as a phantom ...

89.48 Remember how transient I am.
     For what futility you have created all the sons of
     man!

49   What man can live and not see death?
     Will he deliver his life from the hand of Sheol?

90.3   You return man to the dust,
     and you say, 'Return, sons of man!'

5   You sow them year by year;
     they become like grass which sprouts anew.

6   In the morning it flourishes and sprouts anew;
     in the evening it withers and dries up.

10   Our lifespan is seventy years,
     or if we have the strength eighty years,
    but their hurry is toil and trouble,
     for soon they pass and we fly away.

In Pss. 39 and 89 this concern over human transience is not the chief cause of distress. As noted already, in Ps. 39 the psalmist's personal affliction (vv. 11, 14) seems to have engendered these reflections. In Ps. 89 the overriding distress is a battle defeat (see below). The verses noted above simply underline the urgency of the 'How long?' of the previous verse (v. 47). Even in Ps. 90, this musing may reflect a particular period of depression in Israel's history (see the exegesis in Chapter 6).

The image of life as a 'breath' in Ps. 39 connotes the brevity and frailty of life. One can be sure life will not be long lasting, but one cannot be sure of the precise moment it will vanish. The picture of man as a צלם can be elucidated from Ps. 73.20: human existence has as much substance as images in a dream. In Ps. 89 focus is laid upon the brevity and futility (שוא, 'emptiness') of life and the inevitability of death. In Ps. 90 human existence is nothing but a cycle (as implied by the repeated שוב) ending in death. Its duration is fleeting and even those moments leave nothing of permanence behind (cf. also the petition of v. 17b).

f. Death Threatened by an Enemy

7.3	Lest he tear my throat like a lion, dragging me away with none to deliver.
31.14	For I hear many whispering threats from round about; while they conspire together against me, they scheme to take my life (cf. v. 5a). (Physical suffering is suggested in v. 11.)[12]
35.4a	Let those who seek my life be ashamed and humiliated. (The net/pit prepared for the psalmist [v. 7] appears to be one of 'destruction' [שואה, v. 8].)
38.13	Those who seek my life lay traps; those intent on harming me threaten ruin and devise deception all the day. (Vv. 3-11 imply an extreme debilitating illness.)
40.15 = 70.3	Let them together be ashamed and humiliated, who seek my soul to snatch it away;

          let them shrink back in disgrace,
             those who would delight in my ruin.
          (The phrase 'to snatch it away' is absent in
          70.3.)

54.5a   For strangers have arisen against me,
             and violent men have sought my life.

55.5   (In v. 4 the enemies harangue the psalmist.)
          My heart trembles within me,
             and the terrors of death have fallen upon me.

6   Fear and trembling have come upon me,
             and horror has gripped me.
          (Though the remainder of the psalm describes the
          enemies' attack as verbal [vv. 13, 22], these foes
          are also labelled 'men of bloodshed' [v. 24].)

56.7   They conspire, they lurk, they watch my
             footsteps,
             while they wait (to take) my life.

59.4a   For behold, [men of bloodshed] lie in ambush
          (ארב) for my life.

71.10   For my enemies have spoken against me,
             and those watching my life have deliberated
             together,

11   saying, 'God has forsaken him;
             pursue and seize him because there is none to
             help.'

83.5   They say, 'Come, let us obliterate them as a
             nation,
             that the name of Israel be remembered no more.'
          (Ps. 83 is a corporate lament.)

86.14a   O God, arrogant men have arisen against me,
             and a band of violent men have sought my
             life.

The final type of occasion in which death is in view is where foes threaten the life of the psalmist. In most cases the enemies are said to 'seek' (בקשׁ) the psalmist's life (35.4; 38.13; 40.15=70.3; 54.5; 63.10; 86.14). In the Psalter this phrase is used to indicate more than simply the intent to gain possession of the psalmist himself or of his goods—the aim is murder.[13]

Of the 13 psalms in this category only one is a complaint psalm. Thus, there is no connection between the God-lament and the threat of death by enemies, as there is between the God-lament and the preceding expressions relating to death. One may therefore suppose that the intention of, and perhaps even the attempt(s) of, others to inflict injury does not in itself constitute grounds for an expression of complaint.[14] In the psalms listed here there is no suggestion that the psalmist's life is already near to death, as in the other categories above.

g. Conclusion

The occurrences of a God-lament show a high degree of correlation with expressions that depict the psalmist near to death. The external threat of death from adversaries does not appear to evoke such language of complaint. The only individual psalm of complaint not reflecting such an experience is Ps. 35. The only individual psalms of plea to be included are Pss. 28, 69, and 143.

2. The Laments of the Community

The descriptions of distress in the laments of the community are not as stylized as they are in the laments of the individual. With the individual laments the descriptions of distress are usually brief and highly figurative, and thus comparisons of the actual wording prove helpful. Each communal lament, however, seems to describe a distinct type of occasion, or at least a distinct aspect of any given occasion.

a. The Destruction of Jerusalem and the Temple

Ps. 74   The temple and therefore presumably the city around it have been destroyed (vv. 3-8).

Ps. 79   Jerusalem and the temple lie in ruins (v. 1). The people have been slaughtered (vv. 2, 3,10b). In general, the nation has been devastated (v. 7).

No national distress could be more disastrous. With the destruction of the temple the crisis is not merely political but also religious. Its devastation spells the end of the very source of life for the people (e.g. 36.9-10).

b. A Severe Battle Defeat

Ps. 44   The armies of the people are crushed and forced to retreat, while the enemy despoils them, slaughters many of their number, and disperses others (see esp. vv. 10-12, 20, 23).

Ps. 60   The army has suffered a severe rout (vv. 3-5,12).

Ps. 89   The defeat in battle (v. 44) leaves the fortifications in ruin (v. 41), while the enemy plunders (v. 42a) and exults (v. 43).

Ps. 108   Cf. 60.12 above.

While the immediate consequences of a battle defeat may not be as devastating as an invasion of a nation's political and religious capital, the ultimate implications may not be dissimilar, particularly for a nation whose origins are traced back to the traditions of holy war.

c. The Nation is Plundered

Ps. 80   Neighboring nations appear to ravage the towns of Israel as they please (vv. 13-14), burning and destroying (v. 17).

The focus of this psalm does not lie on a specific battle but on the defenselessness of the nation as a whole.

d. Murderous Social Violence

10.8a   ... from hiding places he kills the innocent. (Other verses refer to extreme social oppression (vv. 2-3a, 5-10, 14-15, 18). Note particularly those instances where the innocent are depicted as prey in a hunt.)

Ps. 55   In vv. 10-12 the psalmist describes the city as
full of violence (חמס), strife (ריב) and destruction
(הוֹת). Since this condition brings 'the terrors of
death' upon the psalmist, murder is certainly a
part of the activity of the wicked.

94.5   They crush your people, Yahweh,
and oppress your heritage.

6   They kill the widow and the alien,
and slay the orphan.

21   They band together against the righteous,
and condemn innocent blood.

109.16b   He persecuted the afflicted and needy man and
the brokenhearted to death.

Though the psalms represented here are a mixture of individual
and communal laments, they all display a concern for the social
oppression round about, which in each case goes to the extent of
homicide. In the individual laments of Pss. 55 and 109, however,
the psalmist's social conditions are not of central interest. In these
instances focus is given to those acts perpetrated against the
psalmist himself, particularly deeds of betrayal (55.13-15, 21-22;
109.4-5). The situations reflected in these two psalms are thus
similar to those mentioned previously where death approaches the
psalmist simply as a threat from enemies. As the God-lament was
virtually absent in psalms where death is merely a threat from
enemies, so it is lacking in Pss. 55 and 109.

Both Pss. 10 and 94 do make their social context the primary
object of the lament, but each with a different perspective.
Although taken as a whole Ps. 94 is a communal lament, the
psalmist in the final third speaks through the language of the
'narrative praise of the individual'. He, in effect, singles himself
out among the company of the afflicted. Whereas death strikes the
unfortunate around the psalmist, he announces twice that he has
been protected from this fate (vv. 17, 22). He does raise the urgent
plea, 'How long will the wicked exult?' (v. 3), but does not go so
far to charge God explicitly with failure. (On this psalm, see further
in Chapter 5.) This individualistic perspective contrasts with the
perspective of Ps. 10, where focus is given to social injustices

throughout. This psalm also presents the most elaborate description of this kind of oppression within the Psalter. The appearance of a God-lament in this psalm (v. 1) therefore comes as no surprise.

Within this category of social violence only Ps. 10 contains a God-lament (v. 1); within that of death threatened by adversaries only Ps. 35 has a God-lament (v. 17). It is worthy of note that in both instances the God-lament is limited to one verse and concerns Yahweh's passivity, not his active involvement in the distress.

e. Exile

This event is the background of Ps. 106 ('Gather us from among the nations', v. 47)[15] and Ps. 137 ('By the rivers of Babylon ...', v. 1). Its gravity is evident from a reading of the Prophets.

f. The Nation in Dearth

Ps. 85   This psalm reflects a people and a land lacking 'life' (v. 7) and blessing (vv. 9-14).

Ps. 126   This psalm is probably to be located in the same postexilic situation as Ps. 85.[16]

Both of these psalms begin with praise of the one who has returned the captives back to their homeland, but they also make it apparent that the restoration (שוב, 85.5; 126.4) is not yet complete. The interest in the land and its produce (85.13, cf. ארץ in vv. 2, 10, 12) and in sowing and harvesting (126.5, 6) suggests an occasion of agricultural and economic want.

g. An Absence of Current Saving Deeds

Ps. 77 gives nothing away as to the particular 'distress' (v. 3) behind it. The grief it gives to the psalmist to ponder God and 'the days of old' (vv. 4-7) suggests a contrast between how God acted then and now. Thus the psalmist raises the possibility that God's disposition will henceforth be one of disfavor (vv. 8-10).

h. Conclusion

Among the communal laments, all of the complaint psalms indicate occasions of national disaster. The psalms of plea reflecting such

hardship are Pss. 94, 106, 126, and 137, all of which probably
originate in the exilic and postexilic eras.

C. THE DURATION OF THE DISTRESS

The continuing nature of distress can be expressed in the following
forms.

1. 'How long? ... forever?'

4.3	Sons of men, how long must my honor become disgrace,
	and you love worthlessness and seek delusion?
6.4	And my soul is disturbed exceedingly,
	but you, Yahweh—how long?
13.2	How long, Yahweh? Will you forget me forever?
	How long will you hide your face from me?
3	How long shall I take counsel in my soul,
	with grief in my heart daily;
	how long will my enemy be exalted over me?
35.17a	Lord, how long will you look on?
42.3	My soul thirsts for God, for the living God;
	when (מתי) shall I come and appear before God?
74.1	Why, O God, have you rejected us forever?
3a	Step up to the ancient (נצח) ruins.
9	... there is none among us who knows how long.
10	How long, O God, will the adversary revile?
	Will the enemy spurn your name forever?
77.8	Will the Lord reject forever,
	and will he never again be favorable?
9	Has loving-loyalty ceased forever;
	has 'word' come to an end for all generations?
10	Has God forgotten to be gracious,
	or has he in anger shut away his compassion?
79.5a	How long, Yahweh? Will you be angry forever?

80.5	Yahweh of hosts, how long will you fume against the prayers of your people?
85.6	Will you be angry with us forever? Will you prolong your anger to all generations?
89.47a	How long, Yahweh? Will you hide yourself forever? (See also vv. 48-49.)
90.13a	Return, Yahweh—how long?
94.3	How long shall the wicked, Yahweh, how long shall the wicked exult?

The question 'How long?' implies that the point at issue is not simply the hardship itself but also its duration. It naturally points toward the future, but it is logical that concern over future duration would emerge only if the distress had already persisted for some time. This is corroborated in Chapter 3 by the observation that 'How long?' reflects not a desire for information but a complaint. If the distress were something that had only just occurred, then phrasing the complaint in terms of duration would hardly be appropriate. Rather, the implication of urgency in the question suggests the hardship has gone on long enough.

Questions of 'Will [Hebrew imperfect] ... forever?' appear to bear much the same meaning. In most instances these two expressions appear together, with the interrogative 'How long?' preceding (13.2; 74.10; 79.5; 89.47). Only in 77.8 and 85.6 does 'Will ... forever?' stand alone in the Psalms. In the latter occurrence, the question acts rhetorically as a petition (see the exegesis below). In 77.8, however, the question does not signify persuasion as much as deep personal reflection on the psalmist's part (see the exegesis).

In contrast to the expressions regarding the psalmist's nearness to 'death', these questions focus on the impact of the distress during the span of his life. Thus, in those psalms where both forms of complaint appear, protests concerning the duration of the distress (6.4; 13.2-3; 42.3; 89.47) precede references to (the possibility of) death (6.6; 13.4; 42.8; 89.48-49 [in these verses of this communal psalm the king evidently speaks regarding himself]).

The psalms of plea included above are Pss. 4 and 94. Ps. 4.3 introduces an exhortation addressed to enemies and is thus not to be regarded as a complaint per se. The psalmist rebukes them not simply for their moral bentness but also for their folly. Their behavior is not only wayward; it is futile, as the psalmist's confession of trust in v. 4 substantiates. V. 3 should, therefore, be read as a rebuke against futile action, not as a lament over action that has succeeded. In contrast, Ps. 94.3 is addressed to God as a lament concerning the duration of the ascendency of the wicked. As a 'foe-lament', it does not explicitly lay blame at God's feet.

Most of the 'How long?' expressions in the psalms of complaint occur in the form of a God-lament (6.4; 13.2; 35.17; 74.1; 77.8-10; 79.5; 80.5; 85.6; 89.47; 90.13) and direct attention to Yahweh's disposition (13.2; 74.1; 77.8-10; 79.5; 80.5; 85.6; 89.47).

2. *'Day and night'* [17]

The passage of time may also be suggested by terms such as בקר וערב, יום(ם), ולילה, כל־(ה)יום.

10.5a	His ways are stable at all times (בכל־עת).[18]
	(In addition, one may well suspect that the degree of oppression and violence reflected in this psalm could not develop in a short space of time.)
22.3	My God, I cry by day but you do not answer, and by night but I have no rest.
38.7b	All the day I go about mourning. (Cf. v. 18b.)
13b	And they plot deception all the day.
Ps. 39	There are no expressions that taken individually would convey the notion of prolonged distress, but the general problem underlying this psalm is certainly 'lifelong', namely that of the brevity of human existence (cf. Ps. 90). Moreover, the psalmist describes the dilemma not as something

that has just occurred to him but as a process that
has transpired over a period of time (see Chapter
7).

42.4   My tears have been my food day and night,
while saying to me all the day,
'Where is your God?' (Cf. v. 11b.)

44.16a   All the day my humiliation is before me.

23   But on your account we are killed all day long;
we are considered as sheep for slaughter.

55.11   Day and night they go around [the city],
upon its walls;
trouble and mischief are in the midst of it.

12b   Oppression and deceit do not depart (מוש)
from its square.

56.2b   ... fighting all the day they oppress me.

3a   My enemies hound me all the day.

6a   All the day they distort my words.

59.7 = 15   They return at evening,
they howl like a dog,
and go about the city.

74.22b   Remember how fools taunt you all the day.
(Cf. v. 23b.)

77.3   In the day of my trouble I sought the Lord;
at night my hands were outstretched
but did not languish;
my soul refused to be comforted
(See also vv. 4-7.)

86.3b   For to you I call all the day.

88.2   Yahweh God of my salvation,
I cry by day and night before you.

10   My eye grows dim from affliction;
I call to you Yahweh every day;
I stretch out my hands to you.

14   But I have cried for help to you, Yahweh,
and in the morning my prayer comes before you.

16a   I have been afflicted and gasping for life since
youth.

18a   [Your terrors] have surrounded me like water

all the day.
90.9   For all our days have declined in your fury;
we exhaust our years like a sigh.
10   Our lifespan is seventy years,
or if we have the strength, eighty years,
and their hurry is toil and trouble,
for soon they pass and we fly away.
15   Gladden us, according to the days
you have afflicted us,
the years we have seen misery.
102.4a   For my days have been consumed in smoke.
9a   All the day my enemies mock me.

We shall first consider the psalms of complaint. In contrast to the 'How long?' expressions, of all the 'day and night' laments only 88.18 is a God-lament (cf. however 90.15a). Lament in the 'I' form often mentions prayer being made 'all the day', prayer which Yahweh has presumably not answered (22.3; 77.3; 88.2, 10, 14). Yahweh is thus implicated in these I-laments. Also in the I-laments appear descriptions of the psalmist's personal misery (38.7; 42.4; 44.16, 23; 88.16; 90.9, 10, 15b; 102.4; see also 13.3 above and 6.7 below). These 'day and night' expressions also occur in foe-laments which depict the activity of the enemies, usually directed specifically against the psalmist (10.5; 38.13; 55.11-12; 56.2, 3, 6; 74.22; 102.9).

Among the psalms of plea these 'day and night' expressions appear in Pss. 38, 55, 56, and 86.

3. *'I grow weary'*

6.7   I grow weary (יגע) with my sighing;
every night I drench my bed with weeping;
I soak my bed with tears.
8   My eyes grow dim (עשש) from grief;
they become old (עתק) with all my adversaries.
31.10b   ... my eye has grown dim (עשש) with grief.

11   For my life has wasted away (כלה) with sorrow,
      and my years with sighing;
   my strength falters because of my iniquity,
      and my bones have deteriorated (עשש).

69.4   I grow weary (יגע) with my pleading;
      my throat is parched;
   my eyes languish (כלה)) waiting for my God.

88.10   My eye grows dim (דאב) from affliction;
   I call to you Yahweh every day;
   I stretch out my hands to you.

143.7a   Answer me quickly, Yahweh,
   my spirit has wasted away (כלה). (See also vv.
   5-6.)

Expressions referring to the weariness of the psalmist (יגע, עשש, עתק, and in some cases כלה) also imply a hardship that has weighed upon the psalmist for some time. Hence, they are all I-laments. The language used suggests emotional exhaustion primarily but physical fatigue may well be included. In addition to those listed here, 39.11b and 90.7 should perhaps be noted as well.

Within this category Pss. 6, 39, 88 and 90 are complaint psalms. Pss. 69 and 143, psalms of plea, have been mentioned already as reflecting a near-death distress.

4. Conclusion

The only complaint psalms that do not contain any expression bemoaning the duration of the distress are Pss. 60 and 108. The distress reflected in Ps. 60, a quote from which forms the lament section of Ps. 108, appears to be acute, not chronic. The psalms of plea that speak of a continuing hardship are Pss. 31, 55, 56, and 86. Also to be included are Pss. 69 and 143, which were mentioned above as reflecting near-death occasions, and Ps. 94, which laments violent social oppression. This discussion concerning the duration of distress will be continued in the next chapter where a further distinction must be made.

Recalling that the psalms of plea outnumber the psalms of complaint two to one, it is striking to note that all of the latter (except Pss. 35; 60 = 108b) refer to a distress that is both extreme in intensity and long in duration. Of the 44 psalms of plea, such is the case for only Pss. 69, 94, and 143.

D. ADDITIONAL FEATURES OF THE OCCASION

In addition to the proximity of the psalmist to death/national disaster and the duration of the distress, there are several other factors of the occasion of a lament psalm that correlate with the appearance of complaint. These factors admittedly receive mention in a more incidental fashion than those just referred to, and so should not be taken as definitive in the delineation of these categories. Moreover, with respect to these criteria the balance does not tip so markedly as with those concerning death and duration. Nonetheless, one should recall that the psalms of plea outnumber the psalms of complaint two to one. Thus, even an equal number of occurrences of any given expression among these categories suggests a greater frequency among the psalms of complaint. The first of these concerns only the individual laments.

1. Lack of Solidarity of the Psalmist with His Community

Psalms that betray a sense of alienation are psalms of the *individual* in the truest sense of the word. The psalms of plea suggest this lack of solidarity in the following expressions:

25.16b   I am lonely and afflicted.
31.12   Because of all my adversaries I have become a
        mockery, especially to my neighbors,
        and an object of dread to my friends,
        all who see me on the street flee from me.
69.9   I have become a stranger to my brothers,
        a foreigner to my mother's sons.

21b   I waited for sympathy but there was none,
           and for comfort but I found none.
142.5   Look to my right hand and see that there is none
           who regards me;
           all refuge is taken from me; there is none
           who cares for me.

Pss. 41.10 and 55.13-15 mention the betrayal of a friend, but they nowhere imply that the entire community has abandoned the psalmist.

Among the psalms of complaint the expressions of alienation are:

22.7   But I am a worm and not a man,
           a reproach of man and despised by the people.
8   All who see me mock me ...
           (Vv. 13, 17 make apparent that the only ones
           standing beside the psalmist are opponents.)
38.12   My friends and companions stand aloof
           from my plague,
           and my neighbors stand at a distance.
88.9   You have removed my friends far from me;
           you have made me an abomination to them;
           I am kept imprisoned and cannot go out.
19   You have removed far from me lover and
           neighbor;
           my friends are the dark region.
102.7   I resemble an owl of the wilderness;
           I have become like a screech-owl of the ruins.
8   I lie awake,
           and have become like a solitary bird on a roof.

In Ps. 42-43 the psalmist laments his alienation from the temple and the worshipping community (see 42.2-6; 43.3-5), as he cries 'from the land of Jordan and Hermon, from Mt. Mizar' (42.7).

The appearance of these expressions of alienation among psalms of complaint is not surprising in view of how important the worshipping community was for the individual. Because near-death distresses were often interpreted as divine judgment, friends and relatives would have felt the need to distinguish themselves from the afflicted one, lest they too become subject to the same judgment. Thus, this lack of solidarity should probably not be regarded as a principal cause of complaint, but it certainly must have exacerbated the psalmist's dilemma.

2. Humiliation of the Psalmist

Expressions stating that the psalmist has become an object of mockery appear in roughly one half of those psalms also containing an expression of complaint toward God (first the individual laments):

13.3b	How long will my enemy be exalted over me?
22.7-8	(See above.)
35.15	But when I stumbled they gathered and rejoiced; smiters whom I know not gather against me; they slander [lit. 'tear'] without interruption.
16	When I limped, mockers mocked, gnashing at me with their teeth.[19]
42.11	As a shattering of my bones my adversaries malign me, while saying to me all the day, 'Where is your God?'
88.9b	You have made me an abomination to them.
102.9	All the day my enemies malign me; those mocking me use my name as a curse.

The laments of the community containing such expressions are:

44.14	You make us a mockery to our neighbors, a derision and a ridicule to those around us.
15	You make us a byword among the nations, a laughingstock among the peoples.
16	All the day my humiliation is before me, and shame has covered my face,

17   from the voice of those who malign and revile,
       from the enemy and the avenger.

79.4   We have become a mockery to our neighbors,
       a derision and ridicule to those around us.

80.7   You have made us a contention to our neighbors,
       and our enemies deride us.

89.42b He has become a mockery to his neighbors.

51   Remember, O Lord, the mockery of your
         servant,
       how I bear in my bosom the abuse[20] of the
         peoples,

52   with which your enemies have mocked, Yahweh,
       with which they have mocked the footsteps
         of your anointed.

One may note such expressions of humiliation are rarer and not so developed among the psalms of plea (aside from Ps. 69):

4.3a   Sons of man, how long must my honor
         become disgrace?

31.12 (See above.)

69.10b And the mockery of those mocking you
         has fallen upon me.

11   When I wept with fasting,
       it became a cause for mockery.

12   When I made sackcloth my clothing,
       I became a byword to them.

13   Those sitting in the gate gossip about me,
       and I am the song of the drunkards.

20   You know my mockery, my shame and my
         disgrace;
       all my adversaries are before you.

21a   Mockery has broken my heart ....

109.25 I have become a mockery to them;
       when they see me they shake their heads.

The only lament of the community to be considered here is:

123.3b ... we have had enough contempt.
  4 We have had enough of the derision
      of those untroubled,
    the contempt of the haughty.

At first reading one may read the petition (אל־אבוש(ה (25.2, 20; 31.2, 18; 71.1; cf. 39.9b) as implying that the psalmist has not yet suffered humiliation. But inferences from this imperatival form cannot be conclusive, as Ps. 31 itself indicates. Although this petition appears twice (vv. 2, 18), the psalmist already describes himself as a 'mockery' and an 'object of dread' in v. 12.

As mentioned above, these expressions are more incidental than those referring to a prolonged and/or near-death distress. Surely the psalmists of Pss. 10 and 137, for example, suffer humiliation, but there is no direct reference to it.

Chapter 5

THE INTERPRETATION OF DISTRESS IN COMPLAINT PSALMS

A. INTRODUCTION

Chapter 4 has noted two characteristics of distresses—their intensity and duration—that correlate with the expression of complaint. In ancient Israel complaint psalms appear to have emerged from situations of prolonged hardship and either near-death distress in the individual laments or national disaster in the communal laments.

We shall now look at what traditions these distresses call into question, such that a psalmist would feel justified to complain to God. In other words, what are the traditions that Yahweh is believed to have contravened by permitting such a distress? While these traditions may not always be promises direct from God (as in Ps. 60.8-10: 'God has spoken ...'), they reflect a pattern in Yahweh's past saving deeds that the people of God have recognized and that they expect him to follow in the future.

We shall also attempt to discover why in some complaints God is charged with negligence and why in others he is charged with hostility. This study should also give us insight into how the psalmists interpreted life's distresses in light of their traditions.

Before answering these two questions, it will be helpful to distinguish at what level the extant psalms accuse God. Some do it by questioning the persistence of his disfavor (Pss. 13; 77; 79; 85). Some do it by questioning his idleness (Pss. 9-10; 35; 74). Others do it by actually attributing the distress to God, an action which is shown to be contrary to divine promises (the individual laments: Pss. 6 [implied in the ellipsis]; 22; 39; 42-43; 88; 102; the communal laments: 44; 60 = 108; 80; 89; 90). The latter two divisions may also contain questions directed against Yahweh's disfavor, but these categories have been determined according to those God-laments that are most informative regarding God's involvement in the distress. For example, Ps. 74 complains of God's anger and his withdrawal. Since the latter protest expresses God's relation to the distress more specifically, this psalm is classified in the second rather than the first category.

All three of these categories connote complaint, but the third one does something more. If one encountered distress and felt it was becoming unduly harsh and prolonged, one might say to God, 'Why are you still angry with me?' (cf. 79.5), or 'Why don't you save?' (cf. 74.11). These may simply suggest God is negligent in saving his people. But to assert 'You have brought this affliction upon me!' charges God not simply with failure but with betrayal. The psalmist goes beyond mere complaint—he claims that God caused his distress. This third form of protest would thus require more justification than the first two.

For each of the psalms discussed below, we shall look briefly at its underlying distress, the tradition that is called into question, how the tradition and distress conflict, and why God is given an active or passive role. More detailed analysis can be found in Chapters 6 and 7. We shall first look at how the intensity of these distresses calls tradition into question.

B. THE INTENSITY OF DISTRESS

The traditions that are called into question become most evident from those corporate laments that actually recite the praise traditions that are later contradicted in the lament over distress. We would expect that those psalms that charge Yahweh with active hostility to go to greater lengths to justify this charge, and indeed they do. All of the communal laments that attribute the cause of the distress to Yahweh, Pss. 44, 60, 80, and 89, juxtapose the lament with a lengthy praise section. With these we shall begin. It is interesting to note that in each of these a foreign nation has prevailed over the people of God.

1. Laments of the Community

In Ps. 44 the underlying distress, which is described most clearly in its lament section (vv. 10-23), is a battle defeat. The linguistic affinities between this lament section and the preceding praise section (vv. 2-9) imply that the defeat has been interpreted according to these praise traditions. The tradition called into question is clearly expressed in what must have been a pre-battle confession of the people. The armies had vowed to follow their commanding Warrior into battle and to credit the victory to him (vv. 5-9). That such an expectation was valid is supported by the reports of past generations concerning how Yahweh himself had waged holy war for the armies of Israel as they entered Canaan. The present debacle thus indicates Yahweh's failure to uphold these holy war traditions. The possibility of interpreting the defeat as just divine judgment is excluded by the psalmist's assertion of the people's allegiance to the covenant. Hence the psalmist protests.

The lament section of Ps. 89 likewise reflects a loss in battle (vv. 39-52). The similarity of terminology between this lament and the preceding praise (vv. 2-38) implies that the immediate occasion of the psalm has been interpreted in view of the preceding promise. In this case, however, appeal is made not to the holy war traditions but to the Davidic covenant. The first two-thirds of the psalm rehearses the praise of Yahweh's supreme kingship, especially as demonstrated through his earthly regent. This hymn may have been sung regularly at the enthronement of the Davidic monarch. Since the welfare of the king is bound up with the promise of God, the failure of the king must signify Yahweh's retraction of the covenant. The possibility that Yahweh's withdrawal may be justified on the grounds of human transgression is excluded by the breadth of the covenant itself. Sin would result only in chastisement, not annulment. The covenant as given should be inviolable. Thus Yahweh's retraction must provoke complaint.

The occasion behind Ps. 80 is the plundering of the nation. It depicts the exodus and conquest traditions in the metaphor of a gardener and his vine. The imagery of Yahweh as the gardener places him in a role that entails certain continuing responsibilities. The anomaly that a gardener should destroy the wall protecting his vine, an inference demanded by the present disaster and the role Yahweh has assumed, is expressed as a God-lament. Similarly at the opening of the psalm, the traditions concerning the ark of the covenant leading the people adumbrate the image of Yahweh as a shepherd leading his flock. The tears shed by the people in their distress are thus portrayed as the food given by this faithless shepherd.

Ps. 60 also alludes to a defeat in battle. In its central portion (cf. Ps. 108) is an oracle wherein God establishes himself as the landlord over Israel and her neighbors. Ephraim and Judah are announced to be his instruments of defense and attack. The recent defeat must therefore signal God's failure to wield these divine instruments.

Ps. 74 appears to emerge from the most devastating of catastrophes: the destruction of the temple. According to the people's praise of Yahweh as Creator, he should have militantly opposed all chaotic forces, but now blasphemers triumph in God's own temple. Moreover, Yahweh's choice of dwelling at 'Zion' and his redemption of Israel as his congregation should mean that their defense could be assumed. Seeing that the very heart of the nation has been overrun, God is considered to have failed his people.

Ps. 79 does not make any explicit mention of a praise tradition but the repeated use of the possessive pronoun 'your' in connection with the temple, city, and people (vv. 1-2) must stem from the Zion tradition. The slaughter of God's people certainly indicates Yahweh's failure to uphold the responsibility of defense he assumed by this tradition of election. Moreover, the belief that Yahweh should defend the honor of his name is contradicted by those who continue to mock it.

In these psalms occasioned by a victory of a foreign power Yahweh is sometimes given an active role and sometimes a passive role. Is it possible to uncover any reasons for this? In the psalms that employ the holy war, conquest, or Davidic traditions (44; 60;

80; 89), Yahweh is depicted as the aggressor. Pss. 74 and 79 both reflect the destruction of the temple. In the latter, reference is made only to Yahweh's anger; in the former he is depicted as negligent. One might speculate that in these two psalms the poets thought it inconceivable that Yahweh would raise up foes to destroy his own dwelling. But more probably, Yahweh's role in each distress depends on his role in the tradition employed in the psalmist's argument. The psalms lamenting the destruction of the temple employ the Zion tradition, which places Yahweh in a role of defending his dwelling (e.g. Ps. 48). The reversal of this tradition thus means that Yahweh has neglected to defend the temple. On the other hand, the holy war tradition clearly places Yahweh in an offensive role, and the Davidic tradition as it is presented in Ps. 89 also gives Yahweh an active role:

89:20b	I have given help to a warrior; I have exalted a young man from the people.
24	I will crush his foes before him, and those who hate him I will strike.

25	My faithfulness and merciful devotion
	        will be with him,
	    and in my name his horn will be exalted.

26	I will place his hand upon the sea, and upon the rivers his right hand.
28	I will even make him my firstborn, the most high of the kings of the earth.

Yahweh not only protects the Davidic dynasty and its realm; he promises its expansion and its supremacy over all other kingdoms. The reversal of the holy war and Davidic traditions thus means that Yahweh has acted against his own people. In each of these national disasters, therefore, Yahweh is depicted in a role that is in keeping with the tradition appealed to. If the tradition places Yahweh in an active role, his role in the contrary distress is an active one; if the tradition places Yahweh in a passive role, his role in the contrary distress is a passive one.

Ps. 9-10 sets extended praise and lament sections side by side, but this time the 'wicked' are made the predominant subject of the lament that contradicts the praise. First the psalmist sings of God as the defender of the oppressed. Lament begins with a reproach against Yahweh's remoteness and then continues with a description of the widespread violence of the wicked. Moreover, the persistence of blasphemy leaves the psalmist bewildered. In this reversal of Yahweh as the defender of the oppressed, he is depicted as negligent, not as the one perpetrating disaster against the poor.

Ps. 90, which may reflect the hardships of the postexilic community, focuses on Yahweh as Creator. It opens praising the grandeur of his eternity by contrasting it with the mortality of man (vv. 1-6). The shift from man in the third person (vv. 2-6) to 'we' (v. 7) signals the beginning of the lament proper. It begins from this praise but shifts the focus from God's eternity to his anger and from man's mortality to his generation's travail. The decay of death now overshadows all of existence. Since God is the one who commands death (v. 3), he is considered the cause of the futility experienced by the psalmist and his people.

Another psalm that probably emerges from this same period is Ps. 85. The psalmist, in the language of praise, first recounts Yahweh's 'turning of the fortunes' of the nation, probably referring to the return from exile. But the present circumstances, which appear to be agricultural dearth, indicate that he who controls the fortunes of the people must (still/once again?) be angry with them. Since the 'turning' was viewed as a sign of Yahweh's forgiveness and the withdrawal of his anger, the presence of misfortune is perceived as the persistence of the divine anger.

The specific distress (v. 2) underlying Ps. 77 eludes us, but the overwhelming problem for the psalmist has become the current absence of the kind of saving deeds Yahweh performed in the past. God has become his central problem. The traditions he recites concern the exodus in particular. Complaint in the psalm focuses on the root of the problem: Yahweh's disposition.

2. *Laments of the Individual*

The laments of the individual do not substantiate their complaints so explicitly as the laments of the community. In fact, if one were to consider each psalm in isolation, one could not be certain what praise traditions Yahweh is seen to have contravened. The problem is heightened by the observation that all of the individual complaints, except Pss. 13 and 35, actually depict God in an active role of bringing distress on the psalmist. Among the communal complaints the praise traditions were apparent, by and large, from the structures of the psalms themselves. In this case, however, we must infer them from those features of the distress that correlate with these individual complaints, that is, the psalmist's nearness to death and the prolonged duration of the distress.

If the psalmist's nearness to premature death evokes complaint, then part of Yahweh's responsibility must be to preserve him from premature death. Do we see this tradition spelled out anywhere? A frequent basis for narrative praise is deliverance from death:

> 30.3   Yahweh my God,
>   I cried to you for help and you healed me.
> 4   Yahweh, you brought my soul up from Sheol;
>   you kept me alive that I not go down to the pit.
> 116.8   For you rescued my soul from death,
>   my eye from tears,
>   my feet from stumbling.

(See also 40.3; 103.4; 107.10, 14.) We cannot assume, however, that this praise reflects a belief that it is Yahweh's obligation to preserve each godly Israelite from premature death. It may simply point to the psalmist's delight—and perhaps his surprise—of being delivered from death.

The confessions of trust found in the plea psalms, but absent in the complaint psalms, may give a hint as to what praise traditions complaint psalms cannot uphold (see Chapter 2). A frequent confession of trust is that Yahweh answers when called upon:

> 3.5   I cry aloud to Yahweh,
>   and he answers me from his holy hill.
> 17.6a   I have called upon you for you will answer me,
>   O God.
> 57.3-4 I cry to God Most High ....

He will send from heaven and save me ...

(See also 4.4; 5.4; 55.17-20a; 56.10; 86.7; 142.6 and 8.) In addition to this list there are other confessions of trust which, though omitting reference to the psalmist's calling, state that Yahweh saves his own when trouble comes (e.g., 7.11-12; 25.3, 15; 27.1-6; 31.4-5; 54.6-7; 56.4-5; 58.10; 59.11; 61.7-8a; 64.8; 71.20; 94.18-19, 23; 140.13). The frequency of this pattern—I call, he answers—indicates that this confession forms the bedrock for psalmists in the midst of their individual distresses.

The pervasiveness of this pattern is confirmed by the narrative praise psalms, which view the deliverance from such distresses in retrospect. The pattern, 'I cried, he heard, he drew me out', is fundamental to their structure.[1] Since praise is what living is all about for the psalmists[2] and since this pattern is the structure of that praise, the belief that Yahweh responds to the cry of his people is central to the faith represented in ספר תהלים.

For the psalmists who feel near death, the importance of the tradition, 'Yahweh answers when called upon', is self-evident. The finality of death silences any possibility of the psalmist's calling and Yahweh's answering.Why should it be significant for Yahweh? Because this interplay of the psalmist's calling and Yahweh's saving is the stuff that forms the praise of God. The psalmists saw an indissoluble connection between praise and life. If God allows the psalmist to die, he forfeits his praise. In other words, death would silence the praise of God. Hence, two complaint psalms actually spell out to Yahweh what would be the consequences of the psalmist's death:

6.6   For there is no remembrance of you in death;
       in Sheol who will give you thanks?

88.11 Do you perform wonders for the dead?
       Do the 'ghosts' rise to praise you?

12   Is your merciful devotion recounted in the grave,
       your faithfulness in the place of destruction?

13   Are your wonders known in the darkness,
       or your righteousness in the land of
       forgetfulness?

Praise is something God desires and requires. Therefore God should be zealous to keep the psalmist in life. But if God appears to allow the psalmist to die, the psalmist must interpret this as Yahweh's personal rejection of his praise and so ultimately of himself. This failure to preserve the psalmist from death would thus mean that God has spurned this worshipper and his very reason for being. On these grounds, if premature death appears imminent, then complaint appears warranted. When a psalmist is pushed to the extreme of being at death's door, a corollary to the tradition that 'Yahweh saves when called upon' becomes evident, namely that Yahweh preserves his worshippers from premature death.

We can now pursue the question of why the distress is attributed to Yahweh in the complaint. Aside from Pss. 13 and 35, all of the complaints of the individual not only charge God with failure, they proceed to attribute the actual cause of distress to God:

22.16b	But *you set* me in the dust of death.
39.6	Behold, *you have made* my days as handbreadths,
	and my lifetime is as nothing before you.
	Surely every man who stands firm is breath!
88.7	*You have put* me in the lowest pit,
	in the dark places, in the depths.
102.24	*He has humbled* my strength in the midst of my life;
	he has cut short my days.

Ps. 42.8 depicts Yahweh as the bringer of death in the image of an overwhelming flood (see Chapter 4). Ps. 6.2, 4, 6 also implicates Yahweh as the bringer of death (see the exegesis in Chapter 7). Only Ps. 13 does not connect Yahweh with the action of bringing the psalmist to death, but as noted already, its complaint regarding Yahweh's disfavor simply does not specify the nature of his activity.

The grounds for this attribution probably lie in the belief that Yahweh holds ultimate power over life and death. C. Barth notes that OT statements regarding Yahweh and death lie within three boundaries.[3] First, Yahweh, even when he kills, is never identified as the Power of death. He is never personified as one of the powers of nature. They are simply used by Yahweh so that he may execute his goals (e.g. Ps. 29). Second, Yahweh is never strictly the God of life and blessing, as though curse and death were considered separate powers. Third, Yahweh may exercise both anger and mercy, death and life, but he is never indifferent when he performs such actions. His will is for life. In view of such observations, Barth asks, Is there yet room for an independent power of death? The OT gives no clear answer. But it is clear that the powers of death that do appear in the OT always act under Yahweh's permission. The following texts make clear the belief in Yahweh's sovereignty over death:

1 Sam. 2.6	Yahweh is the one who kills and brings to life,
Deut. 32.39	See now that I, I am he,
	and there is no god besides me;
	I kill and I bring to life ...
Ps. 90.3	You return man to the dust,
	and you say, 'Return, O children of man'.
Ps. 104.29	You hide your face, they are dismayed;
	you withdraw their breath, they expire,
	and return to the dust (cf. Job 34.14-15).

Further particulars as to why Yahweh is depicted as the one bringing the psalmist near death can be found in the 'Interpretation' section for each of the individual complaints discussed in Chapter 7.

Ps. 35, the only individual complaint not discussed thus far, does not reflect such a near-death distress—only the threat of death (see Chapter 4). Its grounds for complaint will be elucidated below.

To sum up this discussion: in the laments of the individual the psalmist's nearness to death signals Yahweh's unfaithfulness to his cries. This entails the anomaly of Yahweh's denying himself praise. Since the issue of life and death can only be in Yahweh's hand, the cause of the distress is traced back to Yahweh.

As already noted, the laments of the individual are much less explicit than the laments of the community regarding the specific traditions upon which they base their appeals. In both the plea and complaint psalms of the individual, the sole reason why Yahweh should act on the psalmist's behalf appears to be an assumed relationship between psalmist and God, which relationship could be encapsulated in the phrase 'my God'.[4] These two words entail a great deal. We can be certain that the phrase implies a mutual bond between psalmist and God and that certain expectations are laid on each, but exactly what is entailed is not clearly spelled out, except in Ps. 22.

The phrase occurs three times in the opening two verses, whose chief concern is that 'my God' is 'far from my crying, the words of my roaring' and that 'my God' does 'not answer'. The following eight verses then spell out the legitimacy of this expectation that 'my God' should answer the cries of those who so address him. (See the exegesis in Chapter 7.)

The expectation upon the psalmist, aside from his crying when help is needed, is that he will 'trust', a term that appears four times in these ten verses. In vv. 5-6 the verb is used three times of those who cried for help and Yahweh delivered. The intimacy of the relationship implied in 'my God' is most evident in vv. 10-11, where Yahweh is described as 'the one who drew me forth from the womb, the one who caused me to *trust* when upon my mother's breast.... Since my mother's womb you have been *my God*.' (In this instance the origin of the psalmist's trust is also traced back to Yahweh!)

The only other obligation upon the psalmist surfaces in vv. 4-6. 'My God' is described as 'enthroned upon the praises of Israel', whose praise apparently consists of the fathers' crying out and being delivered. Thus, once one is rescued after calling upon 'my God' he is to praise 'my God'. Although this phrase is not used after v. 11, it is worth mentioning that the first reference to the psalmist's doing something himself other than trusting and crying for help is to his promise to praise (v. 23), the sum of which consists of 'when he cried to him for help, he heard' (v. 25).

This understanding of 'my God' is not peculiar to Ps. 22. Of the 55 occurrences of 'my God' (אלוהי and אלי) in the Psalter, at least

40 are clearly used in immediate connection with the psalmist's either calling, trusting, or praising.[5] Trust as a fundamental element of 'my God' theology comes to clearest expression in 31.15: 'I trust in you, Yahweh; I say, "You are my God."' Praising as a fundamental obligation upon the psalmist is clear from 30.12-13: 'You have loosed my sackcloth and girded me with joy, in order that I may sing praises to you ...; Yahweh, my God, I will give you thanks forever.' Indeed, a standard motif of the lament psalms, whether plea or complaint, is the vow of praise (not a vow to an ethical life). Most of the other occurrences of 'my God' are used in actual praise, but not in direct connection with the verbs 'to praise' and 'to give thanks'.[6]

It is in times of extremity that one may best discern the bedrock of the faith of individual psalmists. In these complaints of the individual that bedrock appears to be what we might call 'my God' theology. According to this theology, the psalmist lives to trust, call upon, and praise Yahweh. Yahweh is then expected to answer the psalmist when called upon and especially to preserve his worshipper from premature death.

In these complaints there is little reference to specifically ethical obligations. This is not to say that ethics had no role in individual religion, but that when psalmists found themselves at the edge of death, the only obligation that they felt was essential to affirm was their performance of the worship of Yahweh.

C. THE DURATION OF DISTRESS

To this point we have discussed only the intensity of the distresses reflected in the communal and individual complaint psalms. The duration of these distresses, both national and individual, also gives legitimate grounds for complaint. In fact the prolonged nature of these distresses denies the efficacy of the same tradition mentioned above. The belief that Yahweh answers when called upon is frustrated in these distresses where deliverance seems unduly delayed.

We must now note a distinction between a continuing distress and a prolonged distress. In the experiences of the psalmists one cannot assume that a distress of any duration is necessarily one which is unduly long, one where deliverance seems to be delayed. This distinction is suggested by those psalms that refer to the psalmist's distress as persisting for some time but also confidently assert that Yahweh will answer when implored to do so. In Chapter 4, for example, Ps. 86.3b was cited as an expression possibly referring to a continuing distress: 'For to you I call all the day'. In v. 7, however, the psalmist believes, 'In the day of my distress I call to you, for you will answer me'. Thus, though the psalmist must persist in his prayers, this does not imply that he considers Yahweh's response unduly delayed.

Similarly in Ps. 55 the psalmist laments that 'day and night' the wicked encircle the city while oppression never departs from its square (vv. 11, 12b), but he then maintains:

> 55.17   As for me, I shall call upon God
>   and Yahweh will save me.
>   18   At evening and morning and noon I ponder and
>   groan,
>   and he will hear my voice.

Neither the persistence of the oppression, nor the necessity to repeat prayers, need imply Yahweh has failed to answer the psalmist's cries.

In this regard it is remarkable to note that *all* of the psalms of plea that refer to a continuing distress, aside from Pss. 69 and 143, also contain similar confessions of trust. This suggests that the persistence of their distresses does not necessarily indicate Yahweh's deliverance is delayed:

> Ps. 4   The psalmist's exhortation of 'How long ...?'
>   rebukes his foes for their futile endeavors (v. 3),
>   but in the same address he admonishes them,
>   'Yahweh hears when I call to him' (v. 4).
> Ps. 31   Although the psalmist has suffered for some time
>   (vv. 10-11), he is now able to express the
>   conviction that Yahweh has both seen (v. 8) and
>   heard (v. 23). His God has granted partial

deliverance by sheltering him *in the midst of* his
plight (vv. 9, 22). Thus, this psalm represents
the halfway point on the road to deliverance.
Yahweh has heard but he has not yet effected his
salvation.

Ps. 38   In spite of his mourning and his enemies plotting
deception 'all the day' (vv. 7, 13), the psalmist is
assured, 'You will answer' (v. 16b).

Ps. 56   The psalmist's enemies hound him 'all the day'
(vv. 2, 3, 6), but he later confesses, 'Then my
enemies will turn back in the day I call; this I
know because God is for me' (v. 10).

Ps. 59   Though the wicked habitually make their evening
prowl (vv. 7, 15), the psalmist avers that
Yahweh laughs at them (v. 9) and that he will
grant the psalmist his desire (v. 11).

Pss. 94 and 106 express, in ways different from the above, their
certainty that Yahweh will answer. As noted in Chapter 4, Ps. 94 is
the only psalm of plea that contains the question 'How long?'
addressed to God. Hence the psalmist does not express his
certainty of Yahweh's intervention by saying, 'Yahweh will hear
when I call'. Nevertheless, within the teachings of the wise he is
able to see the oppression of the wicked as but a period of
chastisement for the righteous. These 'days of adversity' will
continue 'until a pit is dug for the wicked' (v. 13). Thus, although
the distress persists, the psalmist is able to see a terminus ad quem.

In Ps. 106 the exile was certainly a continuing distress, but the
psalmist by appealing to the past lessons of salvation history avers
that deliverance is as sure as God's mercy and faithfulness to
covenant (vv. 8, 44-46).

Therefore, with the exceptions of Pss. 69 and 143, the
suggestion of prolonged distress, that is, where no terminus ad
quem is foreseen for the distress, is found only in the psalms of
complaint.

Among the complaint psalms the only joint occurrence of a
reference to a continuing distress and a predication of God that he

either has seen or will deliver from distress is found in Ps. 10.14, 16, which is discussed in Chapter 6.

These observations raise the question, At what point does continuing distress become prolonged distress? The answer may possibly be found in those psalms where it comes to expression that prayers were offered prior to the utterance of these psalms but these foregoing prayers have been unanswered:

> 22.2   My God, my God, why have you forsaken me?
>   Why are you far from my crying,
>   the words of my roaring?
>   3   My God, I cry by day, but you do not answer,
>   and by night, but I have no rest.
> 80.5   Yahweh of hosts,
>   how long will you fume against
>   the prayers of your people?

(See also Pss. 77.3; 88.2, 10, 14 and note 6.7-8.) This brings to light the possibility that the problem is not simply the duration of distress but unanswered prayers. Thus, when the psalmist judges that his prayers have been to no effect, he concludes Yahweh has ignored his pleading. This would therefore implicate Yahweh as being involved in the distress, as either an aloof bystander or an active antagonist.

The expression 'How long?' may suggest this phenomenon of unanswered prayer is more pervasive among the complaint psalms than first appears. The question itself connotes a concession that relief may not come soon. But this goes contrary to the expectation expressed throughout the Psalter that Yahweh answers when called upon. We have seen this expectation in the confessions of trust found in the plea psalms. It also appears in other types of psalms, as for example:

> 20.2a   May Yahweh answer you in the day of distress!
> 50.15   And call upon me in the day of distress,
>   and I will rescue you and you will honor me.
> 138.3a On the day I called you answered me.

Although the meaning of 'day' in each case cannot be limited to a 24 hour period, it does designate a certain period of time. The psalmists apparently expected Yahweh to answer without delay. For a psalmist to concede that the normal expectation has been denied, he must have made previous appeals to which there has been no response. At the first signs of distress one simply asks for relief. Only after a period of distress and persistent prayers does one ask, 'How long?' These psalmists thus appear to lack the certainty that prayers are answered 'in the day of distress'.

E. Gerstenberger, after considering this interrogative 'in various literary contexts of the OT' confirms some of these observations. He concludes that the phrase 'introduces reproachful speech, apparently after repeated efforts to amend a situation have failed... The undertone in all these passages is that a change is overdue'.[7]

If this is the case, then nine psalms must be added to the number of complaint psalms that implicitly respond to distresses of unanswered prayer (6.4; 13.2-3; 35.17; 42.3; 74.1, 10; 79.5; 85.6; 89.47; 90.13; Pss. 77 and 80 which also speak of unanswered prayer also pose this question [77.8-10; 80.5]).

The only complaint psalms that do not offer similar hints that previous prayers have been ineffectual are 10; 39; 44; 60 = 108; 102, though this cannot be excluded as a possibility, except for Ps. 102 and perhaps Ps. 10 (see vv. 14, 17). (For Pss. 44 and esp. 60 one could argue the distress is simply acute not chronic.) In Ps. 102 the possibility that the psalmist considers his prayers to have gone unanswered appears to be excluded by the petition, 'in the day I call answer me quickly' (v. 3b), which suggests the psalmist is referring to the present psalm.[8]

Mention should now be made of Ps. 35, the one complaint psalm which does not reflect a 'near-death distress', as defined in Chapter 4. Its complaint, albeit a brief one, 'Lord, how long will you look on?', focuses on the duration of the distress. Verse 10 shows that the psalmist conceives of Yahweh as a God who delivers the afflicted. But as the following verses show, his 'friends' continue to afflict him. Hence the complaint.

In sum, we have noted that some psalms refer to a continuing distress but still express certainty that Yahweh will answer, and others refer to a continuing distress but express uncertainty that

Yahweh will answer. This observation has led us to the distinction between continuing distresses and prolonged distresses. All of the complaints, except Ps. 10, reflect prolonged distress, where there is no terminus ad quem in view. Such is the case for only two psalms of plea (Pss. 69 and 143). This lack of confidence in imminent divine help is probably due to Yahweh's silence in the face of the psalmist's foregoing prayers.[9] These correlations suggest that the psalmists followed common criteria according to which they interpreted life's distresses and Yahweh's relation to those distresses.

As neat as these criteria may appear, the exegete must allow for the subjectivity of a psalmist's interpretation. For example, in the midst of distress a psalmist cries,

22.3   My God, I cry by day but you do not answer;
            and by night but I have no rest.

After deliverance, however, he proclaims,

22.25b   He did not hide his face from him,
                but when he calls to him for help he hears.

Indeed, the psalmists themselves confess that their interpretations of distress in the midst of distress are sometimes rash:

31.23   But I said in my alarm,
                'I am cut off from your sight';
            but indeed you heard the voice of my
                supplication when I called to you for help.
            (Cf. 116.11.)

D. Psalms of Plea Reflecting Extreme Distresses

We shall now turn to those psalms of plea mentioned in Chapter 4 that appear to share the same characteristics of the distress as found in the psalms of complaint. Here we shall try to detect any factors that might help explain why they do not attribute any fault to

Yahweh. The plea psalms of the individual reflecting near-death distress are Pss. 28, 69, and 143. The plea psalms of the community reflecting national disaster are Pss. 94, 106, 126, and 137. Only Pss. 69 and 143 express concern over prolonged distress.

Each of these psalms does contain expressions that may help to explain why their appeal has been tempered. But these reasons must be considered as influential—not determinative. As already noted, we cannot presume that such factors of the distress and of the interpretation of that distress dictated the form of appeal that finally appeared. Thus, in a few cases these same reasons may be reflected in psalms also containing complaint.

Pss. 69, 106, and 143 all express concern over sin. Ps. 143.2 pleads that Yahweh restrain from judging his servant on account of humankind's general sinfulness before God. Such a consciousness of sin may well have led the psalmist to temper his appeal to God. Similarly in Ps. 69 the poet confesses,

> 69.6   O God, You know my folly,
> and my wrongs are not hidden from you.

This psalm also has another feature. The expression here is a lament of a mediator who suffers mockery out of his zeal for Yahweh's temple (vv. 8, 10). This is one of the few psalms reflecting specifically religious—not moral, economic or political—persecution. He thus considers that his own suffering provides no grounds for doubting the value of trusting Yahweh (v. 7), which implies complaint would be an inappropriate form of appeal.

In Ps. 106 the exile is seen as an event similar to others in Israel's history. In the psalmist's rehearsal of God's earlier dealings with his people, he begins with the people's ingratitude and rebellion (vv. 6-7), which is nonetheless followed by a divine act of mercy (vv. 8-12). There then follows a series of seven incidents of Israelite rebellion and divine judgment (vv. 13-43). In spite of their persistence in sin, the climax to this sequence is another divine act of mercy that brings deliverance (vv. 44-46). Without any explicit transition, the final petition (v. 47) brings us to the time of the exile when Israel is yet again in need of mercy.

This awareness of Israel's propensity to sin leaves little doubt that the present exile is a result of divine judgment on this generation's sin (v. 6). Considering the divine mercy in the face of the people's ingratitude and rebellion, the psalmist could hardly appeal for help by charging God with denying the saving traditions.

Ps. 106 exemplifies the impact that the exile had upon Israel. It demonstrated to them that the promises of Yahweh contained in the traditions were not unconditional. Deuteronomistic interpretation of Israel's history and traditions is evident in Ps. 106 and in vv. 40-46 especially.[10] The prophetic and deuteronomistic preaching impressed upon the people that sin and wickedness prevailed *within* the nation. Hence, distresses that were attributed to God were no longer considered inexplicable acts of divine hostility— they were God's just judgments. Complaint soon became an inappropriate form of appeal and was replaced by confession of sin and by praise of God's righteous judgments.[11]

Ps. 137 clearly fits in the exilic or postexilic periods,[12] and Ps. 126 may reflect postexilic hardships (Ps. 85 contains similar language and appears to emerge from a similar postexilic occasion). Although a national disaster underlies each of these psalms, neither voices complaint against God. The psalmist in the latter instance takes heart in the work of restoration that Yahweh has begun and simply requests him to bring it to completion. (Even though Ps. 85 expresses complaint, it does so in a muted form. Moreover, it protests not God's wrath as such, but its duration. See Chapter 6.) The psalmist in Ps. 137 focuses all accusation, not against God, but against his 'captors' who torment the exiles (v. 3).

Ps. 94, a postexilic psalm,[13] though not referring expressly to sin and divine judgment interprets its distress as a form of chastisement. V. 7 contains a confession of the wicked (רשעים), the content of which is similar to that of a God-lament:

> 94.7   And they have said, 'Yah does not see,
> and the God of Jacob does not perceive.'

To such thinking, however, the psalmist gives severe rebuke from the teachings of Wisdom. As certain as Yahweh is the wise Creator, so certain will be his judgment (vv. 8-11). Under the providence of God the oppression of the wicked will prove to be beneficial chastisement for the godly and confirmation of the impending judgment of the wicked (vv. 12-13). In addition, the psalmist's own experience of deliverance in the midst of this violence (vv. 17, 22) may as well have tempered his appeal.

O. Keel has noted two distinct designations for the enemies in the Psalter. One group concentrates around the term אויב (28 psalms), another around רשע (22 psalms). The former group of psalms simply depicts the opposition of the enemies; the latter group gives a moral valuation of the wicked. The רשע-image in the Psalms appears to have belonged to the exilic and postexilic period.[14] Aside from Pss. 9-10 and 39, all of the complaint psalms appear in the אויב category.

Ps. 28, a psalm of plea, belongs to this latter category where people are either צדיק or רשע (v. 3), and God himself personifies צדקה. The conflict in these psalms is thus portrayed on a 'horizontal' level: no discord appears between the צדיקים and the God of צדקה. The focus has been shifted from complaining to God to lamenting the wickedness of the wicked.[15]

In sum, complaint may not appear in psalms that reflect an extreme and/or a prolonged distress because of several factors. An overriding consciousness of sin may temper the appeal. Another related factor is the impact of the exile, wherein the nation became more aware of personal guilt and the justice behind Yahweh's judgments. Such an awareness led to a stronger moral valuation of the opponents of the psalmists. Blame became focused on the 'wicked'. Another factor that tempered the appeals of psalmists was the influence of the teachings of Wisdom. In this light, distress could be perceived as chastisement.

E. THE INTERPRETATION OF DISTRESS IN LAMENT PSALMS GENERALLY

In view of the above, we may speculate that the way psalmists interpreted their distresses followed the following steps.

The psalmist encounters distress. He asks, What light does tradition shed on this distress? How does it help me to make sense of this distress, and what does it instruct me to do? Generally speaking, there are three possibilities.

(1) Usually the tradition most applicable is that Yahweh hears when called upon. The psalmist will then describe his dilemma and call on Yahweh to help. Yahweh, in effect, is treated simply as a third party.

(2) If, however, the psalmist has an acute awareness of sin, he may consider the distress as Yahweh's just punishment. He will then confess his sin, and pray that Yahweh forgive and restore him (as, e.g., in Ps. 51).

(3) If, however, there is a tradition pertinent to this situation and it implies that Yahweh should have acted for the psalmist's benefit (and that tradition may simply be 'Yahweh hears when called upon') and the psalmist does not consider the distress to be fair punishment for any sin committed, then he may complain. He would then describe Yahweh's role in the distress in a way appropriate to that tradition. If Yahweh's role in the tradition is defensive, he will be charged with negligence. If his role is one where he takes the initiative, he will be charged with improper action against the psalmist.

The first two interpretations see the distress within the bounds of tradition. In number one Yahweh is envisaged as the deliverer. Although this tradition assures psalmists that Yahweh will save, it does leave latitude for distress to befall psalmists. Yahweh does not guarantee to preserve psalmists continually from all mishaps. Distress appears to be a given within this tradition and within life in this world. In number two Yahweh is envisaged as the just judge of the psalmist's sin. The distress has a rational cause, and the just judge has provided a means of atonement and restoration.

In interpretations two and three Yahweh bears some responsibility for the distress. In number two he has carried out his responsibility. In number three he has either ignored or misused his responsibility. This third form of interpretation does not rule out the possibility that the psalmist is aware of his own or his people's sin, but it does rule out the possibility that the distress is considered a fair measure of punishment.

Chapter 6

THE COMPLAINTS OF THE COMMUNITY

A. INTRODUCTION

The preceding chapters have delineated the principal distinctives of the complaint psalms within the lament category. Some of the distinctions drawn, however, presuppose a more detailed exegesis, which will now be presented. Moreover, as noted at the close of Chapter 1, literary interpretation must not simply leave the reader with inferences abstracted from the texts but must lead him or her back to the texts themselves. The need for Gunkel's Psalms commentary to accompany his *Einleitung* (both in the Göttinger Handkommentar zum Alten Testament series) illustrates this principle. The text is its own meaning, particularly in the Psalms where poetic interplay sets up an indivisible structure as the conveyor of this meaning. Thus, while Chapters 6 and 7 will endeavor to undergird and further the arguments of Chapters 1-5, their main reason for inclusion is simply this: if we have truly uncovered something 'new' about lament psalms, then our reading, understanding, and appreciation of each psalm should be enhanced. In particular, the next two chapters will endeavor to elucidate how each psalm exemplifies the distinguishing features of the complaint category and how each distinguishes itself within the category.

Chapter 2 examined the lament category and discerned within it two forms of appeal to God: plea and complaint. Focusing upon the more radical appeal, Chapters 4 and 5 asked, On what grounds do the psalmists complain to God? These chapters thus began with the appeal and then sought to elucidate those factors that shaped it.

Now we shall attempt to reconstruct the process of composition presupposed by any given complaint psalm. In order to to present this process in what must have been its 'chronological' order, we shall begin with the distress and then seek to uncover how each psalmist interpreted this distress, and finally how these factors shaped the appeal.

The analysis of these psalms will thus proceed from three vantage points. The first surveys the distress reflected in the psalm, focusing upon its intensity and duration.

The second viewpoint considers how the psalmist used tradition to interpret his distress. First we shall observe who the psalmist considers to be the source of the distress, whether enemies or God, and also their relationship to one another, whether the enemies act as agents of God's purpose (God as hostile) or act simply of their own accord (God as passive). Since these psalms express complaint to God, his role in the distress will be our main interest. Next we shall consider the grounds upon which these complaint psalms attribute some responsibility to God and the grounds upon which they charge him with failure in that responsibility. We shall thus note the traditions employed, their basic claims and the nature of Yahweh's role in them. How Yahweh is depicted in the reversal of those traditions will also be considered. Thus, from this second viewpoint we shall ask three questions, stated here in general terms: (1) Who are considered the sources of this distress? (2) On what grounds does the psalmist attribute the cause of distress to these sources? (3) Are their actions considered warranted?

Keeping in view both the phenomenal and religious dimensions of the crisis, the third vantage point considers the argument the psalmist employs to persuade God to intervene. Since God is not considered as simply a third party in the distress who may be implored to help (as in the psalms of plea) but as one who has either caused or disregarded the psalmist's plight, the poet is naturally at a severe disadvantage in pleading his case. The psalm's rhetoric (in the primary sense of the word, as persuasion) is therefore deserving of special attention. Thus we shall consider how each psalmist charges God with denying certain traditions and how he summons God to maintain these traditions of praise.

The second stage of interpretation must not be overlooked. If one moved immediately from the occasion of the appeal to the appeal itself certain valid questions would be left untouched. We may note that a psalmist accuses God, but we would miss something if we failed to ask, Why does he, in contrast to most other lamenters, consider God to have failed his responsibility? And, why does he, for example, consider God to have actually brought this distress upon him?

The results of this and the next chapter are summarized in tabular form at the beginning of Chapter 8. While the reader is working through the details of the exegesis, the reader may wish to follow the outline format of these tables.

B. PSALM 9-10

1. Distress

Most commentators are agreed that Pss. 9 and 10 form a single psalm.[1] Although the speaker in each psalm appears to be an individual, his concern is a corporate one. Aside from four verses that mention personal distress (9.4-5, 14-15), the psalmist's attention is directed to the 'afflicted' and to the 'wicked' in general. But even in these four verses, the psalmist's own 'just cause' (v. 5) and 'affliction' (v. 14) appear to be indistinguishable from the cause and from the affliction of the 'afflicted' in general.

The underlying occasion of this psalm is expressed most clearly in the lament of Ps. 10 (regarding the function of Ps. 9, see below). The arrogant (vv. 2, 3a, 5-6) and blaspheming (vv. 3b, 4, 11, 13) wicked 'hunt' (vv. 2, 7-10) and 'kill' (v. 8) the oppressed and unfortunate (vv. 14, 17, 18).

The psalm is difficult to date. The use of the acrostic pattern helps little in this problem. According to Craigie, 'the exclusive use of זו as a relative pronoun might be taken as a further indication of antiquity ...'[2] But O. Keel, on the basis of the history of the רשע imagery, places Ps. 10 in the postexilic period.[3]

2. *Interpretation*

The source of the psalmist's distress is clearly the רשע. There is no
hint that God has instigated such adversity against the afflicted.
Rather, the 'wicked' are characterized as arrogant deniers of God
(vv. 4, 11, 13), not as his instruments of judgment. Nonetheless,
the psalmist does reproach God for being idle while the godless
freely pursue their schemes.

The psalmist's grounds for expecting Yahweh to intervene are
evident from the praise that precedes in Ps. 9. According to this
Jerusalem tradition, Yahweh should act as the just Judge protecting
the needy and punishing the wicked.[4] The psalmist's
disappointment in God is made evident, not only from the reproach
contained in the God-lament (v. 1), but also from the foe-lament,
which by simply describing the rampant oppression shows that
God has failed to execute his role as judge. The wicked oppress the
needy, but neither are the needy delivered or the wicked judged.
Because Yahweh's role in the tradition is basically a defensive one,
his role in the reversal of the tradition is seen to be a passive one
(10.1).

The primary categories of people established by the praise of Ps.
9 are the 'needy' (עני, דך, אביון) and the 'wicked' (רשע). The
psalmist refers to 'to my *just* cause' (9.5), but this is simply his
cause against the wicked who attack him. Yahweh is described as
executing '*righteous* judgment' (9.9), but this simply means
protecting the oppressed. The needy should be the beneficiaries of
Yahweh's help, not primarily because they are 'righteous' by their
conduct, but because they are abused by the wicked and more
powerful. For this reason, the issue of whether or not the needy in
Ps. 10 are experiencing a form of just judgment for their sin does
not arise. In support of the reproach of God's aloofness (10.1), the
psalmist gives more attention to describing the arrogance and
blasphemy of the wicked, than to describing innocence of the
needy.

3. Appeal

The appeal of this psalm has been constructed in the form of an acrostic, the constraints of which probably account for the mixture of themes and forms throughout the psalm.[5] This mixture makes a coherent interpretation of the whole psalm difficult. Which genre should determine the function of the whole psalm: the praise or the lament? Kraus takes his lead from 9.15.[6] The psalmist who has been delivered from distress praises God before the congregation. Included in this praise is 'extensive instruction for the listeners' (cf. 34.12), which includes the topics of 'Yahweh's worldwide judgment and kingdom over the nations' and 'the self-assured sinner as a temptation for the faith of the poor'. But contrary to Kraus's interpretation, the lament contained in vv. 1-11 can hardly be placed under the rubric of 'instruction'.

The interpretation that appears most appropriate for the psalm as a whole, and Ps. 9 in particular, is represented by W. Beyerlin.[7] He views 9.2-21 as a *todah* that is given to 'actualize' salvation. This thanksgiving is not praise for a deliverance that has recently been experienced by the psalmist, nor is it a listing of the great deeds of Yahweh. It is rather a compacted overall view, presented within the imagery of Yahweh as judge. Thus, by this praise the psalmist shows that he recognizes from God's deeds in the past that he is a just judge and that he should continue in that role לעולם. The psalmist then unfolds the meaning of Yahweh's role as judge as it applies to the immediate distress. The psalmist believes Yahweh has already undertaken his 'just cause' (עשית משפטי ודיני, v. 5a) because Yahweh 'sits on his throne judging righteously' (v. 5b). Viewing the function of the praise as a call for 'actualization' of tradition is confirmed by the petitions that adjoin this praise (vv. 14, 20-21). The psalmist praises Yahweh, but he is still seeking something from him. Thus, in Ps. 9 the psalmist both affirms the praise of Yahweh's rule in the present and announces proleptically the praise of Yahweh's future 'actualization' of that rule.

In Ps. 10 the psalmist develops his appeal. The shift that occurs with the letter *lamedh* (למה תעמד ברחוק) certainly points to a change of mood in the poem, but it is not wholly discontinuous with what has been voiced from *aleph* to *kaph*. Although its approach is different, this lament also seeks the actualization of the traditions expressed in Ps. 9. Instead of simply affirming these praise traditions, the psalmist brings into clear view how present circumstances are at variance with them. He supports his reproach of Yahweh's aloofness by drawing out the contrast of tradition and present experience. Yahweh should be a stronghold for the oppressed 'in times of trouble' (9.10), but he now appears to hide 'in times of trouble'. Indeed, 'from hiding places [the wicked one] kills the innocent' (10.8). Although praise declares that God 'does not forget the cry of the afflicted' (v. 13), the wicked maintain, apparently with nothing to contradict them, that 'God has forgotten' (10.11). Although Yahweh is called 'the Avenger of blood' (דרש דמים, 9.13), the wicked assert that God 'does not call to account' (דרש, v. 10.13).[8] Instead of being destroyed (9.6-7), the wicked prosper (10.5). Instead of the wicked being caught in their own 'net' (9.16), they drag the afflicted away in their 'net' (10.9).

The psalmist thus sets forth the conflict of faith and experience chiefly by juxtaposing praise (Ps. 9) with an extended *foe*-lament (10.2-11, 13). This makes the psalmist's complaint a manifest feature of the appeal, but it is not so pronounced as it is in those corporate laments that juxtapose praise and *God*-lament (see esp. Pss. 44; 80; 89). Predications of God similar to those found in the God-laments do indeed appear in Ps. 10, but they are placed in the mouth of the wicked:

> 10.11   He has said to himself, 'God has forgotten;
> he has hidden his face; he will never see it.'

(See also 10.4, 13.) The psalmist thus shows that even the wicked recognize the apparent absence of God. He also makes plain that the current prosperity of the wicked and the afflictions of the innocent suggest that the wicked appear to have it right.[9]

The psalmist, however, does not allow complaint to be his final word. In 10.14 and v. 16 especially, he re-affirms his earlier praise of Yahweh's rule (9.8):

10.16   Yahweh is king forever and ever;
          nations have perished from his land.

Therefore, like other corporate complaints, Ps. 9-10 appeals to Yahweh by demonstrating the conflict of tradition and experience, but unlike other corporate complaints, he also affirms the praise of God. The structure of the psalm is not determined by a simple juxtaposition of praise and lament. There is petition in the praise (9.14, 20-21), and praise follows the lament (10.14, 16). Yet it must be noted, that in contrast to the praise contained in Pss. 44 and 89 in particular (44.2-9, esp. 3, 4; 89.2-38, esp. 34-38), the praise contained in Ps. 9-10 is not so categorical. 9.6-7 does refer to the total destruction of the wicked (Hebrew perfect), but 9.18 states that the wicked will return to Sheol (Hebrew imperfect), and then 9.20-21 petition that the nations be judged (Hebrew imperatives and jussives). Moreover, the praise of Ps. 9 itself allows for a certain latitude of distress: Yahweh is 'a stronghold *in times of trouble*' (v. 10) and 'the needy will *not always* be forgotten, *nor* the hope of the afflicted perish *forever*' (v. 19). Thus, since the praise of Ps. 9-10 is 'qualified' praise, the corresponding complaint is not as harsh as what appears in Pss. 44 and 89. In the tension caused by the conflict of faith and experience, the composer of Ps. 9-10 firmly declares both to Yahweh. He affirms tradition, but he also shows that experience denies it. He laments his distress, but he does not allow it to silence his praise.

C. PSALM 44

1. Distress

The people have gone out into battle praising God and expecting victory, but they are instead forced to retreat (vv. 2-11), the shock of which appears overwhelming. Moreover, the enemy has despoiled them, killed many of their number and dispersed others (vv. 11-12, 22).[10] The people are thus humiliated (vv. 14ff.) and utterly downcast (v. 26).

The supposition that the psalm could have originated in the Maccabean period appears unlikely, particularly because it is contained in the Elohistic collection.[11] It may refer to the situation around the death of Josiah or to that concerning Sennacherib's invasion of Judah. Kraus believes the psalm may have undergone various applications during its history of transmission.[12]

2. Interpretation

The concern of the psalm is not limited to the people's devastation and the enemies' triumph. That the defeat entails a crisis of faith is evident from the dominance of the God-lament and the 'assertion of innocence'. As painful as the debacle was, the overriding torment is that the agent perceived behind the defeat is the God of the people. The psalmist's grounds for attributing this distress to God are evident from vv. 2-9. The confession that the people carried with them into combat shows that the battle was staged not between 'us' and 'them' but between 'God' and 'them'. A victory would have been described in terms of praise, but a rout could be spelled out only as a *God*-lament. Since Yahweh's 'favor' leads to victory (v. 4), defeat must spell his 'rejection' (v. 10; cf. 24). Triumph is due to 'the light of his face' (v. 4), failure to the 'hiding of his face' (v. 25). If Yahweh is the one who puts the enemy to shame (v. 8), then the shaming of the people (vv. 10, 14-17) is to be traced back to Yahweh as well. In victory Yahweh 'dispossesses' (הוריש, v. 3; ירש, v. 4) the nations, but in defeat he 'sells Israel over' (vv. 12-13). The lament of vv. 10ff., however, does not mirror exactly the confessions found in vv. 2-9. The focus of interest in the latter is that Yahweh himself wars against the foe (vv. 3-4) or that he acts as the direct agent of victory (vv. 6ff.). But in the lament section the action of God against the people is primarily one of 'handing over' to the enemy. Yahweh has not effected triumph for the enemies (contrast Ps. 89.43), only defeat for Israel. Note, for example, v. 11: since Yahweh causes the people to retreat, the enemy is at liberty to take spoil. Only in v. 20 is Yahweh said to have 'crushed' the people.

Verses 18-23 intensify this complaint by forcibly showing that Yahweh has no grounds for this reversal. Comparing these verses with other assertions of innocence (Pss. 17.3-5; 26.1ff.; 59.4-5, all of which are individual laments) makes clear their distinctive emphasis. Declarations of innocence generally assert the psalmist's conformity to God's moral law, but Ps. 44 confesses the psalmist's loyalty to the covenant. The former contrast the behavior of the psalmist with that of the wicked; the latter contrasts the behavior of the psalmist with that of God. Ps. 44 therefore exhibits not merely an assertion of loyalty but a protest against God. As will be expounded below, what particularly astounds the psalmist is that God seems unaware of the people's allegiance (vv. 21ff.), a mishap that the poet attributes to God's 'sleepiness' (v. 24)! His bewilderment is further underscored by questions of 'Why?' (vv. 24-25).

3. Appeal

In view of the situation just described, the psalmist could not simply plead for God to deliver, for it appears that he is the one the people need to be delivered from! Put most simply the argument runs as follows: the opening section declares the former expectation of the psalmist (vv. 5-9) along with its substantiating basis (vv. 2-4). After describing God's denial of that expectation (vv. 10-17), the psalmist argues that the misfortune amounts to God's contravention of covenant (vv. 18-23). He then pleads for God to awake to the people's loyalty and redeem them (vv. 24-27). In conjunction with the form-critical structure, there works a corresponding pattern of imagery:

2-9 (10 lines: 5 + 5)	Reference to past saving deeds, Confession of trust	The divine warrior fights for his people
10-17 (8 lines: 4 + 4)	Lament	The shepherd sells his sheep
18-23 (6 lines: 3 + 3)	Protest of loyalty	God betrays his covenant
24-27 (4 lines: 2 + 2)	Petition and Lament	God is to awake before his people near death

The compressing of each successive section serves to intensify the movement of the poem. From v. 18 the focus of interest shifts from the battlefield to the covenant relationship.[13]

The psalm opens with a report relying on eye-witness testimony of Yahweh's victories in holy war during the conquest-settlement period (vv. 2-4). Central to this account of holy war is the overriding role played by the divine agency, almost to the exclusion of human effort.

In a confession of trust (vv. 5-9) the psalmist appropriates this tradition of salvation history for his own generation, repeating the emphasis on divine agency. Yahweh is praised as the Warrior-King. In strong anticipation of the ensuing victory, the people publish their praise with the assurance of 'prophetic' perfects (vv. 8-9). In v. 9 the first words of each stich make plain that the people have always and will always attribute their triumphs to their God alone.[14]

After this proclamation of praise one would expect praise itself to follow. But the poet's sudden turn to lament graphically depicts the utter frustration of his expectation. This is evident in the discord between the people's present and promised devotion (v. 9) and Yahweh's rejection in the very next verse. Verses 10-17 portray in vivid terms Israel's humiliating debacle, but the poet's primary thrust is that Yahweh is considered to be the instigator.[15] He describes not only the harshness of Yahweh's cruelty, but he also suggests, in view of the opening proleptic praise, that this action is betrayal. The first six verses of this lament section (i.e. the God-lament portion) form verse pairs, with the second of each pair intensifying the first. The last two verses form a grammatical unit that emphasizes the people's utter loss of confidence.

The protest that the people have been loyal (vv. 18-23) falls into two parts. In the first part (vv. 18-20) the people's loyalty in the midst of opposition is contrasted with Yahweh's crushing of these loyal people. The implication is that the proper divine response to such allegiance would be to honor it, which in this case would mean God's executing the praises of vv. 2-9. Instead, Yahweh performs the reverse: he repays their loyalty with affliction.

Verses 21-23 with their interest in the deep knowledge of God attempt to probe this reversal further. In vv. 21-22 the reference to God in the third person in effect confronts God *with* 'God', that is, with God as he should be and act.[16] Yahweh should be fully aware if the people had indeed been disloyal. If they had 'forgotten' (v. 21), then 'God' would have discovered it; but it has been stated clearly they did not 'forget' (v. 18). If 'God' knows the secrets of the 'heart' (v. 22), then he should know the devotion of the people's 'heart' (v. 19). Verse 23 then moves from this theological argument to the harsh realities that the people suffer—'on account of' God! Thus, the people are slaughtered not because of any disloyalty but because of God himself. In this sense, the psalmist argues that God has not fulfilled his divine role: he seems unaware that the people suffer because of their loyalty to him.[17]

In v. 24 the psalmist presents a curious twist in his description of the divine activity. God is no longer depicted as the selling shepherd or as the treacherous covenant-partner, but as the one asleep. His action thus appears no longer hostile but neglectful. Prima facie this is contradictory. But, as mentioned above, the focus of interest here shifts from the battlefield to the covenant relationship. With this shift of focus there is also a change in the way God is portrayed. In the first half Yahweh is the warrior; in the latter he is the judge.[18] With this change of role comes a change in the depiction of divine activity. The succession of vv. 21-24 implies that Yahweh is unaware of the people's loyalty because he is asleep. The imperatives thus aim to awaken the divine judge to the facts of the psalmist's case and so move him to vindicate.

The dilemma of the judge's disaffection is countered by a negative petition that God not 'reject' (cf. v. 10) 'forever' or

'utterly'. The psalmist then protests God's 'estrangement' (‎למה־
‎תסתיר פניך) of the people and his 'disregard' (‎תשכח) of their
affliction. The use of ‎שכח here is not meant to suggest that the
people's affliction has passed from God's mind but that God no
longer has ány regard for it.

The adjoining description of the people's extreme affliction (note
the connective ‎כי beginning v. 26) heightens the reproach of the
God-lament. Moreover, as the people 'sink down', God is
implored to do what they cannot do for themselves: 'Rise up'.

The petition ‎פדה is pregnant with meaning. Yahweh should both
'buy his people back' and thus demonstrate his possession of them
by 'delivering' them. The former sense receives particular
emphasis with the adjoining motivational phrase: 'for the sake of
your merciful devotion'.[19] This final petition shows that the matter
comes to this: the Shepherd who has sold his sheep must ransom
them and so reaffirm himself as the loyal covenant partner. The
closing verse thus gathers some of the psalm's key images to
combine them into a forceful climax.[20]

In sum, the immediate concern of this psalm, the extreme battle
defeat, becomes the occasion of a larger faith crisis. This
observation is corroborated by the secondary role played by the
enemies, who by the petition section drop from view. The psalmist
argues that the people had expressed a legitimate expectation that
the divine Warrior would prevail over their enemies, but instead
there ensues a reversal that is both unmotivated and cruel. With the
divine Warrior tradition in jeopardy, the psalmist summons
Yahweh to act as Judge.

D. PSALM 60

1. Distress

The text of the psalm itself makes clear that the armies of Israel
have just suffered a rout (vv. 3-6, 12). This is the only complaint
psalm that does not speak of the distress as a prolonged one. The
acuteness of the disaster is what lends the distress its gravity.

According to the superscription, while David was leading a military campaign in the north, Edom struck at Israel's home territories in the south. U. Kellermann considers the historical background of the psalm and concludes that too many factors speak against dating the psalm in Davidic times.[21] He argues for locating the psalm in the catastrophe of 587 BC when the Israelites sought refuge from the invading Babylonians. Such a conclusion is possible but his interpretation of vv. 11-14 seems strained, particularly if these verses represent the prayers of defenseless refugees. For example, he sees in v. 14 a 'blind security of election', which 'corresponds to the attitude of the Jerusalem military in the final years of the kingdom of Judah, against which Jeremiah struggled in vain'.[22] Moreover, his arguments against a Davidic setting are not conclusive. He believes that the 'stormy prayers' depicted in vv. 3-5 do not suit what would have been but a minor defeat at the hands of the Edomites. But in view of the high expectations engendered by the traditions of holy war, any disappointment of them would certainly have occasioned a correspondingly severe lament.[23]

From v. 8 H. Gunkel infers that 'Shechem and the plain of Succoth ... must, since they should here be measured and distributed, at the time of the oracle have been in the possession of a foreign population' (so also Kraus).[24] This argument, however, leans too heavily on the imperfect aspect of the verbs, whose precise nuance in any case is ambiguous. What is clear, however, is that the land to be conquered in this psalm belongs to Edom (v. 11), while 'Ephraim' (= the northern tribes) is depicted as Yahweh's instrument of war, not as territory to be reclaimed.[25] This vivid language thus simply proclaims the right that the people of God may claim to these lands.

After all the known factors are weighed, A.F. Kirkpatrick may have been right when he concluded, 'It may reasonably be maintained that the situation indicated in the title explains the Psalm more satisfactorily than any alternative which has been suggested.'[26] Indeed, as Mowinckel notes, after David's reign 'Judah never stood next to Ephraim as a leading tribe and also the Philistines were no longer a threat'.[27]

2. *Interpretation*

The source of this distress is considered to be God. He is made the grammatical subject throughout until vv. 13b-14, but even here he is presented as the sole determinant. The enemies are never once mentioned as the agents of defeat. Whatever motives God may have had for his actions, they are unstated. He is considered angry, but there is no mention of sin which would have incurred his anger, but neither is there any assertion of innocence (contrast Ps. 44). The reasons for the psalmist's attributing the distress directly to God probably lie in the traditions of holy war which this psalm echoes (this was discussed in connection with Ps. 44). This dominance of divine action is also reflected in the oracle (vv. 8-10), wherein God establishes himself as the sovereign landlord. Thus the fates of the various landholders are entirely subject to the decree of their governor. In this instance, however, the failure in battle of God's appointed instruments of defense and authority is at variance with these traditions, thus creating dissonance. Since this oracle and the holy war tradition in general depict Yahweh as the primary agent of victory, he is—in the reversal—considered the primary agent of defeat.

3. *Appeal*

The psalm opens with a series of simple, direct declarations concerning Yahweh's rejection of and antagonism toward his people. פרץ probably refers to Yahweh's breaking through Israel's battle lines (cf. 2 Sam. 5.20). Each hostile act of God, however, is countered with a petition that he restore the harm he inflicted.[28] Parallel to Yahweh's rejection of the people is Yahweh's shattering of the land, which suggests that, in the eyes of the psalmist, this catastrophe of the people reverberates even to the cosmos. This may indicate the key role Israel believed her election to play in the design of the world (so most commentators). Alternatively, since God's 'shaking' of the land sometimes attended Israel's past victories in holy war (רגז, 1 Sam. 14.15; רעש, 2 Sam. 22.8 = Ps.

18.8; Judg. 5.4), v. 4 may be a reference to God's actually waging war against Israel.

Attention is returned to Israel with the image of God making his people drunk on wine that sends them reeling. So staggering is this military rout considered to be.[29]

One may be tempted to read נתתה as a precative perfect, but there is little evidence that such use was made of the perfect in biblical Hebrew.[30] The versions advocate reading, 'You have given a standard to those who fear you, to take flight from before the bow.'[31] This rendering would indicate Yahweh has given the signal to retreat (cf. Jer. 4.6). In this sense v. 6 continues the lament of vv. 3-5 that Yahweh has reversed his practice of holy war. Instead of leading in victory, he leads in retreat. That vv. 3-6 form a coherent unit is 'confirmed by the position of *Selah*' after v. 6 and 'by the commencement of the extract in Ps. cviii with v. [7]'.[32]

In vv. 6-7 the psalmist employs appellatives for Israel, which in the religious sphere connote loyalty and intimacy, thus reminding Yahweh of the ties that he yet has with his people. This in effect qualifies the meaning of חמה. The first petition of the psalm ('Save with your right hand'), by adopting language reminiscent of holy war (Exod. 15.6; Pss. 44.4; 78.54), calls upon Yahweh to turn and act on Israel's behalf. The second request וענני (Kethib) carries the ambiguity of responding with action (its usual sense when used as a petition in lament psalms) or with words. Here the latter sense is given special emphasis by the oracle which follows.

For reasons stated below, it seems most probable that vv. 8-10 contain an oracle given prior to the defeat reflected in this psalm; thus דבר should be read as a simple past: 'God spoke'. These verses ring with the triumph of a commander who has just conquered and now announces his possession of the land and how he will distribute these spoils among his soldiers. Thus Yahweh is portrayed as the sovereign landholder over Canaan. The boundaries delineated here fit those of the Davidic kingdom (cf. esp. the vanquished nations of v. 10 with 2 Sam. 8). Verses 8-9 refer to Israel's territory and to the prominence given to Ephraim (= all the northern tribes) and Judah as God's agents of defense and rule (see

Gen. 49.10) respectively. Verse 10 refers to Israel's southern
neighbors, depicted as conquered spoils of war.[33]

The petitions for escort to Edom (v. 11) and for help against the
adversary (v. 13) are apparently requests for military escort (cf.
with v. 12b) and thus imply an avenging mission is desired. But
the question following the oracle, 'Who will lead me to Edom?' (v.
11), conveys a note of rebuke against the speaker of the oracle,
which contains a promise—now an unfulfilled promise—that
Yahweh 'will cast his sandal upon Edom'. By repeating the
surprise that God has rejected (v. 12, cf. v. 3), the psalmist
underlines this rebuke. The one who should be their military escort
has rejected them.[34] But as the following petition (v. 13) shows,
the psalmist has no one else he can turn to, 'for vain is the help of
man'.

Noting that v. 12 complains of God's refusal to go out with their
armies, one might be surprised at the simplicity of the petition that
seeks to rectify this anomaly: 'Give us help against the adversary'.
No supporting motivational clauses are given. However, it may be
that the petition is such a simple one because the psalmist has
already made his case clear by echoing God's own promise in vv.
8-10. In the case of the other complaint psalms whose distress is
located on the battlefield (Pss. 44; 89), their citations of earlier
promises make their appeals self-evident, and so their formal
petitions are very brief and nonspecific. The final confession of
trust (v. 14) affirms what can be accomplished when God inspires.

Now having studied the psalm as a whole and the function of the
oracle within its general movement, we can consider whether the
oracle presents itself as Yahweh's immediate answer to the
psalmist's request in v. 7 or whether it is a piece of tradition cited
by the psalmist. I am inclined to take it as older, though not
necessarily much older, than the psalm itself. Though perhaps one
should not draw too much from its distinct meter (3+3+3), the
scope of the oracle is much broader than the concern of this
psalm.[35] Moreover, if the oracle were contemporary to the
composition of the psalm, one would think the psalmist would take
such a fresh word of Yahweh as a clear sign that he will now turn
Israel's fortunes in their favor. The only appropriate response to
this would be the kind of confidence expressed in v. 14. The

intervening verses of lament and petition (vv. 11-13), however, suggest that this oracle was known prior to the defeat. If this is the case, the inclusion of the oracle implies both a complaint and a summons: it shows Yahweh that he has failed his word and it also directs him to execute his word.

E. PSALM 108

The significance that lies in the juxtaposition of Pss. 57.8-12 and 60.7-14 is difficult to ascertain. Ps. 57.8-12 is an extended vow of praise closing an individual lament, probably a 'prayer of the accused'. J. Becker and U. Kellermann offer the most plausible interpretation.[36] Two clues of the text are most significant. First, v. 4, with its vow to praise God 'among the peoples' and 'among the nations', and particularly v. 6 give the psalm a universal scope:

> 108.6   Be exalted above the heavens, O God,
> and your glory above all the earth.

Second, 'Edom' is sometimes used in the OT as the quintessence of nations who are hostile to Yahweh (see Isa. 60.1-6). Thus, it seems likely that Ps. 108, by this association drawn from two psalms, speaks of the eschatological conflict between Israel and the nations. A petition that may have originally sought a theophany demonstrating the innocence of an accused individual (v. 6) now becomes a petition for the final and universal manifestation of Yahweh's כבוד. The oracle, which is also contained in Ps. 60, thus foreshadows Yahweh's establishment of his lordship on earth: it has become an eschatological promise.

We see in this psalm the juxtaposition of praise and lament that is common among the corporate complaints, but this time it is a vow of praise that prepares the way for the petition and the lament. Thus, the juxtaposition of praise and lament, which normally represents the conflict of tradition and experience, here works toward the single purpose of realizing Yahweh's eschatological victory.

F. PSALM 74

1. Distress

The concrete concern of this psalm focuses upon the temple which has lain in ruins (vv. 3-8), evidently for some time (vv. 1, 3, 9-10, 23). Violence now prevails in the land (v. 20), and the very life of the nation appears to be in jeopardy (vv. 19-21). Though the description of devastation is restricted to the temple, it being the physical 'heart' of the nation serves as a synecdoche for the nation as a whole. (Focus is drawn to the temple for the sake of a forcible appeal.)

The most probable setting for this psalm is late in the exilic period,[37] though one may never be certain of a precise location since in the transmission of psalms reapplications often occurred.[38]

Mention should be made of F. Willesen's proposal that this psalm was composed originally as a ritual lament for the cult drama of the supposed New Year Festival.[39] He does not deny that in postexilic times it may have been applied to the historical destruction of the temple. Willesen's article is helpful in showing the possibility that certain expressions of Ps. 74 may have been adapted from cultic conventions common to the ancient Near East, where military imagery may simply illustrate a mythic drama. He does not, however, establish sufficient grounds for projecting Ps. 74 back into a purely cultic setting. His evidence for a ritual of profanation, particularly in Israelite worship, is not substantial. Nevertheless, he does help to elucidate the implied association between the invaders of the temple and the chaotic forces opposing the order of creation. This makes clear that the consequences of the temple destruction are considered greater than the mere loss of a place of worship. The very integrity of creation is threatened. Nonetheless, it seems less consistent with other OT writings that the defilement of the sanctuary occasioned the use of political and military imagery than the reverse. It is more probable the catastrophe of the exile was interpreted in light of its cultic implications.

2. *Interpretation*

As a result of this disaster the psalmist speaks of God's wrathful rejection of the sheep under his care. On the other hand, the psalmist with his graphic depiction of the temple being axed and burned clearly attributes its devastation to earthly enemies. Phrases such as, 'They said in their heart, "Let us ..."' (v. 8), indicate the psalmist envisages this as an act of their own devising. The psalmist's perception of the source of distress is most visible in vv. 10-11. Here the enemies are seen arrogantly blaspheming with their acts of sacrilege, but God is considered ultimately responsible because he fails to defend his sanctuary. Thus, his disposition is considered one of wrathful rejection but his conduct one of restraint.

The psalmist's grounds for believing that Yahweh should have taken action are most evident in the juxtaposition of a lament (vv. 3-11) and a 'reference to God's earlier saving deeds' (vv. 12-17). According to this hymnic praise, God should have militantly opposed all chaotic forces, but now blasphemers triumph in his residence. God triumphant has become God withdrawn. The psalmist thus makes clear the irony of God's past zeal to order creation but his present ineffectiveness to defend his own house.

The psalmist's explicit appeal to the Zion tradition is not as extensive as one might expect from a psalm focusing on the temple (only v. 2b). This invasion of Zion certainly contradicts the belief frequently voiced in the Psalter that Yahweh's defense of his dwelling should make Zion inviolable (e.g. Ps. 48). The psalmist spells out the anomaly of blasphemers invading the temple by referring to it as God's dwelling (vv. 2, 7b) and as his appointed place of worship (מעד, vv. 4, 8b) and to Israel as God's redeemed worshippers (עדה, v. 2). Yahweh should have defended his sanctuary and his name (vv. 7b, 10b, 18b) but since no defense was forthcoming, God is considered to have failed his responsibility. Because God's role in the Zion tradition is primarily a defensive one, he is perceived as having a passive role in this reversal. The foes who mock God's name play the active role of attack. They are thus Yahweh's adversaries and not agents of judgment raised up by him.

In sum, the psalmist's grounds for believing Yahweh should
have taken action are twofold. According to the creation tradition,
God should oppose all workers of chaos. According to the Zion
tradition, God should defend the dwelling place of his name and
his congregation.

3. Appeal

In view of this distress and the faith crisis it entails, the aim of Ps.
74 is to turn God's anger away from his own people and redirect it
toward the invading armies. The pivot for this appeal is the temple.
After reminding Yahweh of how inappropriate it is for his wrath to
be spent on his redeemed (vv. 1-2), the psalmist graphically
describes the enemies as those who have trespassed and defiled
God's holy dwelling (vv. 3-8). A protest against God's restraint in
the face of the foe's insolence then closes the lament section proper
(vv. 9-11). The affirmation of God as the psalmist's king, who at
the beginning had bridled all chaotic forces (vv. 12-17), serves as a
bridge from the lament to the petition section, where God is
implored to contend against the scoffing enemy and for his
(potentially) praising people (vv. 18-23).

The psalm opens with a question probing into the anomaly of a
shepherd's anger burning (עשן, cf. 79.5; 89.47) against his own
sheep.[40] But this is soon 'answered' with a petition that excludes
any possibility of a justifiable response. This petition does so by
reminding God of his possession of the people in the exodus event
(cf. Exod. 15.13, 16)[41] and of his co-habitation with them as
maintained by the Zion tradition. The thought of Yahweh's
rejecting 'forever' (לנצח) is countered with the reminder that his
purchase of the people has been 'of old' (קדם; see also v. 12). The
antiquity of the relationship implies that it should have enduring
value.

Another petition follows which invites Yahweh to inspect the
ruins of the holy place. The psalmist endeavors to present the
people's distress as a personal offense against Yahweh's honor by
describing at length the foe's impudent devastation of Yahweh's
dwelling. They thus become nothing less than his enemies (v. 4;

cf. vv. 18, 22-23). The psalmist throughout makes skillful use of the second person possessive pronoun.

The absence of the divine word (v. 9; cf. 1 Sam. 3.1; Lam. 2.9) compels the psalmist himself to ask, 'How long?'.[42] The lament section proper of the psalm (vv. 1-11) closes as it began with a question of 'Why?' concerning God's demeanor. Thus, encompassing the immediate distress of a ruined temple are the ultimate questions regarding God's hostile disposition and restrained conduct. As with v. 1, this final question also receives a forceful reply, but in this case it is couched in the language of praise where Yahweh is affirmed as victor over chaos.[43]

The absence of any transition between these forms of lament and praise leaves the listener/reader to make the logical connection between the past enemies of the orderly creation and the present enemies of Yahweh's holy sanctuary. This reference to God's earlier saving deeds thus sharpens the reproach of the God-lament (v. 11) by illustrating the contrast between Yahweh's past and present behavior. Verses 12-17 exhibit continuity with vv. 3-11 with regard to the characterization of the enemies but dissimilarity with regard to the characterization of Yahweh. The latter receives particular emphasis with the sixfold repetition of אתה.

This reference to God's saving deeds connects with the following petition as well. When seen adjoining these petitions, however, this hymnic praise acts more positively to summon Yahweh to once again take up his cause against chaos. The psalmist thus makes evident that the deliverance now required is certainly no more than one Yahweh has already performed. The first petition recalls the lament of vv. 1-11. Here and in the petitions that follow there is no explicit reference to the temple. Instead the psalmist speaks of the adversaries' sacrilege against the temple in terms of its theological result, namely the spurning of God's name (already mentioned in v. 10). Thus, the fourfold request for Yahweh to remember is designed to confront him with the dishonor that the adversaries bring to his name (vv. 18, 22-23) and with the helplessness of his people before these 'beasts' (v. 19).[44]

This concluding petition section thus returns to the concern with which the psalm began (vv. 1-2), that is, the people of God. In his appeal for favorable intervention the psalmist places the people in the background behind the invaders' sacrilege. After receiving no mention from v. 3 to v. 18, they appear once again, not as loyal stewards of the temple, but as objects of pity. What makes them deserving of God's attention does not arise directly from their relation to God but from their relation to the enemies. By 'virtue' of the oppression of the 'wild beast' they have become the 'afflicted', the 'oppressed', and the 'needy' (vv. 19,21). They are thus a part of God's cause (v. 22), whose task it is to judge for the poor. As an alternative to the enemies' mockery the psalmist offers the people's praise.

The dishonor the adversaries bring to God's name is given particular emphasis in entreaties that serve as an inclusio for this main petition section (vv. 18-23). This climaxes the appeal to God's own honor which has been of central concern throughout.[45] Verse 20 introduces two new considerations for Yahweh. The psalmist makes an explicit reference to covenant, which probably reflects Deuteronomic theology. To this point the geographical interest of the psalm has been focused on the temple, but now it expands to the 'dark places of the land' where the covenant is violated by acts of violence. The climaxing petition occurs in the one that makes the most explicit call for intervention: 'Arise, O God, contend for your case!' To this point the design of the psalm has been to persuade Yahweh that his contention lies not with his people but with the invaders. Thus Yahweh is now summoned to reverse his action.

This final section thus summons God to call to mind the adversaries' unrestrained sacrilege and to fight for what the psalmist has shown to be his own cause.

G. PSALM 77

1. Distress

The psalmist simply speaks of 'the day of my distress' (v. 3a) with little reference to any particulars. His deepest trouble appears to stem from God's silence in the face of his continual pleading (v.

3). Moreover, since the psalmist's memory of God (v. 4) and of 'the days of old' (v. 6) gives him grief (vv. 4-5), it appears there is a strong contrast between how God acted then and how he acts now. As the psalm develops, it becomes evident that the initial 'distress' that prompted these reflections has become an occasion for confronting a wider issue, namely the absence of Yahweh's saving deeds.

The kind of saving deeds that the psalmist invokes Yahweh to 'actualize' (see below) are those of the exodus tradition. Since these saving deeds were performed on behalf of the nation, it is likely that the 'I' of the psalm speaks on behalf of the nation.[46]

2. Interpretation

God may not be considered the source of the particular 'distress' to which the psalmist refers, but he is clearly held responsible for the absence of any relief from this distress. When the psalmist had called upon God, he expected him to exercise his favor in the present because he had shown it in the past. But the prolonged silence of heaven is now all too evident from the uninterrupted course of his present distress. Hence, God himself has become the psalmist's central dilemma.

3. Appeal

Ps. 77 could not be characterized as a psalm of petition, for it contains none. In fact, God is nowhere addressed in the lament proper (vv. 2-11).[47] The psalm simply *refers* to acts of prayer (vv. 2-3) which have proved unsuccessful. Rather, this 'lament' is simply a description of the psalmist's personal reflections. He recounts his failure in prayer to find 'comfort' (v. 3) and his failure in meditation to 'search out' (v. 7) the ways of God.

In vv. 8-10 appear questions concerning the divine favor. Elsewhere such questions where God is the grammatical subject are used rhetorically to express complaint and to move him to intervene. But in Ps. 77 they are not addressed to God directly—he is referred to in the third person. Instead, these verses are introduced as the ponderings of the psalmist's heart and as the searchings of his spirit (v. 7), which apparently leave him faint (v. 4) and speechless (v. 5). Thus, they are not primarily rhetorical; they are real questions. This interpretation is confirmed by his remark concluding the lament: 'And I said, "This is my piercing wound: the changing of the right hand of the Most High."'[48]

The psalmist then suddenly announces that he will address Yahweh with praise (vv. 12-13)—certainly not because he feels like praising or because he has experienced something to praise God about.[49] What then is the meaning of this praise? Taken in isolation the psalm offers few clues. But, as Chapter 2 has shown, praise frequently occurs within the corporate complaints. The praise contained in Ps. 77, however, is different from the praises contained in Pss. 9-10, 44, 60, 74, 80, 85 and 89 in that it is not set in contrast to a lament describing a contradictory distress, thereby making evident the psalmist's disappointment and grounds for complaint. Hence, the praise of Ps. 77 does not appear to function negatively as the other instances do. But, as also noted in Chapter 2, such praises and references to God's earlier saving deeds also function positively to remind Yahweh of what he can and should be doing. This positive function is most evident when the recitation of praise *follows* the lament, as in Ps. 74.12-17.

Therefore, this turning of the psalmist to praise need not signal a shift in the psalmist's mood (as most commentators assume); rather, it indicates a shift in his appeal.[50] The change of address, from referring to God to speaking directly to God, indicates that the change is from private ponderings to an appeal in the form of 'praise'. Inherent in praise is the desire that Yahweh continue, or in this case, renew his acts that are deserving of praise.

Taken as a whole, the train of thought in the psalm appears to be this: the psalmist first recounts his attempts to reach God in prayer (vv. 2-3) and then his attempts to obtain consolation in memory of the past and to scrutinize the ways of the Most High (vv. 4-11). This description also makes evident the disparity between God in the past and God in the present. The failures of supplication and of reflection lead him to remember *before God*—as indicated by the change of address—the former deeds of God. Such reminders in the corporate complaints aim at bringing Yahweh to 'actualize' (*vergegenwärtigen*) tradition.

Therefore, although this psalm contains no formal petition and the lament proper is never addressed to Yahweh directly, the psalm as a whole functions as an appeal. As the address to Yahweh in vv. 12ff. shows—albeit in the form of praise—the entire psalm has been recounted before Yahweh. The psalmist in vv. 2-11 does not cry to God as such. He simply refers to the fact that he has been doing this. He thus lays bare his own grief and sense of utter disappointment, and so makes plain the intention behind the accompanying hymn: 'Yahweh, make this praise a present reality!'

H. PSALM 79

1. Distress

Ps. 79 points to a national disaster very similar to the one found in Ps. 74, which laments the destruction of the central sanctuary. In this psalm, however, the reader/listener is brought outside the confines of the temple (v. 1) to see the ruins of Jerusalem (v. 1) and the slaughter of the people (vv. 2-3, 10b; both are summarized in v. 7).

The particular historical moment behind this psalm cannot be stated conclusively, but it appears to have strongest affinity with the Babylonians' destruction of Jerusalem in 587 BC. The question regarding the duration of God's anger (v. 5) may presuppose a lapse of some time between the actual destruction and the composition of the psalm, thus placing it later in the exilic period.[51]

2. Interpretation

The psalmist begins by describing the distress as one caused by invading nations. But he then speaks of God exhibiting his anger, which not being directed at the nations (as implied by v. 6) must be directed at Israel. The mention of God's anger here indicates the consequences of that anger are somehow connected to the immediate distress in question. This reference to divine wrath along with the later confession of sin (vv. 8, 9) suggests that the disaster is perceived as some form of divine judgment. But the precise means in which this anger is exercised, whether by actually stirring up the invasion or by simply handing the people over, is not articulated by the psalmist.

The cause of the distress is probably not explicitly attributed to God for the same reasons given with reference to Ps. 74 above. The repeated use of the possessive pronoun 'your' in connection with the temple, city and people (Ps. 79.1-2) suggests that God should bear personal responsibility for the defense of Zion and its citizens. As in Ps. 74, it appears that this psalmist is alluding to the same Zion tradition. In Ps. 74 the destruction of the temple was perceived as a reversal of the Zion tradition, and thus Yahweh was perceived as negligent or passive in the its destruction. The enemies of both Pss. 74 and 79, since they are described as blasphemers of the divine name (vv. 6, 9-10, 12), are not portrayed as Yahweh's agents of judgment—they are *his* enemies.

Since God's anger is seen to have some justification, the psalmist questions not God's wrath per se but its duration, intensity, and as v. 6 suggests, its misdirection. His grounds for questioning God's continued anger are twofold. The vehemence and persistence of God's wrath is considered unwarranted since it now threatens the very existence of his own 'heritage' (נחלה). Secondly, if Yahweh does not soon forgive his people and redirect his wrath toward the godless invaders, then their taunts against Yahweh would go unchecked. Yahweh's reputation, the psalmist argues, is bound up with the people's fate (vv. 9-10, 12).

3. Appeal

Although God's anger has some justification relative to the people's sin alone, the psalmist for the sake of his argument focuses upon other factors that would indicate God is actually acting against his own interests. The psalmist opens his appeal to God with a description of the invader's devastation:

79.1 O God, nations have invaded your property;
they have defiled your holy temple;
they have made Jerusalem a ruin.

2 They have given the corpses of your servants
as food for the birds of the sky,
the flesh of your devout ones to the beasts of the
land.

3 They have poured the blood [of your servants]
like water ...

The intent of this report is, of course, not to inform God of an event he was unaware of, but to portray the scene as personally offensive to God. Thus, although God's wrath and the enemies' destruction are somehow related, it is clear that the enemy bears independent responsibility for his hostilities, at least for the degree of harm he inflicts. The psalmist's frequent use of 'your' characterizes the nations as trespassers against Yahweh's property, not as instruments of just judgment. Though God's wrath against the people's sin is in some measure just, the psalmist for the sake of his argument focuses upon the third party to show that the present course of events is actually working against God's interest.

By referring to the divine wrath after this description of the distress, the psalmist makes plain the irony that God persists to focus his vehement anger toward Israel, while they, God's own possessions, face near extinction. The choice of קִנְאָה in this instance—the only mention of God's jealousy in the Psalms aside from 78.58 (in a recitation of Israel's history)—may suggest that if his jealousy were to continue at this intensity he would have no people to be jealous about! The psalmist forcibly 'answers' this rhetorical question with a petition that summons God to redirect his wrath. In so doing it seeks to resolve the corresponding irony that those who do not invoke Yahweh (v. 6) and who ravage his people (v. 7) go unpunished. As the enemy 'poured out' (שׁפך) the blood of Yahweh's servants (v. 3, cf. v. 10), so God should 'pour out' (שׁפך, v. 6) his rage on the enemy.

The second half of the psalm (the first being marked by the inclusio of the foe's devastation in vv. 1 and 7) consists of two cycles of petitions concerning the divine favor, help and

punishment. The first labors to build a case (vv. 8-10; 5 lines in
BHS) for a sinful and unworthy people, and the second quickly
calls for action (vv. 11-12; 2 lines in *BHS*).

While vv. 6-7 concentrate on directing God's anger to the foes,
vv. 8-9 concentrate on removing his anger from the people. This
request for forgiveness[52] is supported by two reasons: the low
state of the people (כי, v. 8c) and the reputation of Yahweh's name
(על־דבר, v. 9a; למען, v. 9b), which as v. 10 elaborates, is
threatened by rumors of these invading nations. Although the
people have sinned and are therefore deserving of judgment, the
psalmist urges that God's overriding concern should be his honor.
Even though the enemies may falsely interpret God as being absent
or simply ineffectual (when in fact he is very present in jealous
anger), the psalmist considers that God should rather withdraw his
fury and leave no room for misinterpretation since his name is at
stake. Thus the argument runs: if God were to persist in his
jealousy he would threaten his own reputation.

The psalmist then goes on to prescribe how Yahweh can exhibit
the vindication of his reputation: by avenging the slaughter of his
servants. Verses 11-12 repeat the motifs found in vv. 8-10, namely
the pitiful state of the people and the enemies' taunting of
Yahweh's renown. Then in contrast to this mockery the psalmist
vows the people's praise (v. 13). There is here the emphasis on
God's possession ('your people and the sheep of your pasture') as
in the beginning lament (vv. 1-2), but instead of their decimation
the psalmist now speaks of their jubilation. Moreover, instead of
Yahweh's wrath going on 'forever', it is his praise which shall go
on 'forever'. According to Gunkel, this verse rings with a
'confident "certainty"' regarding the future.[53]

In sum, the key appeal of this psalm is to God's honor, which
the psalmist argues is closely tied to the fate of Israel. He
underscores this with frequent use of possessives (vv. 1, 2, 10,
13) and by showing how the people's reproach (v. 4) becomes
Yahweh's reproach (v. 12).

I. PSALM 80

1. Distress

The occasion underlying this psalm appears to be one of extreme national distress: passers-by ravage as they please (vv. 13-14), burning and destroying (v. 17). The people experience sorrow (v. 6) and strife (v. 7). The question 'How long?', associated with prayers that had been offered prior to this psalm, implies that this tragedy has persisted for some time. This psalm thus presupposes foregoing prayers that have been ineffectual.

Commentators have not reached agreement regarding the precise historical occasion behind this psalm, nor regarding its geographical provenance. As noted by Eissfeldt, Ps. 80 has been variously considered to reflect every national crisis from the tenth century division of the kingdom to the time of Maccabees.[54] The most plausible conjectures locate the psalm either in 732-722 BC when the northern tribes were under threat (note esp. vv. 2-3 and the Septuagintal addition in the superscription) or in the time of Josiah and his reform (cf. vv. 18-19).

2. Interpretation

In the description of this distress the enemy is the one who plunders the people (vv. 13-14, 17), but God is the one who exposes the people (v. 13). God also makes the people an object of contention among their neighbors, which may suggest that he incites these neighbors to attack.

As noted in Chapter 5, most corporate psalms speaking from the midst of a grave national disaster attribute the cause of their distress to God. Ps. 80 contains several features, particularly its images, that illustrate the logic of this attribution. The lack of the desired response to the people's prayers indicates Yahweh's disposition is not favorably inclined towards them (v. 5). The image of Yahweh as shepherd—an image probably derived from the ark preceding the people (see below)—along with the continual sorrow of the people evokes the picture of this shepherd 'feeding' his own with their tears. The image of Yahweh as a gardener—an image suggested by the 'transplant' of the people from Egypt to Canaan—along with the nation's broken defenses evokes the picture of this gardener destroying the protective walls. The ironies of a shepherd feeding his flock with tears and of a gardener destroying the protective walls graphically depict the psalmist's disappointment in Yahweh. More concretely, the psalm implies that Yahweh has failed to lead the people to victory in holy war (vv. 2-3), and that he has failed to continue the nurturing of his people, a task that he began in the exodus and conquest (vv. 9-14).

The psalm may betray an awareness that the people have defected from Yahweh (v. 19), and so the psalm does not express perplexity over God's anger per se but over its duration ('How long?') and its intensity ('fume', 'tears in large measure'). Although God's anger may in some measure be just, the overriding conviction of the psalm is that Yahweh appears to have abandoned or even reversed what he began in salvation history. The psalmist's perplexity is underlined by the interrogative 'Why?'—the only instance among the God-laments where God's active intervention is expressed in question form.

3. Appeal

This psalm, besides exhibiting the normal structure of the lament genre, also displays a matching structure of imagery (as in Ps. 44). God is depicted as a Shepherd-King and the people as his flock (vv. 2-4, 6). Then he appears as a vinedresser, the people as his vine, and the enemies as cleared weeds and stones (v. 10) and as beasts (vv. 13-14). The final conception is that of God and his divinely appointed king, 'the man of your right hand' (v. 18). Each image places God in a role of responsibility for his people. This imagery enables the psalmist to present clearly to Yahweh the ironies of the present distress.

The introductory petitions pick up hymnic language which, by its very utterance, serves as praise of God but also functions to 'remind' God of the roles he assumed in past deeds of salvation, here the exodus and conquest. (These are the very traditions drawn upon for the vine metaphor of vv. 9ff.) Yahweh's leading 'Joseph' refers to the exodus out of Egypt.[55] The motif that ties vv. 2 and 3 together, though not named explicitly, is the ark of the covenant and its role in holy war.[56] As this symbolic throne of Yahweh preceded the people (hence the shepherd image) and led them to victory over their enemies in Canaan, so Yahweh is implored to actualize this tradition by a theophanic appearance in their present distress. In the language of the old tribal alliance, he is called upon to renew his warrior strength to bring about salvation.

The psalm continues in petition with a refrain that is repeated with slight variation in vv. 8, 20 (cf. v. 15).[57] The imperative השיבנו, as it were, steps out of the days of the conquest and into the contemporary crisis. Without metaphor or allusion the petition tacitly admits that something has been lost. It does so with what may well be an intentional ambiguity. השיבנו can mean 'cause us to (re)turn', in the sense of repentance (cf. Jer. 31.18; 23.22; Lam. 5.21), and also 'restore us', in the sense of a renovation of fortunes. The latter of course has special reference to a re-establishment of the past glories just intimated.

The petition of the parallel line echoes the Aaronic blessing (Num. 6.25): 'Make your face to shine'. The mere turn of Yahweh's favor results in salvation. As the following verse also shows, God's disposition is a chief concern of the psalm.

The God-lament bemoans the present distress with the assertion that God is its cause. These verses touch upon each sphere of the people's life: religious (v. 5), personal (v. 6) and social (v. 7). This draws the contrast with past glory all the more graphically and infuses the repeated—though not simply repeated—cry for restoration with heightened urgency.

As Gunkel describes it, the sudden turn in v. 9 from 'the misery of the present' to 'the beautiful past' presents a 'heart-rending contrast',[58] which is typical of the dynamic structure of the God-lament psalms. The cycle of reviewing past splendor and present distresses is repeated. As in vv. 2-7, the past splendor is that of the exodus-settlement period and the present crisis is described in a God-lament. In the eyes of the psalmist, God by 'transplanting' the nation from Egypt to Palestine assumed responsibilities like those of a gardener. As a recitation of God's saving history and the splendor he bestowed on the 'vine' (its height and breadth, vv. 11-12), these verses ring with hymnic overtones, but only to be broken by a God-lament. In fact, it appears that this reference to past saving deeds is mentioned only to lead to the God-lament.[59] The body of this psalm (vv. 5-14) is thus dominated by the God-lament.

The petition that begins this closing section offers a twist on the refrain. It pleads for Yahweh to turn not the people this time but himself. This verse displays an anthropomorphic progression of Yahweh turning, looking,[60] seeing, and finally nurturing (פקד) his vine. After again emphasizing the commitment Yahweh has made to his people by a previous action (v. 16a),[61] the psalmist continues the vine metaphor into v. 17 by interjecting a lament into this petition section. The verbs express destruction: in the first half it is directed against the vine, while in the second line it is probably to be understood as a wish directed against the vandals.[62] If so, this psalm then expresses the people's salvation as the enlightening of Yahweh's countenance (פניך), and the foes' destruction as the rebuke of his countenance (פניך).

The next petition breaks with the vine metaphor and turns to another image: Yahweh is invoked to reaffirm his loyalty to the king by placing his 'hand' upon the man of his 'right hand'. Once again, an appositional phrase is added, which draws attention to a previous action entailing present commitment (v. 18b, cf. 16a), perhaps also suggesting that Yahweh has an interest in this himself (note לך).

The vows of loyalty (ולא־נסוג ממך) and of praise (v. 19) tacitly suggest an awareness of the people's past failure. (Note that the imperative השיבנו of the refrain can mean, 'Cause us to return'.) The people desire to cling to the one who has struck them (vv. 5ff.).

Overall, the focus of the psalmist's argument against God's intense, persisting anger lies in his efforts to impress upon God the interest he has invested in the people. This is noted by the imagery employed by the psalm, by references to their past history together, and by the mere fact that in the clear majority of cases Yahweh is the subject of the verbs. Even where he is not the grammatical subject the action follows as a result of divine initiative. The people's dependence on God is made prominent by imagery: they are helpless sheep of the Shepherd, a defenseless vine, and even their kingship is a vassalage. Moreover, the *waws* of v. 19 indicate that the loyalty of the people is also consequent upon prior actions of God. In contrast to Pss. 74 and 79 this psalm employs no relative argument regarding the attacks upon the people by those less godly than they. The poet does not endeavor to stir God's anger by referring to the insolence of the enemy. His interest remains fixed upon Yahweh who has bound himself to his people.

J. PSALM 85

1. Distress

The underlying situation appears to be a people and a land lacking 'life' (v. 7) and blessing (vv. 9-14). No clear references are given to a particular moment in Israel's history. Some commentators therefore believe that the psalm was never designed for a specific historical incident, but that it confronted recurring times of need, namely the need for weather favorable to good harvests.[63] Such a concern is indeed reflected in v. 13. One could therefore interpret vv. 2-4 as a thanksgiving for earlier bountiful harvests that had relieved years of drought. Verses 5-8 would then suggest drought was again prevailing, and the oracle of vv. 9-14 would announce its end and promise coming fertility.

Taking this psalm in isolation, one could not disprove this interpretation. When seen in the light of several prophetic texts, however, the psalm shows a strong affinity to a particular crisis in postexilic times. According to the prophets, Israel's return from exile would be a sign of Yahweh's forgiveness (Isa. 40.2 and esp. Jer. 33.7-8 where the phrase שׁוב שׁבות is used). Thus compare Ps. 85.2-4. Later prophecies, however, show that the people who did return experienced agricultural dearth (Hag. 1.5-11; 2.15-16) and the persistence of God's anger (Zech. 1.12; Isa. 59.9ff.). Thus compare Ps. 85.5-8. But the prophets also assert that God would not be angry forever (Isa. 57.15-19, esp. v. 16, also v. 19 [שׁלום]). The heavens will rain down righteousness, and from the earth salvation and righteousness will spring up (45.8; see also 46.13; 51.5; 52.7-10; 58.8). Yahweh's כבוד will also be revealed (40.5; 62.2). Thus compare Ps. 85.9-14.

Therefore, although Ps. 85 lacks definite historical references, its close parallels of language and concerns suggest that it reflects this postexilic crisis.[64]

2. Interpretation

If one accepts the situation described above as the background to the psalm, the psalmist's interpretation of the distress may be posited as follows.

The source of this distress is considered to be Yahweh. With God being made the grammatical subject in virtually every verse of this psalm, the psalmist speaks of the national welfare hinging solely on the divine favor (there is no mention of enemies or other factors). This conviction of God's control over the fortunes of the nation probably derives from the prophetic preaching. Since the return from exile was interpreted as a divine act (vv. 2-4), so the restoration must be as well (vv. 5-8). However, the return was also foreseen as a sign of Yahweh's forgiveness, but the harshness of life in the land indicates God is persisting in his anger. Although the people's sin may have given warrant for divine wrath in the past, the psalmist asserts that now that the foretold 'turning' (שוב שבות) has been achieved, Yahweh can claim no such warrant. Hence, the psalmist protests the duration of his anger.

3. Appeal

Opening the psalm is a recollection in the language of praise— perhaps styled after the prophecies—of Israel's return from exile (vv. 2-4). The verbs should probably be translated as simple pasts (e.g. v. 4: 'You withdrew...; you turned...'), as distinct from present perfects. The distance in time is suggested not only by the parataxis of 'You turned' (v. 4) and 'Turn!' (v. 5), but also by the pronouns. In vv. 2-4, the reference to an earlier saving deed, the psalmist refers to 'them'; in vv. 5-8, the lament and petition for the current crisis, he speaks of 'us'.[65]

Although the psalm begins by celebrating the restored fortunes of the people,[66] logically this should come in v. 4. After the root problem of sin has been dealt with (v. 3), the divine anger can be withdrawn (v. 4), and then the divine favor can be expressed in terms of material blessing (v. 2). However, by this arrangement the crux of the psalm is brought into sharp focus: God's disposition toward the people.

> 85.4 You withdrew all your fury;
>   you turned from your burning anger.
>   5   Return to us, O God of our salvation,
>   and break off your indignation from us.[67]

With לעולם and לדר ודר enveloping v. 6, emphasis is given to the persistence of God's anger. Only in v. 6 and in Ps. 77.8-9 are such '... forever?' questions asked without 'How long?' preceding. In Ps. 77 these questions appear to convey real personal doubt. The questions in Ps. 85, however, differ in two ways, which point them in the opposite direction. Ps. 85.6 is addressed to God. As noted in Chapter 3, such questions directed to God do not seek information; they are persuasive. Unlike a question directed to oneself where such reflection affects only the individual, a rhetorical question addressed to God seeks to move God. Its aim in this case is therefore to change God's disposition. Secondly, the question that follows clearly points toward a positive resolution, which also indicates that these verses aim to transform God's posture toward the people. Verse 6 pushes Yahweh to the extremes of time, to the point where his wrath would no longer be reasonable, and thus presents a complaint concerning the duration of the divine anger. Verse 7 then moves to the present, and in effect asks Yahweh if it is not more reasonable for him to revive his people so that they can celebrate his kindness. Verse 8 then expresses this request without figures and without rhetoric: 'Show us, Yahweh, your merciful devotion and grant us your salvation!'

Structurally, the crucial transition of the psalm occurs between vv. 6 and 7. Verses 5-6 are joined by their aim to turn God's anger, thus looking back to vv. 2-4. Verses 7-8 are joined by their aim to obtain God's חסד, thus looking forward to vv. 9-14. The complaint regarding God's anger thus climaxes in the God-lament (v. 6), after which the positive summons of the psalm begins.

In v. 9 there is another shift in the psalm. The psalmist no longer speaks to God on behalf of 'us' (vv. 5-8); he is now the individual ('I', v. 9) who will listen (שמע) to God. Verses 9-14 are thus God's response to the appeal, not a constituent part of that appeal. They are words for the congregation and thus not directly a part of the psalmist's argument to God.

K. PSALM 89

1. Distress

This psalm reflects a battlefield scene where the king finds his armies in retreat (v. 44), his fortifications broken down (v. 41) and his nation plundered (v. 42). The scorn of the enemy makes itself felt as a sharp sting (vv. 42, 51-52). The questions, 'How long? ... forever?' (v. 47), imply the abiding nature of the affliction.

Since vv. 47-52 in particular appear to come from the mouth of the king, the lament probably emerged in the pre-exilic era. Considering that the tragedy seems to have occurred in the lifetime of the speaker (v. 48), it is unlikely that the psalm was composed as an expression of post-exilic hope for the restoration of the Davidic monarchy.

Although vv. 2-3, 6-19 have much in common with the so-called 'hymns of Yahweh's enthronement', there is nothing else in the psalm to prompt a 'mythical' or strictly cultic interpretation of the psalm. As argued below, the occasion of the psalm is to be inferred from the lament (vv. 39-52), which responds primarily to the oracle (vv. 4-5, 20-38), not to the hymn (vv. 2-3, 6-19).[68]

2. *Interpretation*

The distress is not perceived simply as a military rout since the welfare of the state, here 'embodied' in the king, is bound up with the promise of God, as the introductory hymn declares. The failure of the head of state thus signals a divine retraction of covenant. Several linguistic and conceptual parallels between vv. 2-38 and 39-52 make plain that the disaster has been interpreted in the light of the preceding promise. The lament is presented as an explicit denial of the praise. Moreover, this contrast indicates not merely a retraction of covenant but a direct violation of it—Yahweh has 'spurned' the covenant itself (v. 40)! The 'anointed' one (v. 21) who was able to call God 'Father' (v. 27) is now rejected as an object of wrath (v. 39). The divinely initiated 'covenant' (v. 4), which even in view of human 'profanation' (v. 32) would not be 'profaned' by God (v. 35), is now spurned and 'profaned' (v. 40). Thus, the 'servant', once the recipient of the promised covenant (v. 4, cf. 20-21), is now the disappointed covenant-partner (v. 40). Yahweh had promised to 'exalt' the people (vv. 17-18), and especially the king (vv. 20, 25), who was to be set as the highest of the kings of the earth (v. 28), but instead Yahweh 'exalts' the king's 'adversaries' (v. 43), whom he had formerly promised to crush (v. 24). 'Rejoicing', by virtue of Yahweh's name, was to characterize the people of God (vv. 16-17), but instead Yahweh gives the foe cause for 'rejoicing' (v. 43). In sum, Yahweh's indestructible 'loyalty' (vv. 2-3, 15, 25, 29, 34) and 'faithfulness' (vv. 2-3, 6, 9, 25, 34), which were once the 'sworn' (vv. 4, 36) guarantors of the Davidic covenant, are now lost from sight (v. 50).[69]

Within the stipulations of the covenant, this reversal could not be explained from the human side. Transgression would be chastised, but it was not grounds for dissolving the treaty (vv. 31-34). Moreover, the closing lines of the hymnic section (vv. 34-38) make clear that God has vowed to stand by his word unconditionally. Human transgression could not break it (vv. 31-34); divine holiness would not break it (vv. 35-38).

3. Appeal

All commentators agree that the immediate occasion behind the present psalm is the distress reflected in the lament. The search for the theme should thus begin here. The linguistic parallels listed above make clear that the disaster on the battlefield has been interpreted within the framework of a word of Yahweh that has been called into question by the defeat. Before expressing his appeal, the psalmist recites the covenant oracle (vv. 4-5, 20-38) along with its basis in the kingship of Yahweh (vv. 2-3, 6-19). After establishing this perspective, he describes the debacle in tones of complaint and petitions for the restoration of the Davidic mercies. In brief, the theme of Ps. 89 is the appeal for Yahweh to restore the Davidic mercies.

The question of how this theme is developed naturally brings us to the problem of the psalm's unity. Ps. 89 has three main sections:

2-3, 6-19	Hymn: Yahweh's right to cosmic kingship
4-5, 20-38	Oracle: the Davidic covenant
39-52	Lament: the king's battle defeat

Were all three sections composed on the occasion of this distress, or did the hymn and oracle exist prior to the distress?

The latter appears to be the most likely possibility. First, we must note that since the oracle coheres strongly to the hymn,[70] it is probable they were composed together. Second, of the some 30 contrasting parallels between the hymn and oracle (vv. 2-38) and and the lament (39-52), only 7 are found in the hymnic section, and all but one of these 7 parallels are also found in the oracle. The lament also lacks any reference to Yahweh's cosmic kingship, the central theme of the hymn. The lament, it would appear, has been composed in light of the oracle, not the hymn. Thus, on strictly literary grounds, one cannot account for the presence of the hymn with respect to its content and especially to its form. This observation would suggest that the hymn was not composed specifically for this distress but has been included solely because of its coherence to the oracle. Therefore, since the hymn was not composed contemporary to the lament and since the oracle and hymn were probably written together, the hymn and oracle should be read as praise sung prior to the distress.

But even if this praise was sung prior to the distress, how should this 'praise' be read now in connection with the lament? In what mood are these verses to be sung: with determined joy or with bitter cynicism? The latter is unlikely since the purpose of the lament is not merely to contradict but to 'actualize' the praise, as the petitions indicate. The former is likewise improbable as it would be difficult to sing these praises with anything more than muted tones since their reality is at best obscured.[71] Moreover, any attempt to read these verses simply as an encouragement to the people's faith or as flattery to God fails to account for the sudden assertions of lament that explicitly deny the praise.

As intimated above, the purpose of vv. 2-38 is to establish the grounds of complaint by reminding Yahweh of his previous commitments. This section might be called confessional, but strictly speaking the intent is not to extol but to remind. It should thus be read as a tearful reminder to Yahweh of the praise which he once received and which the people now wish to see realized anew.

Finally, it may be noted that the psalmist would have a stronger case to argue in the lament section if the hymn and oracle were promises made prior to the defeat, particularly if the hymn and oracle were a familiar piece recited at the king's enthronement.

The hymn's introductory summary (vv. 2-5) presents the main themes of the psalm by means of certain key words: merciful devotion and faithfulness, covenant and David, and terms synonymous with 'forever' (expressed five times in these verses). The dominating notions of vv. 2-38, Yahweh's cosmic kingship (vv. 2-3, 6-19) and his earthly vice-regent (vv. 4-5, 20-38), are carefully woven together by parallel terminology.[72]

Verses 6-13 announce Yahweh's supremacy over the heavens, the sea and the earth. Besides his sheer awesomeness, a feature central to Yahweh's incomparability in the heavens is his 'faithfulness', a term that serves as an inclusio for this second quatrain (vv. 6-9). In the language of the ancient creation myth, vv. 10-11 tell of Yahweh's rule over *yam* and how he crushed the enemies.[73] In vv. 12-13 Yahweh's ownership of heaven and earth is based on his act of creation. Verses 6-13 thus establish

Yahweh's right to universal kingship: he is chief in the heavenly pantheon; he is victor over chaos; he is creator of all.

Verse 14 serves as a transition by providing a summary statement of vv. 6-13 and a fitting preface to the description of Yahweh's kingship in vv. 15-19. In language that is more directly personal, these verses, after characterizing Yahweh's rule with such moral qualities as righteousness, justice, merciful devotion and truth, describe the benefits received by his subjects. The motif of joy (vv. 16-17a) culminates in that of exaltation (v. 17b). This is then substantiated in two כי verses (vv. 18-19), which indicate that the bedrock of the people's exaltation is found in the supreme subject of Yahweh's kingship, the Davidic king.

Most commentators mark off v. 19 as the final verse of the hymnic praise proper, but the second person address continues into v. 20 to introduce the divine oracle as a citation, thus including it too as an expression of the psalmist's praise. The motif of exaltation continues but here focused upon the king, along with references to his election and strength (vv. 20-22). Yahweh promises to crush his adversaries (vv. 23-24) and to make him supreme as the highest of kings (vv. 25-28). Parallels thus appear between the hymn and the oracle, which are presented in a somewhat chiastic fashion under the notions of exaltation (vv. 20b-22 and 17-19), the crushing of foes (vv. 23-24 and 10-11), and supremacy (vv. 25-28 and 6-9). Yahweh thus bestows on his earthly vice-regent the qualities that are characteristic of his own kingship.

This modified chiasm joining the hymn and the oracle is then followed by an inclusio which forms the remainder of the praise section (vv. 29-38). The opening couplet matches the final quatrain with assurances that the covenant is inviolable (vv. 29, 35-36) and that the Davidic dynasty is guaranteed forever (vv.30, 37-38). This divine pledge thus encompasses the promise that human violation of the covenant will result in punishment, *not* annulment (vv. 31-34).

The suddenness of the psalm's reversal is expressed succinctly but emphatically by a *waw*-adversative and two synonyms of rejection. The psalmist leaves the praise at its height and moves without warning into severe lament: the treaty that could not be profaned (vv. 35-38) has been profaned (v. 40). After stating his belief that Yahweh has in effect rejected the covenant (vv. 39-40), the psalmist presents the concrete evidence for his case (vv. 41-44) and then spells out the result of this disaster as the humiliation of the king's glory (vv. 45-16). He patterns this description after the Davidic oracle, as the following parallels show: the 'anointed' (vv. 21, 39) 'servant' (vv. 21, 40) who was chosen but is now rejected (cf. vv. 20-22 and 39-40), the enemies who were once crushed but are now exalted (cf. 23-24 and 41-44), the messiah who was promised exaltation but now sees it overturned (cf. 25-28 and 45-46). Yahweh's explicit denial of the covenant is thus brought to light.

In vv. 47-52 there is a shift in the nature of the appeal. This is noted by a change in meter and syntax. Verses 39-46 are all declarative statements, while vv. 47-52 are either rhetorical questions or imperatives. The two petitions of the psalm do not address the main issues raised in the lament. This is done by the rhetorical questions that begin each half of this final section (vv. 47-52). They appear to take up the function of petition. The grammatical petitions simply add urgency to the summons implicit in the rhetorical questions. The first question confronts Yahweh's disfavor and in effect calls for it to cease. The second confronts the absence of his merciful acts and in effect calls for Yahweh to restore them. This question picks up the key terms of the preceding hymn and oracle (this is the only mention of חסד, אמונה and נשבע in the lament) and thus encapsulates the divine promise. The cogency of the psalmist's appeal is that he asks for nothing more than for what Yahweh has already sworn to give.

L. PSALM 90

1. Distress

Ps. 90 bemoans the brevity and travail of life. Although vv. 2-6 speak of life's transience as a general condition of humankind, vv. 13ff. intimate that a more particular dilemma has occasioned these reflections. The petitions, 'Return, Yahweh—how long?' (v. 13a) and 'Make us glad according to the days you have afflicted us, according to the years we have seen misery' (v. 15), imply that the people's current condition is considered harsher than usual. In addition, G. von Rad has made clear the peculiar character of this psalm, particularly by drawing attention to the near absence of any reference to the saving acts of God in the nation's history.[74] This has been a regular feature of the corporate laments that we have discussed. The lack of attention to the traditions fundamental to the pre-exilic laments, namely the exodus and conquest, the Zion and Davidic traditions, may imply that Ps. 90 best fits the postexilic era. This can be compared with Ps. 85, which, although it alludes to God's gracious act in returning the people from exile, establishes its appeal upon the promises of the late pre-exilic and exilic prophecies, not upon these pre-exilic traditions. Ps. 85, along with various prophetic texts (see above), indicates that the postexilic period was a time of dearth and could still be described as a time characterized by God's wrath (85.5-6). Divine anger is also prominent in Ps. 90 (vv. 7ff.). Thus, for these reasons Ps. 90 may also reflect the hardship of the postexilic period. (Cf. also Ps. 102, an exilic lament of the individual, which appeals not to Yahweh's past mercies but to his promise of future mercies, thus also suggesting that these pre-exilic traditions no longer form the *primary* foundation for the people.)

Ps. 90 originated either as a public prayer of penance[75] or, as von Rad has suggested, as a literary work of the Wisdom tradition.[76]

The intensity of this distress is evident. The work of their hands, for all their toil (v. 10), appears to decay right before them (v. 17). The people themselves feel destined to a life that is futile (vv. 9-10). The duration of the distress is mentioned in the phrase 'the days you have afflicted us, the years we have seen misery' (v. 15) and in the question 'How long?' (v. 13).

2. Interpretation

The distress is traced back to Yahweh throughout—enemies play no part in it; yet he does not appear as the saving and judging God of salvation history but as the Creator (perhaps for reasons suggested above). Ps. 90 apparently draws upon the Wisdom tradition, as distinct from a salvation history one. Although the distress is a particular one, it is perceived against the backdrop of the transience of the generations before their Maker (vv. 2-6). Since the Creator is the one who commands death (v. 3) and since the people's life is now characterized by that decay which leads inexorably to death, the psalmist expresses with no uncertainty that the people's affliction comes from Yahweh.

The psalmist does not avoid the issue of the people's sin, which has aroused God's anger (vv. 7-8), but his purpose in mentioning it is not to express penance but to show that he perceives that God is intent on, even preoccupied with, measuring the people's sin:

> 90.8   You have placed (שׁית) our iniquities before you,
> and our secret sins in the light of your face.

The psalmist's disappointment in God is also adumbrated in his question 'Return, Yahweh—how long?' Thus, the psalmist raises no complaint about God's anger per se but about its intensity (vv. 7ff.) and duration (v. 13, cf. 15).

3. Appeal

All commentators regard the opening verses as hymnic. Kraus reads vv. 1-4 as containing 'elements of hymnic address', while S. Schreiner considers only vv. 1-2 as being 'similar to the hymn'.[77] Such interpretations appear to be based on the content of these verses. There is, however, a formal transition in the psalm that may indicate that the hymn continues through v. 6. Between vv. 6 and 7 there is a shift from referring to 'man' in the third person to referring to 'we' in the first person. If one takes this change of person as one's guide, then vv. 1-6 should be read as a coherent piece praising the eternal God by contrasting him with mortal humanity. Moreover, the contents of vv. 1-6 and of vv. 7ff. maintain different focal points. Verses 7ff. do not concentrate on the shortness of life referred to in vv. 1-6; they lament the decay and poverty the people experience within that life, however brief it may be. Thus, at v. 7 the psalmist shifts his focus from God's eternity to God's anger and from humanity's mortality to the travail of his own generation.

Ps. 90 therefore has this in common with other corporate complaints: it uses the praise of God as a platform from which it can express a persuasive appeal. As B. Vawter notes:

> The 'motivation' which the psalmist proffers to the Almighty to urge him to spare his people is not, as in other psalms of impetration, a reminder of the great divine acts that formed the people, the merciful election that established a precedent for continuing mercy; it is, rather, an appeal to the One who need not count his years to show generosity to those whose end is always in sight, whose little play on life's stage extends at best to the duration of a sigh.[78]

The psalmist appeals to the eternal God to show pity to his perishing people. One notes as well, however, that this praise is not set *in contrast to* the lament, as is the case among other corporate complaints. Their complaints are evident because the psalmist shows how God's present action conflicts with this former action. But in Ps. 90 the nuance of complaint is implied in the tenor of the lament itself.

The opening words of this praise read: 'Lord, you have been a refuge for us in all generations'. Verses 2-6 give attention to the temporal aspect of this verse: 'in all generations'. But the closing petitions (vv. 13-17) give attention to the positive relationship between God and the people: 'Be sorry for *your servants*' (v. 13) and 'Let your work appear to *your servants*' (v. 16). In vv. 2-12 the psalmist makes no allusion to this relationship. It is this conviction of solidarity with the preceding generations of Israel[79] that arrests the lament of vv. 7-11 before it becomes mere lamentation. On the grounds of this solidarity with preceding generations the psalmist summons Yahweh to renew his saving deeds:

90.16   Let your work appear to your servants,
         and your splendor to their children.

As G. von Rad makes clear, it is characteristic of Israel's faith that
it be founded not upon 'philosophical speculation and religious
mysticism', but upon events 'in history in which God would
manifest himself'.[80] Hence, the psalmist shows that the only relief
from the futility that the people experience before their holy Creator
can be found in a renewal of God's work of favor in their history.

In sum, the opening praise of God (vv. 1-6) refers to the
temporal distinction between God and humanity. The lament
heightens this distinction even further by introducing the moral
distance between them. By themselves vv. 1-6 could be read as
coherent praise of God, but juxtaposed with the following lament
these opening verses simply bring to the fore the wide gap that the
Creator has put between himself and his creation. Thus, by
drawing upon this praise of God and by intensifying the separation
it refers to, the psalmist makes clear to Yahweh that the people's
only hope is a revelation of his saving work in their own
experience.

Chapter 7

THE COMPLAINTS OF THE INDIVIDUAL

A. PSALM 6

1. Distress

Perhaps of all the psalms we are considering this one gives the fewest references to a specific form of distress. It is clear that the psalmist is emotionally exhausted (vv. 7-8) and that enemies are involved (vv. 8-9, 11), but precisely how they are involved and whether any suggestion is made regarding the psalmist's physical condition (v. 3, 6) are questions to which this psalm is particularly elusive. The only other feature which can be stated with certainty is that the distress is a prolonged one (v. 4).

One could interpret the psalmist's suffering as principally emotional and spiritual. The physical exhaustion of vv. 7-8 may well derive from emotional stress. The same may thus be said of the statements in v. 3. The meaning of אמלל ('frail, feeble', from אמל, 'to dry up, wilt, languish') cannot be limited to either the emotional or the physical level. נבהל ('be terrified, hasty') is normally an emotive word, but it is here used with 'bones'. In Ps. 35.9-10, however, 'bones' and 'soul' are parallel expressions used as grammatical subjects in the verbal act of praising. They thus signify how the psalmist's whole being will respond in expressing Yahweh's gracious deliverance.

Neither is the meaning of v. 6 clear. Does the psalmist here indicate that he is actually at death's door, or is he simply comparing himself to the dead, in that neither is able to praise God (note the elaboration of the psalmist's condition in vv. 7-8)? This will be discussed further below.

K. Seybold includes this psalm among those with probable reference to sickness, chiefly because of the appearance of רפא.[1] After discussing other possible interpretations, he concludes that limiting the affliction to inner turmoil would not be justified in view of the analogy of Ps. 41 and the identical opening petition found in Ps. 38, which has clear references to physical illness.

The role played by the enemies will be considered below in connection with the psalmist's interpretation of his distress.

2. *Interpretation*

The precise source of the psalmist's affliction is likewise difficult to ascertain. The opening imperative is ambiguous as to whether God's chastening is actual or simply possible. As an example of the latter, P. Craigie suggests for v. 2 that 'the psalmist prays not to be rebuked or chastised for bringing this problem to God in prayer'.[2] Such a reserved posture for the psalmist, however, appears unlikely in view of the ensuing complaint, 'But you, Yahweh—how long?' Rather, it seems more likely that God's chastening is already felt by the psalmist. The emphatic position of the adverbial clauses in v. 2 ('Do not *in your anger* reprove me, and do not *in your wrath* chasten me!') indicates that the focus of the psalmist's concern is that Yahweh's chastening not become excessive, thus implying it is already present to some degree. Another clue can be found in Ps. 38, where the identical petition is followed by a statement which makes plain that God's anger is already at work.

Yahweh's role in the distress may be further elucidated from the complaint, 'But you, Yahweh—how long?' Though elliptical, its inclusion here shows that the psalmist's dismay (נבהל) is somehow contingent on Yahweh. He has the power to terminate the psalmist's affliction. Because נבהל is used frequently in the OT to describe responses to the chastisements and judgments of Yahweh,[3] it seems best to understand this ellipsis as, 'How long [will you continue to chastise]?'.

The role of the enemies, though not made explicit, can be discerned with greater ease. The 'assurance of being heard' (vv. 9-11) indicates that the adversaries will be ashamed when Yahweh answers the prayer of this psalm. Since this prayer was not directed against these foes, it appears that their harassment of the psalmist was contingent upon and not the cause of whatever affliction befell the psalmist. Their influence must therefore be considered secondary,[4] and probably took the form of accusing the psalmist in his infirmity (so Seybold, Kraus, Gunkel and Kirkpatrick).

Does the reference to reproof and chastisement suggest that the psalmist perceives his affliction as divine judgment on his sin? An awareness of sin is probably presupposed by these terms, but the absence of a confession of sin or of any allusion to sin should caution the exegete from reading this simply as a psalm of penance. (Contrast Ps. 38 which begins with the identical petition.) One cannot assume that psalmists regularly considered sin to be a sufficient explanation for their distresses. Some psalms have no reference to sin whatever, while others do (e.g. Ps. 41.5), which indicates its treatment was not assumed to be a matter of course.

The chief concern of this psalm is not with the mere fact of chastisement but with its persistence (v. 4) and its intensity (v. 2). Verse 6 makes clear that it is the psalmist's conviction that Yahweh should preserve his worshippers from premature death (see below). The psalmist complains that if this chastisement continues further, Yahweh would lose a worshipper. Such extreme chastening thus works against Yahweh's best interest. A prolonged distress that brings the psalmist to the brink of death is considered grounds for complaint. This psalm is more accurately understood as a psalm of complaint regarding excessive chastisement, than as a psalm of penance for sin.

3. Appeal

Weiser's remarks on the structure of this psalm are typical of some commentators:

> The style of the psalm is characterized by the use of
> traditional phrases, as can be gathered by the number of
> sayings which are similar to those used in other psalms
> and partly even verbally accord with them. The metrical
> structure of the strophes is not the same throughout,
> and the ideas expressed in them do not exhibit a strict
> sequence of thought.[5]

Prima facie his judgment appears fitting, but N.H. Ridderbos's
thorough analysis seems to justify his conclusion that 'the structure
of the psalm is well thought out'.[6]

The psalmist's appeal is twofold. First, appeal is made to
Yahweh's mercy (vv. 2-4a)—the only instance among the
complaint psalms. He opens pleading against *wrathful*
chastisement. This and the plea for mercy and healing are
supported by motivational clauses that describe the 'unnerved and
languishing' condition of the psalmist, and so aim to evoke pity.

Second, with the *waw*-adversative in v. 4b the tone changes
toward complaint, and the appeal is shifted to God's interest in
maintaining his 'merciful devotion'. Instead of spelling out the
predicate of this complaint ('But you, Yahweh—how long ...?')
with what Yahweh should not be doing, the psalmist interrupts
with what Yahweh should be doing. The question 'How long?'
and its interruption by the petitions, that Yahweh return in favor
(cf. 80.15; 90.13) and save, inject a tone of urgency into the poem.
The ensuing reference to the silence of the Sheol implies that if
Yahweh does not act quickly this will soon be the fate of the
psalmist. Verses 7-8 then portray the psalmist's near likeness to the
dead. One could not assert it with complete certainty, but this
element of urgency does seem to intimate that the psalmist's
allusion to death is more than a mere comparison. The continuance
of divine chastisement would spell the final silencing of the
psalmist's praise.

The psalmist's argument as to why his life should be a concern
of Yahweh begins with למען חסדך, 'in order to maintain your
merciful devotion'.[7] As elaborated in v. 6 (note the כי), this phrase
refers to the commemoration and praise of his 'merciful devotion'.
This and the indefinite subject show that the issue is not solely the

psalmist's interests but also Yahweh's praise. On the other hand, it would be presumptuous to read v. 6 as a kind of 'spiritual blackmail', as though the psalmist were referring merely to God's own interests. The crux is the praise of God, which the psalmist also has a concern to continue. This verse thus reflects a mutual concern for the praise of God, which is a central feature of the relationship between psalmists and Yahweh. The content that forms the praise of God in the Psalms is God's mighty acts of deliverance, to which praise is the verbal response of thanksgiving. But since the praise of God is thus contingent upon the welfare of God's worshippers, their well-being is presented as being of central concern to God.[8]

The psalmist's descriptions of his own grief in vv. 7-8 do not revert back to an appeal for pity as found in vv. 3-4a: they draw a parallel between the inability of the dead and of the psalmist to praise God. Instead of praise he can offer only tears. Thus, rather than pleading for pity, this description protests the psalmist's inability to praise.

In view of this analysis of the psalmist's appeal, it appears that he argues his case by pitting Yahweh's 'merciful devotion', or more specifically its proclamation, against his wrath.

The sudden reversal seen in vv. 9-11 is explained most plausibly by J. Begrich's theory of the salvation oracle.[9] If this is so, these verses constitute the psalmist's response to Yahweh's answer to the appeal, and thus do not form part of that appeal. Although there is thus an interval between vv. 8 and 9, the psalm is no less a unity. Verses 2-8 and 9-11 show strong linguistic ties, and the introduction of the enemies in v. 8b provides a suitable transition into this assurance of being heard.[10]

B. PSALM 13

1. Distress

The psalmist's experience appears to be one of deep sorrow (v. 3) in the midst of enemies who have gained the upper hand (v. 3) in their endeavor to oppose him (v. 5). The crucial issue, however, is the psalmist's proximity to death (v. 4). K. Seybold places this poem among those psalms with probable reference to sickness.[11] The fourfold 'How long?' makes evident the prolonged nature of the distress. E. Gerstenberger notes, 'As the reproachful questions in vv. 2-3 suggest, previous attempts to secure health and well-being have failed'.[12]

2. *Interpretation*

The opening series of questions addressed to God embrace not only God's own activity but also that of the psalmist and his foes. Being directed to God these questions presuppose he has the power to determine their answer, saying in effect, 'How long must you allow this to happen?' Thus, God is considered ultimately responsible for the psalmist's grief and the enemies' dominance. But the exegete cannot assume that the psalmist identifies God as the cause of the distress. Verse 2 speaks of the absence of God's favor, not necessarily of his active disfavor. Compare Pss. 74 and 77 which lament God's disfavor (74.1; 77.8-10) but object to his passivity in distress (74.11; implied in 77.3-7, 11). On the other hand, the language of God 'hiding his face and forgetting' need not suggest God has simply withdrawn himself from the psalmist. Other psalms use similar expressions of disfavor (22.2; 42.10; 44.25; 88.15) and yet these psalmists complain of God's active hostility against them (22.16; 42.8; 44.10ff.; 88.7ff.).

On what grounds does the psalmist complain that Yahweh is disinclined toward him? This cannot be answered from the psalm itself. One may not assume that the personal relationship between the psalmist and his God was such that his despair and his impotence before adversaries compelled him to trace the distress back to the displeasure of his God.[13] There are numerous psalms wherein the psalmist appears disheartened (see, e.g., 31.11 where יגון also occurs) and enemies prevail, but they do not charge God with neglect or betrayal.

This question can be answered only from the comparisons made in Chapter 4, which revealed a correlation between expressions of complaint and prolonged and near-death distresses. Thus, the extreme nature of the distress, namely that the psalmist is at death's door and deliverance seems unduly delayed, gives him grounds for complaint. More specifically, as the argument runs in this psalm (see below), the psalmist objects that God should permit one of his worshippers to be overcome by those who would rejoice at his death. His appeal is therefore based on the assumption that Yahweh should preserve from death those who trust in his merciful devotion and glory in his salvation (v. 6).

3. Appeal

H. Gunkel considers this lament to be 'the model of a "lament of the individual" ..., in which the individual components of the genre step forth most clearly'.[14]

One must be amazed at the turnaround the psalmist undergoes in five verses. He moves from 'Will you forget me forever?' to 'I have trusted in your merciful devotion' and 'I will sing to Yahweh'. In ordinary conversation such remarks could be regarded as insincere or as a contradiction. However, upon closer examination one can detect a certain logic as the psalmist moves from one statement to the next.

2	God-lament: disfavor: '*Yahweh*'
3a	I-lament: '*I*'
b	Foe-lament: '*my enemy*'
4a	Petition: favor
	Motive: '*Yahweh*, my God'
b	Petition: intervention
	Motive: 'lest *I* sleep in death'
5	Motive: 'lest *my enemy* ... *rejoice* when I totter'
6a	Confession of trust & vow of praise:
	'*But* I will *rejoice* in your salvation'
b	Vow of praise & anticipatory praise

The psalmist begins complaining of the duration of Yahweh's adverse disposition, and then laments his own personal grief and the dominance of his enemy. To resolve this distress he petitions

Yahweh to heed his concern and so to restore him. Undergirding these requests are several motivational clauses that echo the three subjects found in the opening lament. To counter Yahweh's disfavor toward him, the psalmist affirms Yahweh as 'my God'. While this affirmation buttresses the petitions soliciting God's favor, the request for intervention is supported by clauses that spell out what would be the consequences if Yahweh failed to intervene: the psalmist would die and his enemy would rejoice (גיל) at his downfall. To argue why Yahweh should act on behalf of the psalmist and not allow the foe to have his way, he contrasts the object of his foes' rejoicing with the object of his own rejoicing (גיל), namely Yahweh's salvation. During this distress his trust has been and is in Yahweh's merciful devotion; thus his rejoicing would be in Yahweh's salvation, and so when granted, he will sing to Yahweh. His enemy simply looks forward to the downfall of one who worships Yahweh. Therefore, although there is a wide disparity between the beginning and the end of the psalm, there is an inexorable logic from one step in the sequence to the next. An appeal which might be thought to show discontinuity, in fact, displays an inner continuity. Thus the psalmist succeeds in presenting both a complaint and a desire to turn from complaint to praise.

The key to this interpretation lies in the ואני of v. 6. The *waw* attaches it to v. 5, but its attachment to the subject indicates it is joined as a contrast to the preceding.[15] Thus since vv. 4b, 5 cohere as motivational clauses subordinated to the petition, v. 6 must also be considered as such. Form critically v. 6 is a confession of trust and a vow of praise,[16] but it functions as a reason for why Yahweh should intervene on the psalmist's behalf.

In view of the above, the psalm does exhibit a progression from lament to petition and finally to anticipatory praise. Nonetheless, though the psalm ends on the high note of a vow of praise, it must be regarded as just that, a promise and not necessarily a 'change of mood'. There is nothing to suggest that the psalmist has dropped his protest against God's adverse disposition (see Chapter 1). Simultaneous with the psalmist's confession of present trust is his complaint of God's hiddenness. Apparently a God-lament need not signal a lack of trust, nor does trust obviate lament. In fact, such trust may well give freedom for the expression of lament. The faith represented in this psalm has not tried to resolve religious antimonies; if anything, it has heightened them for the sake of appeal.[17]

C. PSALM 22

1. Situation

The genre and liturgical setting of Ps. 22 are difficult to determine. We will therefore consider both its distress and its social setting. Three possibilities will be discussed here. Each of them is distinguished according to one's understanding of the extended praise in vv. 23-32. (1) This praise section may be a vow of praise with actual praise given *in anticipation* (so S.B. Frost, R. Kilian, F. James, A.F. Kirkpatrick, and E. Gerstenberger[18]). (2) If one supposes an intervening salvation oracle was given after the expression of lament and petition, vv. 23-32 may be an extended 'assurance of being heard' (so P. Craigie and H.-J. Kraus[19]). In each of these cases the lament would refer to a present distress. (3) Verses 23-32 could be read as actual narrative praise sung during the performance of a *todah* offering. If these verses were added subsequent to the deliverance, then the lament (vv. 2-22) would have originally been recited contemporary to the distress. If, however, this praise was an integral part of the original psalm, then the entire psalm must be read as narrative praise, in which case the lament would function as a 'recollection of the time of need' recounting a past distress in the 'historic present' (so A. Weiser and H. Gese[20]). The question of whether vv. 28-32 were a subsequent expansion need not concern us now.

None of these options is without difficulties. Verses 23-32 appear to reflect an actual occasion of thanksgiving for deliverance.[21] An imperative call to praise (v. 24) summons the congregation present to praise God. The expression 'Let your heart live forever' also appears to address worshippers actually sharing in the *todah* meal with the psalmist: 'The afflicted shall eat and be satisfied' (v. 27). Such expressions are not found in vows of

praise, 'assurances of being heard', or anticipatory praises found in
other lament psalms. Moreover, the contradiction between vv. 2-3,

> 2   My God, my God, why have you forsaken me?
>   Why are you far from my crying (שׁעה),[22]
>   the words of my roaring?
> 3   My God, I cry by day, but you do not answer,
>   and by night, but I have no rest.

and v. 25,

> 25   For he has not despised,
>   nor detested the affliction of the afflicted,
>   and he did not hide his face from him,
>   but when he cried (שׁוע) to him, he heard.

suggests that v. 25 is to be recited not contemporary to the crisis
but in retrospect, after deliverance has actually been obtained.

We should also note that vv. 23-32 do not appear to stand as a
'narrative praise' psalm in their own right. The strong linguistic
and structural ties between this praise and the preceding lament
imply that vv. 23-32 never formed and independent unit.[23] In
addition, the 'recollection of the time of need' (v. 24) is too brief
for an independent *todah* psalm.[24] But if vv. 2-22 were always
connected to vv. 23-32, then there would be no need for the praise
section of the psalm to repeat in detail the report recalling the time
of need.

On the other hand, Ps. 22 does not fit the pattern of 'narrative
praise' psalms that we have in the Psalter. It does not open with a
'proclamation of praise' and an 'introductory summary' of the
deliverance. Moreover, its detailed description of distress far
exceeds any 'recollection of the time of need' that we have in the
narrative praise psalms, which highlight the deliverance, not the
distress (e.g. Pss. 30.7-11; 116.3-4, 10-11).

None of the proposed solutions is conclusive. Perhaps we have
in vv. 23-32 a genuine addition of narrative praise appended to the
lament after deliverance was obtained. In any case, Ps. 22 is still a
suitable object of study for our purposes. The lament (vv. 2-22),

whether an actual cry out of distress or a report looking back on the distress, retains those motifs that qualify it as a lament psalm.

Taken at face value this psalm presents us with a psalmist who is despised and mocked (vv. 7-9) by enemies who surround him and are about to overcome him (vv. 13-14, 17-19). He suffers physical deterioration (vv. 15-16) and so is near death (v. 16). His continual prayers bring no relief (vv. 2-3).

The reader must be struck, however, by the way everything happens in the most extreme form imaginable. The enemies who encircle the psalmist are ferocious in the extreme, described with images bearing demonic connotations.[25] The psalmist is completely desiccated, set upon the ashes of death by God and treated as already dead by his enemies (v. 19).[26] And God remains aloof from his persistent cries. In addition, the subsequent deliverance is a matter not simply for the immediate friends and family but for all Israel (v. 24)—indeed it reverberates even to the ends of the earth and culminates in nothing less than the conversion of all peoples (vv. 28ff.).[27] While it cannot be disproven that such language was originally intended to refer to a particular experience and its repercussions, it seems most consistent with the lament genre to read this psalm as that which embraces *any* distress and its ensuing deliverance. The implication of this type of language is that no hardship is beyond Yahweh's salvation. Indeed, Yahweh matches the depths of the distress with a rescue and testimony of the highest order. In a word, Ps. 22 is paradigmatic for the individual in dire straits.[28]

2. Interpretation

The predominant subject of the statements in the lament is the enemies. They hurl abuse at the psalmist (vv. 7b-9) and surround him (vv. 13-14, 17-18) as for an execution (v. 19). The subject of the opening lament, however, is God. Tradition teaches that when those who trust in Yahweh cry for help, he responds with deliverance (vv. 5-6). Even the psalmist's adversaries affirm this tradition in their mockery of him (v. 9). But this psalmist cries from day to night with no answer from Yahweh. Hence he concludes Yahweh has been ignoring him.

As is customary in the individual laments, however, the cause of the psalmist's nearness to death is traced back to God (v. 16b): 'You have set me in the ashes of death'. We should probably not press this poetic language further to try to determine whether the psalmist actually envisages Yahweh as the agent causing his death or he reckons that Yahweh's abandonment of him is tantamount to leaving him at death's door.[29]

The psalmist evidently believes Yahweh has no warrant for his conduct. The tradition of Yahweh answering those who trust in him and call him 'my God' has been well established for generations, such that even his foes are aware of it (v. 9). He then reminds God that he has been 'my God' since the psalmist's birth—indeed God himself initiated the relationship (v. 10). Since God actually engendered the psalmist's trust (מבטיחי), the psalmist should surely be counted with the 'fathers' who trusted (בטח) and were delivered. The psalmist underscores his disappointment by noting that the one upon whom he was 'cast' at birth (v. 11) has 'placed' him into 'the ashes of death' (v. 16b).

3. Appeal

The dilemma of Ps. 22 goes beyond the concrete distress to the problem of God himself. The psalmist must cry to God who does not answer. He must implore God who is remote not to be remote. He must seek deliverance from death from God who laid him in the ashes of death.

The psalmist presents this conflict of faith and experience by alternating descriptions of the distress with arguments of faith. The psalm moves from a complaint over God's abandonment (vv. 2-3) to a reference to God's deliverance of the fathers (vv. 4-6), from a lament concerning the foe's mockery (which contains a sting of truth, vv. 7-9) to a reference to God's nurture of the psalmist since birth (vv. 10-11), from a lament over the sense of an impending execution (vv. 12-19) to a petition summoning the Helper to draw near and save (vv. 20-22). All of these transitions are introduced by a grammatical marker (*waw*-adversatives in vv. 4, 7, 20, כי in v. 10, and the psalm's first petition in v. 12, אל־תרחק, which also appears in v. 20).

Although only two and a half of the verses constituting the lament proper (2-22) are formal complaints (i.e. with God as subject), the opening two verses announce the psalmist's central dilemma through two motifs: Yahweh's remoteness (רחק) and his silence at the psalmist's cries for help. The latter in effect calls into question the efficacy of the confession 'my God'.

The second motif pervades vv. 3-11. Despite unceasing prayers Yahweh gives no answer to the one who calls him 'my God'. But, as the psalmist is quick to show, such behavior contradicts the experience of generations (vv. 5-6) and indeed the very nature of God's kingship, whose praise consists of the people's thanks for deliverances (vv. 4-6). Verses 7-9 describe the ridicule of the enemies, but three features suggest that it is given mention not simply to present the psalmist's social predicament but to emphasize his religious one as well. First, these successive sections (vv. 4-6 and 7-9) open with similar constructions (ואתה in v. 4, ואנכי in v. 9) that produce a contrast which, as Ridderbos notes, is 'breathtaking': 'And you, you are the holy one', but 'I, I am a worm'.[30] Second, the fathers who called were not ashamed because Yahweh delivered them (v. 6), but the psalmist who calls becomes an object of scorn because Yahweh fails to deliver (vv. 7-9). Third, vv. 7-9 climax in a citation, thus focusing attention on the content of their reproach:

> 22.9   He entrusted himself to Yahweh,
> let him deliver (פלט) him;
> let him rescue (נצל) him,
> because he delights in him.[31]

But this is precisely what Yahweh did for the fathers: he 'delivered' (פלט) them. (נצל is used as a petition in v. 21.) The psalmist actually quotes his enemies' words, though intended for mockery, to pass on their challenge to Yahweh and to make the point that even his enemies have it right: it is Yahweh's duty to rescue the psalmist. Moreover, the psalmist endeavors to show by referring to his own 'salvation history' that Yahweh has in fact delighted in him, even since birth (vv. 10-11; note the connecting כִּי). In a word, the poet substantiates his claim that Yahweh is 'my God', who is obliged to rescue the one who has day and night called upon him.

Therefore, the 'my God' of v. 11b appears to form an inclusio with the opening 'my God' to mark off the first half of the lament section. A second inclusio is evident from the repetition of 'Don't be far off' at the beginning of the second half of the lament (v. 12) and at the beginning of the main petition section (vv. 20-22). The second instance thus serves double duty by both closing this lament section and opening the petition section.[32] Most commentators place v. 12 with vv. 2-11, but its content appears rather to be a summary statement introducing the following lament in vv. 13-22.

The terms forming this second inclusio, 'Don't be far off', present the central motif of the second section of the lament (vv. 12-22), namely God's remoteness. God's aloofness becomes a problem precisely because 'trouble is near' and no other helper is available (v. 12). Hence, this lament concentrates on the grave threat of this trouble and the absence of any helper. The psalmist depicts his enemies as ferocious beasts ready to tear and devour. The repetition of synonyms meaning 'to surround' emphasizes that the psalmist sees no helper among this company and no hope of escape (vv. 13, 17).

In the middle of this second section the psalmist describes his own condition. The images of dryness and heat in vv. 15-16—melting wax, a dried up potsherd, a parched tongue—may explain the psalmist's choice of verb in v. 16b. According to BDB, שׁפת is a denominative derived from שְׁפֹת, which in the light of its cognates denotes one of three stones which are used to support a kettle on the fire (cf. the derived noun, אַשְׁפֹּת, 'ash-pit'). Hence, the verb שׁפת may stem from the notion of placing something on these stones over a fire. עֵפֶר can refer to 'ashes' (Num. 19.17; 2 Kgs. 23.4). If this is the case, vv. 15-16 form a consistent picture of the desiccation of the psalmist and so trace the ultimate cause of this affliction back to Yahweh. It may not have been by chance that v. 16b is exactly at the center of this second lament section (vv. 13-16a = 5 lines, 17-20 = 5 lines in *BHS*).[33]

Thus, although God himself is made the grammatical subject in but one of these verses (v. 16b of vv. 12-22), each part serves to undergird the protest against Yahweh's remoteness.

אל־תרחק (v. 20) is repeated in the opening petition of the final section of the lament psalm proper (i.e. vv. 2-22), but as J.S. Kselman notes, there has been a subtle progression from v. 12. The lament of v. 12, 'there is none to help' (עוזר), is replaced by 'O my help, hurry to my help' (אילותי לעזרתי חושה, v. 20).[34] Thus, after the psalmist has given full expression to his complaint, he summons Yahweh to draw near and intervene. The animal images are repeated (in reverse order) to underline the dire urgency of the psalmist's distress (vv. 20-22).

D. PSALM 35

1. Distress

The attempt to piece together the particular occasion presupposed by this psalm is, as with most laments, beset by the problems of language that at times appears to be metaphoric and at other times literal. Since J. Eaton and P.C. Craigie interpret the opening military language as referring to a real battle, they read this as a royal psalm.[35] But one must note that the psalm projects a diversity of images. All at once the psalmist appears to be engaged in a military conflict (vv. 1-3), pursued in a hunt (vv. 7-8), falsely accused in a lawsuit (vv. 1a, 11, 23-24), threatened by lions (v. 17, cf. 25) and also by robbers (v. 10).[36] Some of the images are more clearly figurative than others. The royal interpretation tries to read most of the psalm's language as literal by positing a treaty background for the various episodes of the psalm. Such an attempt, however, appears strained.

The clearest and most elaborate description of the distress afflicting the psalmist appears, as is usually the case with lament psalms, in the lament proper (vv. 11-16).[37] All of the allusions in this section, even though some of them are highly figurative, point to a company who have betrayed the psalmist by false witness. The images used in the petitions—alluding to a battle, a hunt, and threatening wild beasts—can be easily incorporated into the setting projected by the lament since each portrays threat and conflict. The frequent use of legal language in the petitions (vv. 1a, 23, 24, 27) suggests that the traps set by these foes (v. 7) are prepared to ensnare the psalmist by 'legal' means. Hence most commentators read Ps. 35 as a prayer of the accused. The language is too vague, however, to assign this psalm to an institutional process where the accused appears before the temple and hopes for acquittal, nor can one be certain the psalm refers to actual legal proceedings.[38] Kraus suggests that it may represent a composition from earlier formulae.[39]

The enemies' grounds for accusation may derive from a sickness the psalmist *may* have had. The psalmist refers to a time when those who are now his adversaries were sick themselves (v. 13) and he interceded for them. But now when he 'stumbles' (צלע, v. 15), they presume he must have committed some offense, and so they slander and mock him. Since the psalmist expected them to offer a response similar to his (vv. 12-14), the distresses of both may have also been similar.[40] K. Seybold, however, does not place Ps. 35 within his third category of psalms with probable reference to sickness since these allusions are not unequivocal, nor are they central to the main theme of the psalm.[41]

Irrespective of the psalm's particular setting, we can be certain that the psalmist feels threatened by persecutors (v. 3) who seek his life (vv. 4, 7). They bear malicious witness (v. 11, cf. 20), slander and mock him (vv. 15-16).

As noted in Chapter 4, this is the only complaint psalm that does not allude to 'near-death' distress. The feature of the distress most pertinent for this study is its prolonged nature: 'How long ...?' (v. 17; see Chapter 4).

2. Interpretation

The psalmist's false accusers are presented throughout as the source of the psalmist's distresses. Yahweh has no active involvement in the distress, but his delay in delivering the psalmist makes him in some measure responsible for it.

The psalmist's grounds for expecting this of God appear to be as follows. Since Yahweh's deliverance of the 'afflicted' from oppressors forms part of the content of Yahweh's praise in general (v. 10), this implies that it is Yahweh's business to look after those being afflicted. Since the treacherous bear malicious witness against the psalmist (vv. 11-16), he expresses no doubt that Yahweh is indeed 'looking on', but the persistence of this affliction, as presupposed by the complaint, gives the psalmist reason to believe that Yahweh is unduly idle (v. 17).

3. *Appeal*

This psalm falls into three sections, each containing lament, petition, and a vow of praise, and each presenting the distress from a different viewpoint. It is depicted as a battle and as a hunt (vv. 1-10), as an occasion of false witness and betrayal (vv. 11-18), and as a lawsuit (vv. 19-28).[42]

The appeal of this psalm may be characterized as a cry for justice. In the opening strophe the psalmist pleads that his adversaries simply receive what is due them: that Yahweh contend with his contenders (ריב), fight against his fighters, pursue his pursuers, and trap his trappers—in their own snares. In the second strophe the psalmist testifies of false witness, betrayal, slander and mockery. In both strophes the psalmist asserts his innocence: his adversaries attack 'without cause' (חנם, vv. 7, 19). In the third strophe he draws a clear divide between those who revel in a man's ruin and those who revel in his prosperity—those who gloat and those who praise.[43] Yahweh is called upon to give just deserts to each.

The actual complaint of this psalm is brief: 'Lord, how long will you look on?' (v. 17a). It is directed against Yahweh's apparent idleness. (On this use of ראה see Gen. 42.1.)[44] The psalmist, by spelling out the content of what his praise will consist (vv. 9-10) and then by describing what opposition prevents its realization (vv. 11-16), prepares the way for this pressing complaint. After this expression of protest the psalmist renews his vow of praise, thus making clear that the intent behind his protest is not to scorn Yahweh but to urge him to give the psalmist occasion to praise. The final strophe of the psalm (vv. 19-28) is concerned largely with ensuring that Yahweh will see to it that the psalmist will be able to offer his praise. In v. 18 the psalmist renews his vow of praise, but he once again speaks of the danger that his foes may be the ones who will have the final shout of triumph.[45] Thus, the petitions pray to this end. Verse 22 echoes the complaint of v. 17 but presents it in the form of a declarative ('You have seen it') and negative petitions ('Do not be silent [or 'deaf', חרש] and 'Do not be far from me'). In language familiar to such prayers of the accused, the petitions of vv. 23ff. seek to move the Judge to execute his judgment.

E. PSALM 39

1. Distress

The psalmist's determined effort to muzzle himself in the presence of the wicked implies that he wants to say something. But apparently, if he were to give himself free course to talk, he would sin (v. 2). This indicates that the wicked by their very presence, and not necessarily by direct attacks, somehow provoke the psalmist. His only other reference to the wicked speaks of them as potential mockers (v. 9). But, in each case where he mentions 'every man', he describes him as amassing wealth (v. 7, reading המון[46]) and as one whose pleasures—perhaps those things he amasses—Yahweh dissolves (v. 12). After each of these verses the psalmist distinguishes himself from those whose desires are set on material things:

39.8   And now, for what do I wait, Lord?
My hope is in you.

13   Hear my prayer ...,
for I am a sojourner with you,
an alien like all my fathers.

There is here implied a distinction between those who possess wealth and those who lack it, or at least are not attached to it. Since the psalmist draws this distinction while he determines to restrain his speech (see further below), it appears that the matter about which he was so anxious to talk concerns the dilemma of the wicked prospering and the godly envying that prosperity.

If this is so, the predicament of this psalm appears very similar to that of Ps. 73:

> 73.3 For I was envious of the deluded,
> when I saw the prosperity of the wicked.

We also note the psalmist's restraint in speaking:

> 73.15 If I had said, 'I will speak thus',
> I would have betrayed the generation of your children.

Remarkably, both psalmists describe their own misfortune in the same way:

> 73.14 I have been plagued [נגע] all the day,
> and my reproof [תוכחת] comes every morning.

> 39.11a Remove your plague [נגע] from me.
> 12a With reproofs [תוכחת] you chasten a man for iniquity.

Should these 'plagues' be regarded as physical or emotional? With 'relative certainty' K. Seybold treats Ps. 39 as a psalm of sickness. He points particularly to the terms נגע (v. 11) and כאב (v. 3). Moreover, an illness of the psalmist may have occasioned his reflections on the frailty of life and the imminence of death (vv. 6, 12, 14). On the other hand, since כאב is something aggravated by the mere presence of the wicked, it may refer more to mental anguish than to physical pain. נגע is also not unambiguous, as Seybold is himself aware (see 1 Sam. 10.26).[47] Moreover, the chain of thought in vv. 9-11 may indicate that the psalmist's 'plague' relates to his 'dumbness' before the wicked (see further below). Perhaps his plague—at least in part—consists of a forced preoccupation with the injustice and futility of life (cf. Eccl. 8.14; contrast 5.19). The psalmist of Ps. 73, as a result of his envy of the prosperous wicked, speaks of his heart turning bitter (יתחמץ) and of his kidneys being pierced (אשתונן, v. 21), both of which are physical images that refer to an emotional response to guilt (cf. also vv. 16, 22).[48]

The specific form of divine chastisement (vv. 9-12) may include both both physical and emotional anguish. It is clear, however, that foremost among the psalmist's concerns is the imminence of death. While it is a fate that all will meet (vv. 7, 12), the psalmist feels himself particularly near death, as the petitions of the psalm make clear:

> 39.11   Remove your plague from me;
> I am perishing (כלה) from the blow of your hand.
>
> 14   Look away from me, so that I may smile again, before I go and am no more.

2. Interpretation

The wicked are not depicted as actual, personal adversaries against the psalmist, but simply as potential mockers (v. 9). Yet it is clear that their very presence (v. 2) compels the psalmist to maintain silence (vv. 2-3, cf. 9-10), which in turn aggravates his pain (v. 3). Although they somehow provoke the psalmist's dilemma, the ultimate source of his troubles could not be expressed more clearly:

> 39.10   I am dumb; I do not open my mouth, because you have done it.
>
> 11   Remove from me your plague; from the blow of your hand I perish.

(See also v. 14.)

As in Ps. 90, the psalm is dominated by two characteristics of Yahweh, which help to explain why the psalmist attributes his hardship to Yahweh. Yahweh is unquestionably the sole creator, the one who 'gives' to the psalmist and to 'every man' his 'days' (v. 6). The evanescence of life is thus to be traced back to him. A second characteristic is that Yahweh chastens men for their iniquity (v. 12). The psalmist, being aware of his own transgressions (v. 9), recognizes his affliction as divine reproof. But in view of a life that is already too brief he implies that this reproof is excessive:

> 39.11b   From the blow of your hand I am perishing.
> 14   Turn your gaze from me, that I may smile,
>   before I go and am no more.

3. Appeal

Unlike most of the other individual laments we are discussing, this one does appear almost autobiographical.[49] It exhibits the psalmist's reflections and shows his progression of thought. Much of this reflects the OT wisdom tradition. The psalm is less clearly an 'argument' that is presented to Yahweh than are most of the complaint psalms. An argument, nevertheless, is expressed but primarily through the psalmist's presentation of his reflections.

Ridderbos appears to be correct when he argues that vv. 2-4 should be read as a description of the psalmist's 'state of mind' underlying the following prayer, not as a description of his determined, but failed, effort to restrain from speaking.[50] Some commentators regard דברתי בלשוני (v. 4) as the psalmist's admission that he is breaking his vow of silence (vv. 2-3). But the repetition of נאלמתי (cf. v. 3), along with 'I do not open my mouth', in v. 10 indicates that his vow was not unqualified and that he has in fact maintained his vow. דברתי בלשוני therefore does not appear to signify a violation but a breakthrough: 'I muzzle myself *before the wicked;* instead I speak *to God*'.[51]

In vv. 2-4 the psalmist thus lays his soul bare to God. This functions as a motive for divine intervention in that 'the poet shows how much effort it cost him, so to pray, as he does in vv. 5-14'.[52]

The psalmist begins his prayer not with a description of his immediate need, but with a request to see from God's perspective how transient his life really is. His following statement regarding the transience of his and of all human life frames the thinking for the appeal that follows. This statement appears to serve three purposes: (1) it shows that it does not suit man to lash out against God, especially since his transience follows as a result of his iniquity (v. 12); (2) it makes clear that even the wicked and their riches will perish; (3) it should move God to pity.[53]

Verses 8ff. are difficult to interpret. If one regards 'what Yahweh has done' (v. 10b) as a sickness, then vv. 9-11 could be understood as follows. First, the psalmist deals with the root cause of his sickness, namely his sin, by asking Yahweh to deliver him from it (v. 9a). His second petition seeks to avoid the mockery to which his illness has made him vulnerable (v. 9b). The psalmist is 'dumb' because he in fact has no defense to plead before the wicked, for *Yahweh* has made him sick (v. 10). Finally, he makes his petition for healing explicit: 'Remove your plague'.

Alternatively, there is another interpretation that may be more appropriate to the parallelism of these verses. In view of the futility of life, the psalmist declares that his only hope is God (v. 8). He then pleads, not for forgiveness of, but for deliverance from his transgressions. Parallel to this request, is one that Yahweh not make him (or allow him to become) a mockery of the wicked. This may imply that the psalmist prays to be delivered from his propensity to speak of his envy before the wicked and thus, in effect, admit that his faith is vain. This is corroborated in the following verse where the psalmist again speaks of his dumbness and then states: 'You have done this'. His dumbness may therefore result from Yahweh's bridling of the psalmist. This bridle is then called 'a plague', which the psalmist petitions Yahweh to remove. Hence, the psalmist may be praying that instead of chastening his sin, Yahweh would deliver him from the sin itself.

The psalmist's predications of God do not connote complaint as clearly as do the predications of God in other complaint psalms. He asks no questions of reproach. He does not complain of God's adverse action by contrasting it with references to his praiseworthy deeds of the past (e.g. Ps. 22.2-6). He simply states God's adverse action against him and appeals for its removal. As noted above, however, there is the implication that this chastisement has become too extreme (vv. 11, 14). The subdued nature of this complaint is probably due to the psalmist's consciousness of sin and to his restraint of speech, as his opening confession makes clear. Moreover, it is likely that this psalm emerges from 'a relatively late age', as the 'late sapiential and early Jewish thoughts ... undeniably present' would imply.[54] As noted in Chapter 5, complaint as a form of appeal to God faded after the exile.

F. PSALM 42-43

1. Distress

Most commentators argue for the unity of Pss. 42-43. In addition to the principal reasons listed in ANDERSON, we should note how 42.4b and v. 11b tie strophes one (vv. 2-6, as marked out by the refrain) and two (vv. 7-12) together, and how 42.10 and 43.2 tie two and three (43.1-5) together.

In Ps. 42-43 it is clear the psalmist is alienated from the temple (esp. v. 7). The circumstances of this separation, which some commentators believe to be sickness (cf. v. 11, 'with a shattering in my bones'),[55] recede behind the one circumstance upon which all else hinges: the psalmist needs to obtain access to the temple, his source of life (v. 2-3, 5-6, 12; 43.3-5). Mention is made of an enemy oppressing the psalmist (vv. 10b; 43.2b), but it is not clear whether this exceeds verbal derision of the psalmist's faith (v. 11; this verse appears to spell out the form of 'oppression' mentioned in v. 10b). The petition of 43.1 may suggest that the psalmist is somehow restrained by 'a faithless nation'.

This intense distress is also a prolonged one. The question 'Where is your God?' haunts the psalmist 'all the day' (vv. 4, 11). In the context of growing thirst he asks, 'When shall I come and appear before God?' (v. 3).

2. *Interpretation*

In this psalm the enemies appear to be a secondary source of distress for the psalmist. As already noted, v. 10 contains the first reference to their activity, which is then elucidated in the following verse where it is characterized as ridicule of the psalmist's faith. The question 'Where is your God?' implies that his faith is vulnerable because there has been no divine intervention on the psalmist's behalf. His faith has been denied its realization. This reference to enemy oppression is repeated in 43.2. That the psalmist perceives his troubles to be primarily religious can be seen in the following petition. The relief to this oppression is sought in the request to be brought to God's mountain. The poet's desire will then be fulfilled by his appearing at the altar of God (43.4). The petition of 43.1 thus may not point to any institutional detainment, whether political or legal. The psalmist may simply be seeking religious vindication against those who have falsely supposed that his separation from the temple is deserved divine judgment.

The primary source of distress for the psalmist therefore appears to be God. If 'tears' is the subject of the infinitive construct in v. 4b, then the psalmist's sorrow, or more particularly his unquenched thirst for God provokes the haunting question, 'Where is your God?' Thus the prolonged absence of intervening help that would grant the psalmist access to the temple causes him to ponder the possibility that his God is either hostile or indifferent towards him. His memory of the temple worship (זכר, v. 5) leads to an expression of despair (literally a 'melting away', השתוחחי, v. 6). His memory of God (זכר, v. 7) leads to accusation (v. 8; *God's* waves drown the psalmist) and complaint (v. 10). With despair and complaint already present, the psalmist makes his first reference to the 'enemy' (v. 10b). Their abuse (v. 11) and faithlessness (לא־חסיד, 43.1) drive the psalmist to repeat and perhaps intensify his complaint: instead of complaining of God's 'forgetting' he complains of his 'rejecting' (43.2).[56]

The psalmist not only expresses apprehension regarding God's disposition (v. 10; 43.2), he asserts that God has actually brought this distress upon him:

42.8   Deep calls to deep at the sound of your
        waterfalls;
        all your breakers and waves have passed over
        me.[57]

Since the temple is believed to be the source of life (vv. 2-3), the psalmist's alienation from it is depicted as a form of death (on the image of drowning, see Chapter 4). As Yahweh the Creator alone provides food and water to animals (vv. 2-3; cf. 104.27-30), so the Lord of the temple alone provides access to the life made available at the temple (43.3-4). Perhaps the same reversal of tradition that we saw with the corporate complaints is evident here. Since according to tradition Yahweh provides life-giving 'water' at the temple (42.2-3; cf. Pss. 36.9-10; 46.5; Ezek. 47.1-12), in a distress where the psalmist is alienated from the temple Yahweh is depicted as 'drowning' the psalmist (v. 8).

In sum, underlying this psalm are the beliefs that, (1) God dwells at his temple; (2) here in particular God is worshipped and life is received; (3) God delights in receiving worship and granting life. But the psalmist's separation from the temple calls the third belief into question. God's apparent refusal to grant life spells death for the psalmist.

3. Appeal

Several verses of this psalm refer to God in the third person (42.3-6, 9, 12; 43.5). But this does not mean that these verses are not part of the psalmist's appeal addressed to God. Thus, for example, although 42.3 speaks of God in the third person, it elaborates on and continues the simile of the panting deer in v. 2, which is addressed to God. Verse 4 is also 'linked by the motif of water; the one who longed for a refreshing drink, tasted instead the bitter water of tears'.[58]

Aside from the refrain (42.6, 12; 43.2) the only other verses referring to God in the third person are 42.5, 9. The verbs in each instance are imperfect. In v. 5 עבר in the imperfect 'portrays past events with vivid sympathy'.[59] The tense of יצוה in v. 9 has troubled commentators. But since both אעבר and יצוה are closely preceded by 'I remember' (42.5a, 7), it is possible this second imperfect also 'portrays past events with vivid sympathy'. In the first instance the psalmist remembers the temple festivals and so recalls when he 'used to pass along' (עבר) with the procession. In the second instance the psalmist remembers God and so, since God's waves have now 'passed over' (עבר) him, he recalls when Yahweh 'used to command' his merciful devotion on behalf of the psalmist.[60] The first recollection of worship at the temple makes Yahweh's absence ('Where is your God?') all the more evident and thus leads to expressions of despair (42.6, 7). The second recollection of God granting his merciful devotion makes the anomaly of Yahweh's overwhelming the psalmist (42.8) all the more evident and thus leads to an expression of complaint (v. 10).

Although both of these memories make clear the dilemma of the present, they also appear to provide grounds of hope for the future, as expressed in the second half of the refrain. These vivid recollections of offering worship at 'the house of God' (42.5) and of receiving the benefits of worship from 'the God of my life' (42.9) compel the psalmist to exhort his 'soul' to hope.[61] It must be observed that these self-exhortations occur in the midst of this integrated appeal to God. Therefore, the psalmist's addresses to himself, both in recollection and in exhortation, appear to have the effect of laying bare to God his inner struggle for faith in God. Like Pss. 39 and 77, this is one of the rare instances where a description of this subjective turmoil forms a constituent part of the psalmist's appeal to God. Hence even one of the questions complaining against God's disfavor is introduced as a determined effort of the psalmist's faith: 'I *will* say ..., "Why have you forgotten me?"' (אומרה, v. 10).

The inner longing of the psalmist for God is nowhere more evident than in the opening simile: as a deer pants for water, so he longs to 'appear before God'. Although this phrase is used in Yahweh's command that all males must appear before him three times a year (Exod. 23.17; 34.23, 24; Deut. 16.16; 31.11; cf. Exod. 23.15; 34.20), the psalmist nowhere employs Yahweh's own words to move him to act on the his behalf. The mere expression of the psalmist's longing suggests that for him the *command* to appear before Yahweh has become a *promise*, which he yearns to see fulfilled. But the psalmist then expresses his disappointment in God in the same graphic way that he expressed his personal longing for God. In a comparison of 42.2-3 and v. 8 L. Alonso Schökel notes:

> ... the poet who desperately seeks water, finds it, but it is not life-giving water—it is destructive. God *sends* water, overwhelming, destructive of life. God, who was to have been the life of the psalmist, has become his death; he has become an elemental force, oceanic, irresistible. The possessive 'your' is emphatic; it invites us to conclude that the psalmist suffers his exile because of God. The two contrasting images of water provide us with the substance of the poem: a dramatic tension in the soul between God and God.[62]

The psalmist also expresses his disappointment by juxtaposing divine titles with incongruent predicates: God his 'rock forgets' him (42.10) and his 'fortressing God rejects' him (43.2). Another contrast sharpens his complaint further: 'I *remember* you' (42.7), 'why have you *forgotten* me?'

After the psalmist states his case in the form of lament and complaint, he petitions Yahweh to act as judge and as prosecutor (43.1). The psalmist's ground for expecting a favorable answer to this request appear to be similar to those expressed in Ps. 26.8ff., which begins with a petition identical to 43.1. In both psalms the psalmist's affinity to the sanctuary marks him out as distinct from his enemies. (Thus, the preceding lament should be regarded as essential to the petitions found in Ps. 43. Ps. 42 should not be read as timid introspection and Ps. 43 as the place where the psalmist finally turns from self-pity and gathers the pluck to petition God.)

The terms composing the second petition (43.3) may hint that the psalmist is requesting his own exodus experience. He asks for Yahweh's light to 'lead' him, as Yahweh had 'led' (לְהַחֹתָם) Israel by the light of the fiery pillar (Exod. 13.21). As Yahweh led his people to his 'holy habitation' (15.13), so the psalmist seeks to be brought to God's holy hill. 'Light' and 'Faithfulness' appear to be

personified as ambassadors sent out from Zion to escort the
psalmist to God's dwelling (cf. Pss. 57.4; 85.10-14; 89.15).[63]

G. PSALM 88

1. Distress

Death is the subject of this psalm. The psalmist employs numerous
images of death to describe his condition (vv. 4-8, 11-13, 16-
18).[64] Hence his specific sickness cannot be identified, but his
nearness to death is clear enough. According to the criteria K.
Seybold established to distinguish psalms of sickness and healing,
Ps. 88 appears among those with 'certain reference to sickness'.[65]
As a result of his stricken condition, the psalmist is completely
alienated from companions (vv. 9, 19). Though his distress is
extreme, it has not muted his prayers. He appeals 'every day'
(בכל־יום, v. 10, also vv. 2, 14), but the terrors of death continue to
envelop him 'all the day' (v. 18).

2. Interpretation

In a few verses the psalmist describes the mere fact of his distress
(vv. 4-5, 10a, 16a) but in most instances he attributes its cause
directly to God (vv. 7-9, 15, 16b-19). There are no hostile enemies
in the psalm, but the psalmist does suffer estrangement from
companions, which however is also believed to be Yahweh's
doing.

The principal reason for the psalmist considering Yahweh to be
the cause behind his affliction appears to stem from the lack of
response to his prayers. The psalmist has cried 'day and night',[66]
yet Yahweh has evidently given no answer (v. 2). This silence
leads the psalmist to compare himself with the dead (נחשבתי עם ...,
הייתי כ ..., v. 5, כמו, v. 6) since they too are not 'remembered' by
Yahweh and are 'cut off' from his hand (v. 6). The psalmist then
pushes this to its logical conclusion and asserts, '*You* have put me
in the lowest pit, in the dark places, in the depths' (v. 7). The

conviction that Yahweh should preserve his worshippers from premature death (vv. 11-13) provides further grounds for complaint. Hence, the psalmist again asserts that he has cried to Yahweh for help (v. 14), but since no help is evidently forthcoming, he concludes Yahweh has rejected him and hidden his face from him (v. 15). The terrors of sickness and death he suffers are thus from Yahweh (vv.16ff.).

3. Appeal

In view of this divine hostility the central concern of the psalmist's appeal is God himself. Even his social relationships are determined by God.

The structure of the psalm is established by the psalmist's repeated references to persistent prayer (vv. 2-3, 10b, 14). Hence there are three 'strophes', each beginning with this mention of preceding appeals for help.[67] The implied complaint that Yahweh has failed to respond to these cries thus introduces each section of the psalm.

The opening address, 'Yahweh God of my salvation', is really the only note of hope in the entire psalm, aside from the very persistence of the psalmist's crying.[68] This epithet may at first not seem surprising, but its significance as a sign of the psalmist's hope becomes more evident after one reads what follows, namely that God is the very cause of his distress. The only formal petition of the psalm follows, where he simply asks that Yahweh give this 'prayer' (תפלה) and 'cry' (רנה) a proper hearing. The absence of any petition for intervention may suggest that the form of deliverance required is self-evident from the lament itself.

The diversity of images that the psalmist employs to depict his nearness to death combine to convey the horror that presses in upon him. He approaches 'Sheol', the realm of the dead, and likens himself to one going down to the 'pit' (בור), which suggests the image of one in a cistern, a place dark and mucky with no means of escape.[69] Related to the cistern image is the figure of drowning: Your terrors 'surround me like water all the day' (v. 18), and 'all your waves oppress me' (v. 8). The succession of nouns describing the realm of the dead intensifies this sense of horror: the lowest part, dark places (cf. v. 13), the depths (v. 7). It is identified further as the 'grave' (vv. 6, 12),[70] Abaddon (the 'place of destruction', v. 12) and the 'land of forgetfulness' (v. 13). Further, those inhabiting this region are called 'men without strength' (v. 5) and Rephaim ('shadows', v. 11). Like a man without strength, the psalmist uses various phrases to refer to his exhaustion: his eyes languish (v. 10a), he is expiring, he bears Yahweh's terrors and becomes feeble or numb (v. 16, reading אָפוּנָה; see also v. 4a). The psalmist refers to himself as being 'silenced' (v. 17), which is also characteristic of the dead,[71] particularly because they are disqualified from singing the praise of God (vv. 11-13). This last aspect becomes the most horrifying of all: the dead are cut off from Yahweh (v. 6) and from the worship of Yahweh (vv. 11-13), because beyond the boundaries of death he ceases to perform saving wonders (v. 11).

The enigmatic phrase, 'I am shut up and cannot go out' (v. 9b), probably continues to describe the psalmist's condition as one confined to the grave, the pit, etc.[72] As one considered dead, he cannot join his companions in the land of the living. Each reference to the psalmist's alienation thus appears to climax in the psalmist's confinement to the place of the dead. Verse 9 speaks of his inability to associate with the living, v. 19 of his only companion: 'the dark place'. (One wonders if this awkward reference to a place as his 'friend' is not a way of underlining his sense of total estrangement from people.)

As horrifying as 'death' is in itself, one must note that the force judged to be afflicting the psalmist is none less than 'the God of my salvation'! The psalmist aims not simply to describe his condition in such pitiful terms that would move Yahweh but also to assert that he considers his condition to be a result of Yahweh's hostility. Moreover, behind this hostile treatment the psalmist perceives an adverse disposition. Hence he complains of Yahweh's personal rejection of him and of Yahweh's 'hidden face' (v. 15). The psalmist experiences the consequences of his wrath as those (burning!) waters of death which overwhelm him (vv. 8, 16-17).

An additional element of the appeal is the rhetorical questions which argue that 'the dead do not praise Yahweh' (vv. 11-13; see

Chapter 4). Here the psalmist points to Yahweh's praiseworthy attributes and deeds—his wonders, his merciful devotion, his faithfulness, his righteousness—and asks, If you permit your worshippers to die, who then will you save and who will extol your kindness? These questions are phrased in general terms but the psalmist quickly applies them to his own case: '*But I* [ואני] have cried to you for help' and (presumably) have received no such 'wonder'. Hence another rhetorical question follows: 'Why, Yahweh, do you reject my soul?'[73] The enigma that the God who should desire to save and receive praise denies the psalmist such an experience permeates the texture of this psalm.

A final, though much less explicit, appeal concerns the 'rights' of the afflicted before God.[74] (See the discussion of Ps. 9-10.) The psalmist does this simply by identifying himself as עני (v. 16, see also v. 10a).

In sum, the psalmist appeals to God by addressing God as his only source of help, by referring to his persistent but unanswered prayers, by depicting his extreme hardship as an act of Yahweh himself, by posing questions to God that argue for his best interest, and by appealing to the rights of the afflicted.

H. PSALM 102

1. Distress

K. Seybold places Ps. 102 among those psalms that 'with relative certainty' can be labelled 'psalms of sickness'.[75] The psalmist's illness (see esp. vv. 4-6) evidently brings him near death (vv. 12, 24-25a). The intensity of his bodily suffering ('My bones are scorched like a burning mass') is matched by the duration of his suffering ('My days are consumed in smoke', v. 4). He portrays his loneliness by comparing himself to an unclean bird of the wilderness (vv. 7-8).[76] His only reference to contact with others is to enemies who mock him 'all the day' (v. 9).

Seybold infers particularly from vv. 13ff. that the psalmist is distant from Zion.[77] The references to Yahweh's answering the 'destitute' (v. 18), the 'prisoners' and 'those doomed to die' (v.

21)—people all alienated from the cultic worship—suggest that the psalmist likewise seeks to gain a hearing from Yahweh in a distant land. Most commentators locate this psalm in the exilic period. The convergence of four references suggest this: Zion appears to be in ruins (v. 15) and the people oppressed (vv. 18, 21); but Yahweh will build Zion (v. 17, 'prophetic' perfects) and will soon reveal his 'glory' (vv. 16-17, cf. 22-23).

2. *Interpretation*

Most of the verses referring to the psalmist's distress simply describe his condition (vv. 4-8, 10, 12). One verse mentions enemies taunting the psalmist (v. 9), but their role is clearly secondary since they are simply taking advantage of his wretched state (note the connective כי beginning v. 10).

Behind his affliction the psalmist perceives the wrath of God (v. 11). Yahweh is the one who drains him of vitality and 'has shortened his days' (v. 24). The description of Yahweh that follows may contain a hint why he is given this active role in the distress. In parallel to the petition, 'do not take me away in the midst of my *days*', the psalmist asserts in hymnic language, 'your *years* are from generation to generation' (v. 25). Further hymnic language follows that 'your *years* will not come to an end' and that 'the children of your servants ... will be established before you' (v. 29). The parallelism of v. 25 suggests that the primary purpose of this hymnic language is to support the petition of v. 25a. He whose years are endless and whose servants enjoy stability and security is asked to grant this psalmist the ability to live out his generation of life. Since Yahweh possesses endless years and since the psalmist feels his days are being cut short, he attributes his lack of days to Yahweh.

One should not assume that the psalmist's affliction could be explained simply within a sin-punishment scheme. A confession of sin does not surface in the psalm. Rather, the psalmist focuses simply on his pathetic condition. The phrase 'for you have picked me up and cast me away/down' (נשאתני ותשליכני, v. 11b) may indicate not simply rejection but also cruel treatment, which would connote a sense of protest from the psalmist, not an acknowledgement of just action.

3. *Appeal*

The prophecies that the psalmist recites speak of Yahweh as the compassionate one who hears the cries of the needy.[78] Hence, it is not surprising that the psalmist's lament concentrates on describing his affliction as a pitiful one. Complaint plays a relatively minor role. The first God-lament (vv. 11) occurs within the larger I-lament (vv. 4-8, 10, 12). The second God-lament (v. 24) does not confront God directly but refers to him in the third person. Nonetheless, a petition follows immediately, which implores Yahweh to reverse his act of weakening the psalmist.

Along with this depiction of the psalmist's misfortune, the prophetic citation forms the substance of the psalm's appeal. Some commentators believe the psalmist takes consolation in God's future restoration of the people of Israel, and thus his own personal need for healing fades from being so important.[79] But the repetition of lament over his own immediate hardship *after* this recitation of what Yahweh will do for Israel indicates otherwise. Rather, he appears to associate his own fate with that of the people of Israel. He implies that his תפלה (vv. 1, 2) is one of the תפלות of the 'destitute' (v. 18) to which Yahweh has promised to respond. He suggests that he is one of 'the sons of death' (v. 21) whom Yahweh has promised to set free. This juxtaposition of prophecy that promises Yahweh's salvation to the afflicted of Israel and a lament that describes the psalmist's own peril in effect calls Yahweh to apply these corporate promises to the lamenter's particular need.[80]

Hymnic praise follows this final complaint and petition. In parallel to the petition 'Don't take me away in the midst of my days', this praise begins: 'Your years endure through all generations'. The psalmist does not abandon interest in his own condition and seek refuge in God's eternal nature, as though the second line of the verse nullifies the first. Rather, he appeals to the one whose years are unending that he may enjoy the few days that he is allotted (note the contrasting parallelism of ימי and שנותיך).

The appeal of this psalm is based on future expectations for the people of God, not on their past history together. The psalmist establishes his appeal not on tradition but on promise. Complaint in the psalms usually emerges from tradition which has been formulated over generations and which establishes a certain constancy (with which the term חסד is associated) in God's demeanor. Thus, a psalmist may infer from what God has done in the past what he probably will and will not do in the future. The expectations engendered by promise, however, can never be so specific. The particular form in which the fulfillment will appear must remain elusive until it is actually fulfilled. Therefore, although complaint can and does emerge from promise, as it does in Ps. 102, it is a subdued complaint.

Chapter 8

CONCLUSIONS AND IMPLICATIONS

The charts on the following pages summarize some of the findings of Chapters 6 and 7. The first two charts (pp. 214-15) outline the laments of the community, the second two (pp. 216-17) the laments of the individual. The following abbreviations are used:

->	implies
=	is/are, is/are depicted as
w/	with
[]	material not stated explicitly (see Chapter 5)

Interpretation

T	Tradition: the tradition employed in the psalm, its claims and Yahweh's role in it
R	Role: the reversal of the tradition and Yahweh's role in the distress
S	Sin: the issue of sin and appropriate judgment

Appeal

L	Lament
G-L	God-lament
I-L	'I'-lament
F-L	Foe-lament
Ref	Reference to God's earlier saving deeds
CT	Confession of trust

(Abbreviations are continued on p. 218.)

Psalm	9-10	44	60	74	77
Distress	·Blasphemers oppress & murder ·Date?	·Battle defeat ·Pre-exilic	·Battle defeat ·Pre-exilic	·Temple in ruins, violence in land ·Late (?) exilic	·Absence of Yah's saving deeds ·Date?
Interpretation	T) praise of Yah as just Judge, defender of oppressed & punisher of wicked R) Yah's failure to defend -> Yah remote (passive) ·Foes = arrogant deniers of God	T) Holy war: Divine Warrior vs. foe R) Defeat -> Divine Warrior vs. people (except 'handing over' to foe) (active) S) Expectation based on testimony of fathers & people had promised praise ·People loyal	T) Holy war & oracle: Yah as Divine Warrior who wields his weapon, Israel, & claims his spoil, Edom R) Defeat w/Edom -> Yah wars against people (active)	T) Zion: Yah should defend his dwelling & congregation ·Creation tradition: Yah should oppose chaos R) Foes: blasphemous & thus Yah's foes; Yah angry but withdrawn (passive)	T) Yah should bring relief when called upon R) Yah perhaps not source of original distress but duration of distress -> Yah is silent (passive)
Appeal	·Praise of Yah as judge contradicted by lament re: oppressors ·Praise allows for some distress & accompanied by Pet (praise to be actualized) ·Lament concerns foes & accompanied by praise of Yah ·Thus, complaint (G-L) not so extensive	·Ref: Divine Warrior fought for fathers ·CT: Pre-battle praise of Divine Warrior ·G-L: contrast of Yah's rejection & handing over ·Protest: people loyal to covenant but crushed because of Yah ·Pet: Divine Judge to awaken to their loyalty & redeem (Since Yah as Divine Warrior acts w/hostility, appeal is made to him as Judge)	·G-L of Yah's warring against people countered w/Pets to restore ·Epithets show Yah's bond w/people ·Oracle: citation of promise that Israel = Yah's weapons & Edom = his spoil establishes ground of complaint & summons to fulfill oracle ·Pets simple because request obvious from promises & contrasting lament	·Aim: to turn God's anger from people (G-L) to invaders ·Pet: people = Yah's redeemed, temple = dwelling of 'name' ·F-L: Foes' act = sacrilege, thus foes = Yah's foes ·Ref: God's past victory over chaos contrasts w/present idleness toward blasphemers; Ref also supports Pets: deliverance has precedent ·Pet: confront Yah w/foes' blaspheming his name &	·L: failure of finding resolution by prayer & meditation ·Ref/Praise: Yah to actualize praise traditions ·No Pet

Distress	Jerusalem wasted / Late (?) exilic	Passers-by ravage / Pre-exilic	Agricultural dearth / Postexilic	Battle defeat / Pre-exilic	Travail of life / Postexilic hardships
Interpretation	T) Zion: Yah should defend his dwelling & congregation ·Yah should uphold honor of his name R) foe = godless butchers; Yah angry (active/passive?) S) People sinned but wrath excessive & misdirected: existence of Yah's people threatened & wicked go unpunished	T & R) Ark before people -> Yah as shepherd, their tears = his food ·'Transplant' of people from Egypt to Canaan -> Yah as gardener; broken defenses -> Gardener broke walls (reversal of salvation history) ·Yah exposes (active), foes devour S) People sinned (?) but wrath excessive	T) Return = sign that Yah has forgiven & turned from anger R) Harsh life -> Yah persists in anger (active/passive?) (Return & restoration seen as acts of God prob. because of prophets)	T) Yah's kingship & Davidic covenant: Yah rules thru & fights for king R) King's defeat -> Yah defeats king (active) S) Since sin should bring chastisement not annulment, Yah has violated the covenant	T) Yah as eternal creator over transient generations (Wisdom?) R) People's fading life -> afflictions are from Creator (active) S) Awareness of sin, but complaint that Yah preoccupied with it & his anger excessive
Appeal	·F-L: Foes' devastation portrayed as offensive to Yah (3rd party acts on own initiative) ·G-L: Yah's anger ·Pet: shift anger from people to foes ·Reasons: low state of people & Yah's name threatened ·References to Yah's honor & frequent use of possessives -> foes are Yah's foes ·People have sinned, but near extinction & godless go unpunished	·Argument: imagery used of Yah & people derived from their history together to impress Yah w/his continuing responsibility ·Shepherd-King & flock: Pets w/ hymnic language: renewal of theophany; G-L: fed w/tears ·Vinedresser & vine: Ref & G-L: exodus-settlement & its reversal ·God & king: Pet: reaffirm loyalty to king	·Ref: praise of past act of forgiveness & turning from anger ·G-L & Pet: persistence of anger & call for favor (rhetorically pushes God to extremes: to revive the people is more reasonable than to be angry w/them) (Since exile = judgment & return = mercy, complaint muted)	·Hymn: Yah's right to universal kingship ·Oracle: Davidic kingship bestowed on basis of Yah's kingship; covenant unconditional (reminding Yah of his promises & establishing grounds of complaint) ·G-L: distress as cruel reversal of praise ·Rhetorical questions: appeal for restoration ·Pet: add urgency	·Praise of eternal Yah by contrasting him w/mortal humanity (temporal distinction) ·Lament heightens distinction by showing moral distance: Yah's anger & travail of this generation ·Pet: revelation of Yah's work in the experience of those who have been his servants

Psalm	6	13	22	35
Distress	·Emotional exhaustion, near-death (illness?), foes present (accusers?) ·Prolonged distress	·Sorrow, near-death (illness?), foe dominant ·Prolonged distress	·Foes mock & about to prevail, near-death (illness/execution?) ·Unanswered prayers	·Malicious witnesses seek psalmist's life, sickness(?) ·Prolonged distress
Interpretation	T) Yah disciplines ·Yah [hears when called upon &] preserves his worshippers from premature death R) Distress = Yah's chastisement (active), but it should be beneficial, not so prolonged & not to death	T) Yah [hears when called upon &] preserves those who trust in his *hesed* & rejoice in his salvation [from premature death] R) Yah ignores psalmist (active/passive?)	T) Yah answers people who call him 'my God' [& preserves them from premature death] ·Yah = 'my God' from birth; Yah initiated & nurtured psalmist's trust R) Yah is remote & abandons psalmist to 'dust of death' (active/passive?)	T) Yah's praise is based on his delivering oppressed R) Lack of intervention -> Yah idle (passive)
Appeal	·Pet: against wrathful chastening; for mercy & healing ·G-L: duration ·Pet & Mo: Yah should preserve his worshippers for the sake of his *hesed* & its praise ·I-L: emotional exhaustion: as the dead are unable to praise, so the psalmist is unable	·G-L: duration of Yah's disfavor ·I-L: personal grief ·F-L: dominance of foe ·Pet: to heed & restore ·Mo: Yah = 'my God', psalmist might die, foe might rejoice ·CT & VP: those who would rejoice at the death of a godly person should not prevail over the godly person who would rejoice at Yah's salvation	·2 inclusios frame lament 1) 'My God': Yah's silence toward prayers ·Alternating laments & arguments: ·Unanswered prayers of psalmist contrasted w/prayers & rescue of fathers (not ashamed) ·Foes mock psalmist, 'Commit to Yah, let him rescue', but Yah = 'my God' since birth 2) 'Don't be far': Yah's remoteness ·God upon whom he was cast at birth has placed him in death ·Foes surround but no helper ·Pet: draw near & save	·3 sections, each w/L, Pet, & VP, each w/distinctive setting: 1) Battle & hunt: foes to receive their due 2) False witness & betrayal: psalmist testifies & asserts innocence ·Spells out content of praise, describes what opposes its realization, resulting complaint, VP (psalmist seeks occasion to praise) 3) Lawsuit: clear distinction between those who gloat & those who praise; just deserts to be given to each

Psalm	39	42-43	88	102
Distress	·Wicked prosper & godly envy that prosperity; death imminent (plague = emotional/physical?) ·Prolonged distress	·Alienation from temple (illness?); foes harass ·Prolonged distress	·Near-death; alienation ·Unanswered prayers	·Exiled from Zion; near-death (illness?); loneliness & mocking foes ·Continuing distress
Interpretation	T) Yah assigns few days to all ·Yah chastens for sin R & S) Distress = Yah's chastening (active), but—in view of a life already too brief—considered excessive ·Wicked = potential mockers who aggravate	T) As Creator provides water to animals, so Lord of temple provides the (river of) life that issues from temple ·In past, psalmist was a participant in temple worship R) Yah 'drowns' the psalmist (active) ·Foes mock absence of divine help	T) Yah hears when called upon & preserves his worshippers from premature death R) Psalmist compares himself to the dead, then pushes to logical conclusion: Yah has put him in death & has estranged him from friends, as dead have no friends (active)	T) Yah's 'years' are endless & he preserves his servants R) Psalmist's weakness & lack of days -> Yah 'has shortened' his 'days' (active) ·Foes taunt
Appeal	·Confession of avoiding sin ·Pet & L: life brief & riches vain ·Pet & L: Yah should not merely chasten for sin but should deliver from sin (Complaint is restrained because of awareness of sin & determination to restrain speech)	·I-L: thirsting for God & memory of temple festivals ·L: God, who used to grant hesed, now drowns psalmist ·Complaints that his shielding God ignores & rejects ·Foes mock his God's absence ·Pet: for escort to temple (Refrain: psalmist's inner struggle for faith)	·Yah = only source of help ·References to persistent prayer establish psalm's structure ·Imagery depicts hardship as a horrible act of Yah ·Rhetorical questions show inappropriateness of Yah's hostile disposition: the God who should desire to save & receive praise denies the psalmist (argument for Yah's best interest) ·Appeal to the 'rights' of the afflicted	·Prophetic citation: Yah compassionate to people of Zion (corporate promise applied to psalmist's need) ·I-L: psalmist's pitiful condition ·Complaint subdued: Yah, whose years are unending, appears to deny the psalmist his full course of days ·Pet &HP: he who possesses endless years not to take psalmist in the midst of his life

Protest   Protest of innocence/loyalty
Pet   Petition(s)
Mo   Motifs to move God to intervene
VP   Vow of praise

In the 'Distress' category of the corporate laments are listed the occasions of the psalms and their approximate dates. In the same category of the laments of the individual are listed the occasions of the psalms and their duration.

Listed first in the 'Interpretation' category are the traditions employed in these psalms. Noted here are their basic claims and the nature of Yahweh's role, whether he actively takes the initiative or acts in a defensive role. The second item notes how Yahweh is depicted in the reversal of that tradition. Where relevant, the role in which the enemies are perceived is also mentioned. The third item of sin is noted when it arises in a psalm. The point made here is that while the people may have sinned, the distress is considered as either excessive or inappropriate judgment.

The 'Appeal' category highlights the key features of the psalmist's argument to God.

A few observations may be drawn from the preceding tables. Among the laments of the individual, the enemies are not the explicit cause of distress (except perhaps in Pss. 22 and 35). They simply harass and mock the psalmist in his plight.

In the corporate complaints the roles of the enemies are more complex. (The only psalms not discussed here are Pss. 77, 85, and 90, where enemies are not in view.) In those psalms where Yahweh is perceived as *passive* (Pss. 9-10, 74, and probably 79), the enemies are portrayed as godless. They set themselves up against God, either by arrogantly spurning him (10.3-4, 11) or by abusing his name (74.10, 18, 22-23; 79.6, 10a, 12), desecrating his sanctuary (74.3-8; 79.1), and slaughtering his people (74.19-20; 79.2-3, 7, 10b). Such a portrayal shows that these enemies are Yahweh's enemies, thus making clear to Yahweh that he has a personal interest in intervening in the distress.

In those laments where Yahweh is perceived as *active* (Pss. 44, 60, 80, 89), Yahweh's activity consists in exposing and handing his people over to enemies who attack them (44.11-13; 80.13-14; 89.41-42, 44).

> 44.11 You cause us to turn back from the adversary,
> so that those who hate us take spoil for
> themselves.

Ps. 60 makes no mention of the enemies' action; only Yahweh is referred to as an agent of disaster (vv. 3-5). Ps. 89.43 comes the closest to saying that Yahweh actually promotes the activity of the enemy against his people:

> 89.43 You have exalted the right hand of his
> adversaries;
> you have given all his enemies cause for
> rejoicing.

For the most part, these complaints do not go as far as the prophets, who assert that Yahweh has 'raised up' an enemy, such as Assyria (Amos 6.14; cf. Isa. 10.5, 6) and Babylonia (Hab. 1.6). In the prophets these enemies are perceived as instruments of 'just judgment', a category which the lament psalmists would not feel appropriate for their disasters. In the complaints where Yahweh is considered an active agent bringing the distress, the enemies may have inflicted serious harm on the people, but they are not the primary concern—Yahweh is. The psalmists' chief interests lie in confronting Yahweh for exposing the people to the enemies' devastation.

Among the ten corporate complaints, the issue of sin surfaces in five or perhaps six psalms. Ps. 44 staunchly affirms that the people have upheld their allegiance to Yahweh and his covenant (vv. 18-19, 21-22). Pss. 79, 85, 89, and 90 all mention (at least the possibility of) the people's sin, but for these psalmists the people's failure to obey completely does not account for the extreme disaster that has befallen them. The distresses cannot be considered just judgments commensurate with their transgressions. Ps. 79 does contain a prayer for forgiveness (vv. 8-9), but the conviction of the psalmist is that Yahweh's wrath is excessive (v. 5) and misdirected. Should his anger continue, the very existence of his people is threatened and the wicked who mock him would go unpunished (vv. 8-12). Ps. 85 reckons that the issue of the people's sin had been dealt with decisively in the past, when Yahweh forgave their sin and turned from his anger in the return from exile (vv. 2-4). According to the oracle cited in Ps. 89, should the Davidic son sin, this would result in chastisement, not the annulment of the covenant (vv. 31-38). But the current catastrophe cannot be regarded as mere discipline; it runs counter to the covenant itself (see Chapter 6). Ps. 90 acknowledges the people's sin, but in the psalmist's view Yahweh seems preoccupied with it (v. 8), and his wrath is considered excessive—the Creator's creatures are left with a futile existence (vv. 7, 8-11). Ps. 80 may allude to a defection of the people (v. 19), and so complaint is based not on God's wrath as such but on its excess (vv. 5-6). His severe wrath appears to have reversed what he began in salvation history.

Among these ten corporate complaints, only the psalmist in Ps. 44 asserts the people's innocence as a basis for his argument. The others argue exclusively from the commitments that Yahweh had established in the past. Sometimes they elaborate on the evil of the enemy, with no mention of the conduct of the people (Pss. 9-10, 74, 79). Ps. 79, for example, employs a relative argument: your people have sinned, but the enemies are thoroughly godless. And in Ps. 9-10 the people are deserving of God's help not because they are the 'righteous' but because they are the 'afflicted'.

Finally, it should be clear from the exegetical work in Chapters 6 and 7 that, as argued in Chapter 1, the lament psalms must be read as arguments to Yahweh. A lament psalm is not primarily a 'reflection of the psalmist's soul', as though one could read from it how the psalmist struggled to hold on to faith. The 'references to God's earlier saving deeds' and the hymnic praises do not find their way into these psalms for the psalmists' sake, as a way to bolster his own faith. Nor are they present in the psalm simply for 'cultic' or 'liturgical' reasons. They function as reminders to Yahweh of his promises. They establish the grounds for complaint and also serve as a summons for Yahweh to actualize these earlier saving deeds and praises. They present a precedent for Yahweh to save the contemporary generation as he saved past generations. In a sense, these 'references to God's earlier saving deeds' and hymnic praises can be regarded as a form of petition.

We may now summarize some of the key observations of the preceding chapters and note their implications. Upon closer examination of the lament category we have discerned two distinct forms of appeal: the psalms of 'plea', which affirm the praise of God, and the psalms of 'complaint', which charge God with failing certain traditions normally expressed as praise. In the former subcategory, praise appears as a motif in its own right; in the latter, praise is presented as that which the lament denies. The complaint psalms in effect reflect a conception of God different from that found in the praise psalms and the plea psalms: God is approached as either an aloof bystander or an active antagonist. The aim of these psalms, however, is never simply to complain, for this protest is always directed toward the purpose of summoning God to conform to his promises, as contained in these traditions.

The factors that influenced the form of appeal assumed by any given psalm are several. The more radical appeal of the complaint psalms appears to emerge from either near-death distresses (in the individual laments) or national disasters (in the communal laments) wherein deliverance seems unduly delayed.

These distresses deny the efficacy of certain praise traditions. An underlying expectation disappointed in almost every instance is that Yahweh answers when called upon. A prolonged distress implies Yahweh has ignored the psalmist's prior pleading. This therefore implicates Yahweh as being involved in the distress in either an active or a withdrawn form.

Among the laments of the community, the psalmists appear to have drawn upon a variety of traditions which were met with contradictory experiences through Israel's history. In times of battle defeat (Pss. 44, 60, and 89) the traditions of holy war, rooted in the exodus and conquest traditions, were in jeopardy. In Ps. 60 Yahweh's ownership of the land is threatened, and in Ps. 89 the whole Davidic covenant appears to have failed. In times of invasion (Pss. 74 and 79) the Zion tradition is violated and Yahweh no longer appears to be the restrainer of chaos. In times of social violence (Ps. 9-10) the tradition of Yahweh as the Judge defending the oppressed and punishing the wicked is contradicted. In the postexilic period the belief that the return of the people from exile signalled Yahweh's turning from anger is disappointed (Ps. 85).

Compared to the corporate laments, the individual laments are much simpler in their interpretations of distress and in their appeals to God. This observation is probably due to the relative simplicity of the traditions upon which the individual psalmists' draw. The fundamental tradition upon which most of them are based is that Yahweh hears when called upon and preserves his worshippers from premature death. We may call this the 'my God' tradition. Such deliverances should form the content of the praise of God, the expression of which gives the psalmists their very reason for living. When premature death looms large, this gives warrant for complaint.

Several other traditions or beliefs also surface. Yahweh sometimes disciplines those who call on him (Pss. 6 and 39). (Only Ps. 39 mentions sin explicitly.) Such chastening is assumed to be for the psalmist's benefit; it should not result in his death or make his existence unbearable. Explicit reference to the temple or to Jerusalem occurs only in two psalms, Pss. 42-43 and 102. But in each case, the psalmist is clearly separated from the temple site. In Ps. 39 the psalmist's reflections on the brevity of life—a motif held in common with Ps. 90—appear to stem from the Wisdom traditions. Ps. 102 applies the corporate promises of Yahweh's compassion toward 'Zion' to the distress of an individual. The psalm also appeals to Yahweh as the everlasting God who should ensure the stability of the generations of his people.

Such findings give us deeper insight into the faith represented in the Psalter. In these psalms we see Israel's faith in a position of extremity, when circumstances test that faith with challenge and lead to a critical examination of faith's foundation. In the psalms of plea when distress is encountered it is met with petition, which seeks to actualize expectations engendered by praise traditions. These psalms give no evidence that expectation has been disappointed. God is not accused of having had a role in the distress. Thus, for example, when enemies threaten, God is simply called upon as a third party to come to the rescue. That one (even if he be 'righteous') may encounter distress and subsequently call on Yahweh appears to be a given in Israelite faith. This is confirmed by the conception of God as a refuge, so often seen in the Psalms. Yahweh is the Deliverer, which means that one may not presume that he is a guardian who preserves his own from even the sight of evil. His salvation is known by a series of saving acts, not by a continual state of salvation. He is the God of the heights who reaches down to the depths (cf. Ps. 113).

In the complaint psalms, however, expectation is disappointed. It is not distress itself which causes dissonance (as the psalms of plea make clear); something else must have happened—or have failed to. We have observed a correlation between the distress reflected in lament psalms and the expression of complaint. The expression arises because the distress has been prolonged, which means Yahweh has not heard previous petitions; or because the distress is about to take the psalmist's life, which in the thinking of the psalmists means nothing but the termination of life with God. Since this calls into question the conception of Yahweh as a rock of refuge, expectation is disappointed.

The distress itself may cause the psalmist physical pain and social ostracism, but the faith dissonance results in intensified psychological turmoil and religious questioning. With the security of the 'Refuge' called into question, the traditional conception of God the Deliver becomes God the absent Deliverer (in cases where his role is viewed as passive) or God the Cause of distress (in cases where his role is active). It is this altered conception of God which demonstrates the radical nature of these psalms. The psalms of plea affirm God to be who he is in the praises: he is Savior and Deliverer. In the complaint psalms, however, such traditions are called into question.

According to the cognitive dissonance theory as outlined by R.P. Carroll, there are three possibilities for the resolution of dissonance. The first is avoidance of disconfirming evidence.[1] This means, by definition, could not be employed in a complaint psalm, which by its very nature addresses God with an apparent anomaly. The second category of dissonance resolution is that of social support. In the case of individual laments, however, the absence of social support and the harassment from adversaries would naturally aggravate dissonance. This is frequently the case in these psalms because the distress from which the psalmist is suffering is often interpreted as a judgment by God.

The third means of resolution offered by the theory is that of reinterpretation. Thus, there may be a reinterpretation of the disconfirming evidence, but in most cases there is a reinterpretation of the beliefs received, which would thereby lead to altered expectations. Dissonance could be reduced if the 'new' expectations did not conflict as strongly with the events. The composers of the complaint psalms, however, clearly rejected this form of dissonance resolution. In these psalms the conflicting elements are plainly open to view, as can be seen in the juxtaposition of praise and lament in the same psalm (e.g. Pss. 9-10; 44; 89). Instead of seeking to attain a synthesis, these psalmists set side by side the praise traditions and the disconfirming evidence. The conflict is thereby brought into focus for the sake of the appeal to God. These psalms, by their very nature as prayer, abandon all attempts at resolution from the human side: the disappointment is in God and so the resolution must be from him as well. The psalmists seek to paint the picture of their distresses in such a way as to show that their dilemmas are not simply their own—they threaten the integrity of God's own character. These psalms present clearly the reality of the traditions and the reality of their distresses to bring to light the anomaly of Yahweh's present disposition and behavior. It is, thus, 'for his name's sake' that resolution becomes imperative.

It is striking that the community of worshippers in Israel should have preserved psalms of such unresolved dissonance. On the divine side, such mystery was not 'explained away' by notions of transcendence; and on the human side, the mystery of sin and its consequent judgment did not offer sufficient grounds for resolution.

Whereas in the psalms of plea, God and the psalmist are, as it were, on the same side, in the complaint psalms the psalmist must appeal to a God who appears to have abandoned loyalty. Their case therefore becomes exceedingly more difficult to argue. The psalm must appeal to God against God. Ironically, however, the God-lament itself becomes the first step toward resolution. By attributing the cause of the distress to God, it is also a confession that he is the one who can reverse that distress.

NOTES

Notes to Chapter 1

[1] G. von Rad, *Old Testament Theology* (1965), I, pp. 355-56.

[2] Cited in J. Becker, *Wege der Psalmenexegese* (1975), p. 9 n. 2.

[3] So B.S. Childs in 'Reflections on the Modern Study of the Psalms', *Magnalia Dei* (1976), p. 391, and in *Introduction to the Old Testament as Scripture* (1979), pp. 513-14.

[4] S. Mowinckel, *Psalms in Israel's Worship* (1962), I, p. 23.

[5] M.J. Buss, 'The Meaning of "Cult" and the Interpretation of the Old Testament', *JBR* 32 (1964), p. 325.

[6] One may define a 'motif' as 'a word or pattern of thought that recurs in a similar situation ... to evoke a similar mood, within a work, or in various works of a genre' (J.T. Shipley, ed., *Dictionary of World Literature* [1968], p. 274, cited in D.J.A. Clines, *The Theme of the Pentateuch* [1978], p.121 n. 11). Gunkel himself used the term 'Motiv' to denote these components of psalms (*Einleitung*, pp. 25ff.).

[7] This analysis has an obvious debt to C. Westermann. For a more complete listing and discussion of these generic marks of the lament, see Westermann, *Praise and Lament in the Psalms* (1981), pp. 52-55, 64-70, 173-94; Gunkel, *Einleitung*, pp. 121-33, 212-51; Mowinckel, *Psalms in Israel's Worship*, I, pp. 195-219, 229-35; II, pp. 9-11.

[8] H. Gunkel, *Einleitung in die Psalmen* (1933), p. 231.

[9] See Gunkel, *Einleitung*, pp. 218ff., and E. Gerstenberger, *Der bittende Mensch* (1980), pp. 119-27, esp. pp. 125-26.

[10] Gunkel, *Einleitung*, p. 216.

[11] See, e.g., Mowinckel, *Psalms in Israel's Worship*, I, pp. 2-12.

[12] Gerstenberger, *Der bittende Mensch*, p. 4.

[13] On the intricacy of psalmic structures see esp. N.H. Ridderbos, *Die Psalmen: Stilistische Verfahren und Aufbau mit*

besonderer Berücksichtigung von Ps 1-41 (1972). The assertion that psalms generally have an author, not authors, does not exclude the possibility of redactional work, wherein psalms are reinterpreted, verses are added, and originally separate psalms are spliced together. For 'psalmist' to be a helpful term we need not necessarily identify him or even the century and social group in which he lived.

14 Mowinckel, *Psalms in Israel's Worship*, II, pp. 92-93.

15 Cf. W. Brueggemann, 'From Hurt to Joy, From Death to Life', *Int* 28 (1974), pp. 3-8.

16 Though this function is especially true of sacred literature, it is also shared with literature in general: 'A poem, we have to conclude, is not an individual experience or a sum of experiences, but only a potential cause of experiences' (R. Wellek and A. Warren, *Theory of Literature* [1956], p. 150).

17 W.K. Wimsatt, *The Verbal Icon: Studies in the Meaning of Poetry* (1954), p. 49.

18 H.-J. KRAUS, *Psalmen* (1978), I, pp. 40-41.

19 W. Beyerlin, *Die Rettung der Bedrängten* (1970); K. Seybold, *Das Gebet des Kranken im Alten Testament* (1973); O. Keel, *Feinde und Gottesleugner* (1969).

20 Some interpreters following a more cultic approach to the Psalms have accused of literalism those taking a more historical approach, but each school practices its own kind of literalism. Commenting on a verse such as Ps. 46.9 ('Come, behold the works of Yahweh ...'), S. Mowinckel writes, 'Knowing how thoroughly the cult in ancient times was a "drama" for the purpose of presenting visibly what faith knew to be happening, and considering the prominent part played by ritual fighting games in the cult of ancient peoples, we can hardly help interpreting the words in the above passages as references to ritual acts, through which was presented in a more or less realistic or symbolical way the victory of Yahweh over the united nations' (*Psalms in Israel's Worship*, I, pp. 181; cf. A. WEISER, *The Psalms* [1962], p. 43). Though a cult drama interpretation is possible, arguments from ancient Near Eastern parallels would not be sufficient without a full reckoning with the use of imagery in Hebrew poetry. We need not necessarily suppose that such language reflects a cult drama any

more than assuming that in every case where the psalmist turns to
address his enemies, or the sea and mountains (as in Psalm 114),
they were represented physically in a drama.
    21 See, e.g., J. Becker, *Israel deutet seine Psalmen* (1966); P.R.
Ackroyd, *Exile and Restoration* (1968), pp. 45-46, 225-26.
    22 H. Gunkel, 'The Religion of the Psalms', *What Remains of
the Old Testament* (1928), pp. 70-71. Although Gunkel did not see
most of the extant psalms as composed for the cult, he viewed the
cult as the birthplace of the genre.
    23 See, e.g., Gunkel, *Einleitung*, pp. 117-21; Mowinckel,
Psalms in Israel's Worship, I, pp. 193-94; C. Westermann, *The
Psalms* (1980), pp. 30-31.
    24 See, e.g., Mowinckel, *Psalms in Israel's Worship*, II, pp. 4,
16ff.
    25 See, e.g., Gerstenberger, *Der bittende Mensch*, pp. 134-60;
R. Albertz, *Persönliche Frömmigkeit und offizielle Religion*
(1978), pp. 25-27; Seybold, *Das Gebet des Kranken* (1973), pp.
171ff.
    26 In connection with the historical-critical method, B.S. Childs
remarks, 'Whereas during the medieval period the crucial issue lay
in the usage made of the multiple layers of meaning *above* the text,
the issue now turns on the multiple layers *below* the text' ('The
Sensus Literalis of Scripture', *Beiträge zur alttestamentlichen
Theologie* [1977], p. 92). As an example of how some form critics
are reconsidering the relations of texts to their social settings, esp.
regarding cause and effect, see R. Knierim, 'Old Testament Form
Criticism Reconsidered', *Int* 27 (1973), pp. 436-49, 463-66.
    27 For an example where the supposed 'cultic actualities' of a
psalm prevail over its function as prayer, see J.H. Hayes, *An
Introduction to Old Testament Study* (1979), pp. 305-306.
    28 R. Wellek and A. Warren, *Theory of Literature* (1956), p.
139, see further pp. 73-74.
    29 J. Muilenburg, 'The Gains of Form Criticism in Old
Testament Studies', *ExT* 71 (1959-60), pp. 231.
    30 D.A. Knight, 'The Understanding of "Sitz im Leben" in
Form Criticism', *SBL 1974 Seminar Papers* (1974), I, pp. 105-25,
esp. pp. 107-109; Knierim, 'OT Form Criticism Reconsidered',
pp. 436-49.

31 On Psalm 6 for instance see KRAUS (1978), I, p. 184; P.C. CRAIGIE (1983), p. 92; A.F. KIRKPATRICK (1902), p. 26.

32 See O. Keel, *Feinde und Gottesleugner* (1969), pp. 107-108.

33 The difficulty of uncovering how psalmists interpreted their distresses should not be understated, but this task is no more speculative than the many attempts scholars have made in reconstructing festal liturgies from the Psalms.

34 Knierim, 'OT Form Criticism Reconsidered', *Int* 27 (1973), p. 436.

35 As S. Ullmann states, '...the meaning of a word can be ascertained only by studying its use' (*Semantics* [1972], p. 67), and 'the true meaning of a word is to be found by observing what a man does with it, not what he says about it' (cited from p. 64).

36 See D.J.A. Clines, 'Psalm Research: Genres', *TB* 20 (1969), p. 109; Mowinckel, *Psalms in Israel's Worship*, I, pp. 37-39.

37 Mowinckel himself makes the point that our best window into what worship was like in pre-exilic Israel is the Psalms, not for example the Priestly material of the Pentateuch (*Psalms in Israel's Worship*, I, pp. 35-36).

38 Knierim, 'OT Form Criticism', pp. 448-49.

39 Koch, *Growth of the Biblical Tradition* (1969), pp. 3-5.

40 Cited in Koch, *Growth of the Biblical Tradition*, p. 66; cf. p. xiii.

41 Buss,'Understanding Communication', *Encounter with the Text* (1979), p. 10. The scope of the class depends on how specific the expectation is. Buss's conception of genre appears to do the best job of handling genre as a heuristic means of classification (nominalism) and as an entity in its own right (realism).

42 After having composed this analysis of genre, I came across two other definitions that confirm this understanding: see N.R. Petersen, 'On the Notion of Genre in Via's "Parable and Example Story: A Literary-Structuralist Approach"', *Semeia* 1 (1974), p. 137; and F. Lentzen-Deis, 'Methodische Überlegungen zur Bestimmung literarischer Gattungen im Neuen Testament', *Bib* 62 (1981), pp. 13-14. The latter emphasizes that genre appears as concrete features in texts, whereby these signals serve as instructions to the reader/listener (p. 14). The speaker, to make himself understood, chooses an appropriate form of

communication held in common with the listener, which will fulfill his intention (p. 12).

43 Cf. Knierim, 'OT Form Criticism Reconsidered', *Int* 27 (1973), p. 454.

44 OT studies frequently uses genre criticism to reconstruct the (usually institutional) context of a given passage. In contemporary use the context of any text is usually self-evident. As when reading a newspaper, readers make decisions about the various genres to determine how the texts should be read, not to determine their context, which is plainly known. Ancient texts, however, often lack an explicit context, which genre studies can help to determine. That, nevertheless, is a derived use of genre, not its essential use. Therefore, in the strict sense of the term, the main purpose of form criticism is not 'to relate them [texts] to their sociological context', but to study 'their conventional forms' so as to elucidate their 'meaning and intention' (G.M. Tucker, 'Form Criticism, OT', *IDBSup*, p. 342; and *Form Criticism of the Old Testament* [1971], p. xi). Genre is primarily a literary feature, not a contextual one. This, however, is not intended to belittle the search for *Sitz im Leben*, for genre is undeniably one of the most helpful means for inferring this context.

45 However, regarding the limitations of any classification system, esp. when the essential one is the aim, see M.J. Buss, 'Understanding Communication', *Encounter with the Text* (1979), pp. 9-16.

46 Mowinckel, *Psalms in Israel's Worship*, I, pp. 23.

47 Mowinckel, *Psalms in Israel's Worship*, I, pp. 23-24.

48 See, e.g., Mowinckel, *Psalms in Israel's Worship*, II, pp. 126ff., on 'Traditionalism and Personality in the Psalms'.

49 Cf. WEISER (1962), pp. 74-75.

50 See further Knierim, 'OT Form Criticism Reconsidered', *Int* 27 (1973), pp. 458-59, on mixed genres.

51 An exception to this tendency, K. Seybold warns against the 'Pauschalierung' of the laments of the individual (*Das Gebet des Kranken*, p. 82).

52 R.J. Clifford, 'Rhetorical Criticism in the Exegesis of Hebrew Poetry', *SBL 1980 Seminar Papers* (1980), p. 19.

53 On this distinction see Caird, *Language and Imagery of the Bible* (1980), pp. 38, 40ff., 49ff. This corresponds to F. de Saussure's terminology of *la langue* (the prelinguistic activity of the mind) and *la parole* (the actual activity of language).

54 See G.B. Caird, *The Language and Imagery of the Bible* (1980), pp. 117-21.

55 Hence, interpreters should pay more heed to Gunkel's component of 'mood' when talking about the makings of genres.

56 W. Nowottny, *Language Poets Use* (1965), pp. 106-107.

57 See further Ridderbos, *Die Psalmen* (1972).

58 WEISER, p. 163.

59 This interpretation is by no means new. Luther, commenting on this psalm, speaks of the 'state in which hope despairs, and yet despair hopes at the same time' (cited in J.L. Mays's excellent exposition of this psalm, 'Psalm 13', *Int* 34 [1980], p. 281).

60 On this popular feature of ancient Hebrew poetry, see Caird, *The Language and Imagery of the Bible* (1980), pp. 117-21.

61 Nowottny, *Language Poets Use* (1965), p. 142.

62 See, e.g., D.J.A. Clines, 'Story and Poem: The Old Testament as Literature and as Scripture', *Int* 34 (1980), pp. 115-27.

63 J. Barr, *The Bible in the Modern World* (1973), p. 70. In a footnote on the same page Barr quotes R.M. Frye: 'A literary work is its own meaning, and its meaning cannot be univocally abstracted from it. This is the one literary principle upon which all competent literary critics now agree.' Barr states these principles for those parts of the Bible which exhibit themselves as literature, without arguing for any view of the Psalms at this point. M. Weiss, with specific regard for Psalm poetry, argues for the indispensability of their poetic structure. See 'Die Methode der "Total-Interpretation"', *Uppsala Congress Volume 1971* (VTSup, 22; 1972), pp. 91, 92.

64 L. Alonso Schökel, 'Hermeneutical Problems of a Literary Study of the Bible', *Congress Volume: Edinburgh 1974* (VTSup, 28; 1975), pp. 9-10. A lesson in reading can often be an intricate affair: 'When the linguist, studying the common tongue, can declare that "each word when used in a new context is a new word" the literary critic may hope to find more general acceptance of the

elaborateness of his discourses on the highly organized linguistic structures encountered in the word of poets ...' (W. Nowottny, *The Language Poets Use* [1965], p. 20). This awareness, however, needs to be balanced with another observation: "'The true use of interpretation", said Jowett, "is to get rid of interpretation, and leave us alone in the company of the author". It is impossible not to feel after reading much modern interpretative criticism that the author and his work have disappeared and that it is the interpreter's insistent company which we are left alone with' (H. Gardner, *The Business of Criticism* [1959], pp. 132-33). Cf. R.M. Frye, 'A Literary Perspective for the Criticism of the Gospels', *Jesus and Man's Hope* (1971), pp. 195, 217 n. 7.

65 'Exegesis', *IDBSup* (1976), p. 297.

Notes to Chapter 2

1 Gunkel, *Einleitung*, p. 284. Cf. also his remarks in 'The Religion of the Psalms' (1928), p. 111.

2 Westermann, *Praise and Lament*, p. 11. Cf. p. 152.

3 Westermann, *Praise and Lament*, p. 154. Cf. p. 74.

4 Westermann, *Praise and Lament*, pp. 27-28.

5 See A. Jepsen, 'Warum? Eine lexikalische und theologische Studie', *Das ferne und nahe Wort* (1967), pp. 106-13.

6 Pss. 4.3 and 94.3 are exceptions, the latter of which will be discussed in Chapter 4. Ps. 13.3 works in parallel to the preceding verse, a God-lament which is also prefaced with 'How long?'

7 The psalms that qualify as 'God-laments' are Pss. 6; 9-10; 13; 22; 35; 39; 42-43; 44; 60; 74; 77; 79; 80; 85; 88; 89; 90; 102; 108. The 'non-God-lament' psalms are thus Pss. 3; 4; 5; 7; 12; 14 = 53; 17; 25; 26; 27; 28; 31; 36; 38; 40b = 70; 41; 51; 54; 55; 56; 57; 58; 59; 61; 64; 69; 70; 71; 83; 86; 94; 106; 109; 120; 123; 126; 130; 137; 139; 140; 141; 142; 143.

8 The confessions of trust that are predications of God occur frequently in the non-God-lament psalms. In the psalms of the individual they are 3.4-6; 4.4, 9; 5.4; 7.11; 14.5b, 6b (cf. 53.5-6); 17.6a, 7; 25.5; 27.1-5, 10b; 28.5; 31.4ff., 15-16a; 38.10, 16b; 40.18b = 70.6b; 41.12-13 (or is this actually a thanksgiving

psalm?—see commentators); 54.6-7; 55.17-20a, 24; 56.9a, 10b (note 4-5, 11-12 where אוֹהִלל is used); 57.2b-5; 58.10-12; 59.9-11; 61.4, 6-8a; 64.8ff.; 71.3b, 5-8, 20; 86.5, 7; 130.4, 7b-8; 140.7a, 8, 13; 142.6; 143.10a. In the corporate psalms they are 12.6-8 (it is difficult to determine whether this oracle is actually given as a response to the preceding lament, or the psalmist cites it to remind Yahweh to perform his own words); 123.1, 2b.

[9] Westermann disagrees with this interpretation (*Praise and Lament*, p. 74), but he offers little to support his assertion. His argument from the parallelism of Ps. 38.15 is hardly sufficient. (On the problems of drawing semantic inferences from poetic parallelism see J.F.A. Sawyer, *Semantics in Biblical Research* [1972], p. 75.) Moreover, his conclusion stands at variance with another essay of his where he draws the opposite conclusion regarding grammatical subjects in the first and second persons ('The Structure and History of the Lament in the Old Testament', *Praise and Lament*, p. 185). Finally, one of Westermann's strongest affirmations regarding the nature of praise in the OT concerns the grammatical subject.

[10] Westermann, *Praise and Lament*, p. 55.

[11] These observations on the reference to God's earlier saving deeds, and on the other motifs which follow, show that the mere identification of form critical motifs is not sufficient. One cannot assume the function of even identical phrases is the same in every context.

[12] Narrative praise occurs in 3.8 (?); 4.2, 8 (?); 31.8-9, 22; 86.13, 17b (?); 94.17-23; 120.1 (a thanksgiving psalm?); 126.1-3. Hymnic praise occurs in 3.9; 5.5-7, 13; 7.9a, 12; 25.8-10, 12-15; 31.20ff.; 36.6-10; 41.2-4; 51.6b, 8; 57.11; 69.17a; 71.19 (cf. 15); 86.8-10, 15; 94.8-15; 106.1-3 (cf. 7-46, which is both a confession of sin and praise of Yahweh's just and merciful dealings with Israel); 109.21b (cf. 31); 139.1-18.

[13] Reading אֶחְזֶה instead of נֶאְוָה

[14] Gunkel, *Einleitung*, p. 224.

[15] See KRAUS, II, pp.754, 757.

[16] Ps. 69 does close with a number of verses of praise but these are attached to the psalmist's vow of praise. This feature also

occurs, though restricted to one line of a verse, in Ps. 13, a God-lament psalm.

[17] 'The opposite pole of praise' is not merely 'this supplication in time of need' (as according to Westermann, *Praise and Lament*, p. 34) but the complaint.

Notes to Chapter 3

[1] I have stayed with the Hiphil for reasons stated in the section 'God Passive' below.

[2] Read מְשַׁעְתִּי for the sake of parallelism.

[3] The third person plural has little textual support.

[4] כל preceding הבל is to be deleted for the reason of dittography.

[5] Read בְּלְאֻמִּם.

[6] The כִּי, following the negative of v. 19, is translated as an adversative. On תצים see D.W. Thomas, *Text of the Revised Psalter* (1963), p. 16. On צלמות as an expression of the superlative see D.W. Thomas, 'צַלְמָוֶת in the Old Testament', *JSS* 7 (1962), pp. 191-200.

[7] Read הרעשׂת הארץ.

[8] With the LXX וימינך is placed in the second line. Read בקרב instead of מקרב (cf. Thomas, *Psalter*, p. 31). כְּלֻאָה (the passive participle of כלא, 'to keep back') is preferred to כַּלֵּה because of the parallel line and because an imperative is not so appropriate at this place in the psalm (see Chapter 6). J.A. Emerton ('Notes on Three Passages in Psalms Book III', *JTS* 14 [1963], pp. 374-81), claiming probable support from the Peshitta, reads קְהָלְכָה for חוקך כלה. Thus 74.11b would read, 'even your right hand from the midst of your assembly'.

[9] I translate 77.5 as, 'I have grasped my eyelids; I am disturbed and cannot speak'. The MT אָחַזְתָּ is improbable since God is nowhere else addressed in the second person in the lament section of this psalm, the character of which decidedly resembles a soliloquy (esp. vv. 6-10). God is not addressed until the hymn begins in v. 12. In addition, the versions show variation of the person of this verb: the LXX and the Syriac version translate it as a third person plural (the codex Vaticanus of the LXX also has *ol*

ἐχθροί μου, thus reading עֹיְבָי instead of עֵינִי), Symmachus and Jerome imply a first person singular, אֲחֻזְתִי. D.W. Thomas (*Psalter*, p. 32) and M. DAHOOD (II, p. 227) propose אָחֹזוֹת. שְׁמֻרוֹת may be a hapax legomenon for 'eyelids' or it should perhaps read אַשְׁמֻרוֹת, 'watches (of the night)' (see BRIGGS, II, p. 177 for textual support; cf. Pss. 63.7; 119.148), which is certainly possible (cf. *GKC*, § 85b and DAHOOD, II, p. 227).

10 Since אלהים is not actually in its construct form, it should probably be considered, as *GKC* calls it, a 'mechanical substitution' (§ 125h).

11 לֹא makes better sense of the parallelism and receives support from two Hebrew MSS, the LXX, Symmachus, the Syriac version and Jerome.

12 The MT חָפְשִׁי is acceptable if understood either as irony or as meaning 'separated', with possible support from 2 Kgs. 15.5. Nonetheless, reading נִפְשִׁי is perhaps more likely. הֻשַׁבְתִּי ('I am made to dwell'; cf. Lam. 3.6) and חֻפַּשְׂתִּי ('I am searched for', implying 'I am hidden') are other conjectures.

13 The LXX suggests reading אֲנִיתָ ('You have let all your breakers fall [upon me]'), which as KRAUS notes (II, p. 772) would be a scribal error due to the dictation process.

14 Read probably צִמְּתוּנִי. For translating this verb as 'to reduce to silence', see G.R. Driver, 'Notes on the Psalms. II. 73-150', *JTS* 44 (1943), pp. 17-18.

15 The Peshitta and Jerome suggest reading מֶחְשֵׂךְ, 'withholding', which is in keeping with the parallel line (cf. also v. 9). Another possibility is to read מְיֻדָּעִים חֲשֵׁכָה. In each case the מִמֶּנִּי would have to be understood from the parallel line. Nonetheless, if one assumes the end of this psalm has not been lost then 'My friends are the dark region' is a suitable climax for a psalm that to this point has shown no ray of hope (note esp. v. 7). Cf. Job 17.13-14.

16 צוּר ('rock of his sword') is taken as צַר ('the flinty edge of his sword'), so Driver, 'Notes on the Psalms. II. 73-150', *JTS* 44 (1943), p. 18. Cf. BDB, p. 866a.

17 מַזֶּה הֲדֹו is read instead of מִזְהָרוֹ since it gives better metrical balance to the verse and a more fitting parallel to the other metonym for royalty: the crown. Cf. Ps. 45.7 where כִּסֵּא is parallel to שֵׁבֶט.

Note Ps. 110.2 where מַטֵּה־עֻזְּךָ is used of the king ruling from Zion.

[18] D.W. Thomas (*Psalter*, p. 37) suggests reading שֵׂיבָה ('gray-headedness') instead of בּוּשָׁה, thus making better sense of the parallelism and the progression of thought from v. 46 to v. 49.

[19] The MT may be translated:
You flood them away; they become sleep.
In the morning like grass that sprouts anew.
Such a rendering is awkward and lacks parallelism. Verse 5b shows closer connection with v. 6. Most commentators see textual corruption here. What secures better parallelism and a fitting prelude to v. 6 is:

זְרַעְתָּם שָׁנָה שֵׁנָה

יִהְיוּ כֶּחָצִיר יַחֲלֹף

Thus זרעתם is read, as implied by the Syriac version. שׁנה is pointed שָׁנָה, as suggested by the LXX and the Syriac version, and haplography is conjectured. יהיו is placed in the second line and בבקר is presumed to be a dittograph from v. 6. Cf. KRAUS, II, pp. 795-96.

[20] The Qere, כֹחִי, has the widest textual support.

[21] This verse is identical to 60.12, but most MSS here omit אֱלֹהֵה from the first line.

[22] Westermann, *Praise and Lament*, p. 64; cf. pp. 54, 67, 69, 108-9.

[23] B. Wiklander, 'זָעַם', *TDOT*, IV, p. 110. Contra G. Van Groningen, 'קָצַף', *Theological Wordbook of the Old Testament* (ed. R.L. Harris, et al), II, p. 643.

[24] See E. Johnson, 'אָנַף', *TDOT*, I, p. 352.

[25] Cf. G. Sauer, 'קָנָאָה', *THAT*, II, p. 649.

[26] See E. Johnson, 'אָנַף', *TDOT*, I, pp. 352, 354.

[27] K.-D. Schunck, 'חֵמָה', *TDOT*, IV, p. 462.

[28] K.-D. Schunck, 'חֵמָה', *TDOT*, IV, p. 463.

[29] See Schunck, 'חֵמָה', *TDOT*, IV, p. 464 for references.

[30] E. Johnson, 'אָנַף', *TDOT*, I, p. 353.

[31] E. Johnson, 'אָנַף', *TDOT*, I, p. 353. Cf. G. Sauer, 'חרה', *THAT*, I, p. 634, who translates it '*Zornglut*', and G.J. Botterweck, 'חרה', *TWAT*, III, p. 183, who translates it '*Zorn, brennende Wut*'.

32 L.J. Wood, 'חָרָה', *Theological Wordbook of the Old Testament* (ed. R.L. Harris, et al), I, p. 322.

33 G. Van Groningen, 'עבר', *Theological Wordbook of the Old Testament* (ed. R.L. Harris, et al), II, p. 643.

34 S.R. Driver, *Deuteronomy* (1902), p. 60.

35 Cf. G.R. Driver, 'Some Hebrew Roots and Their Meanings', *JTS* 23 (1922), p. 69.

36 J.A. Emerton, 'Psalms Book III', *JTS* 14 (1963), p. 381; 'Notes on Jeremiah 12.9', *ZAW* 81 (1969), p. 189.

37 G.R. Driver, 'Hebrew Roots', *JTS* 23 (1922), p. 69; 'Problems in the Hebrew Text of Proverbs', *Bib* 32 (1951), pp. 185-86.

38 Johnson, 'אָנַף', *TDOT*, I, p. 352.

39 Wiklander, 'זָעַם', *TDOT*, IV, p. 108.

40 See F. Stolz, 'כעס', *THAT*, I, p. 841.

41 Stolz, 'כעס', *THAT*, I, p. 840.

42 For references see J. Fichtner, 'ὀργή', *TDNT*, V, p. 399.

43 A.T. Hanson in *The Wrath of the Lamb* (1957), pp. 1-4, discusses certain passages from Samuel.

44 For further discussion of this see Fichtner, 'ὀργή', *TDNT*, V, pp. 408-9 and Eichrodt, *Theology of the Old Testament* (1961), I, pp. 260ff.

45 Contra G. Sauer who cites Ps. 102.11 as an example of God's angry response to disobedience and sin ('קצף', *THAT*, II, p. 665).

46 Cf. Fichtner, 'ὀργή', *TDNT*, V, p. 400. Though the complaint psalms leave little doubt that God's wrath has already been manifested and experienced, one must not presume that in Israel the knowledge that God was angry was necessarily coincident with its realization. God's wrath may be known even before punishment is inflicted. See Eichrodt, *Theology of the Old Testament*, I, p. 264.

47 The one declarative praise psalm of the Psalter that in its description of the past distress retains a God-lament expression (30.8) gives thanks that God's anger is momentary and that his favor is imminent and lifelong (v. 6).

48 In Hos. 8.5 the verb is either an imperative directed to Israel, זָנַח, or a statement of God, זָנְחְתִּי. וַתִּזְנַח of Lam. 3.17 has either נפשׁי

as its subject or God (in the second person) as its subject. The LXX suggests reading וַיְמַן, the Syriac and Vulgate וַתְּמַן.

49 R. Yaron, 'The Meaning of *ZANACH*', *VT* 13 (1963), pp. 237-39.

50 The omission of an explicit accusative is quite common in Hebrew poetry. M. DAHOOD lists examples of double-duty suffixes with verbs (III, pp. 431-32).

51 H. Ringgren, 'זָנַה', *TDOT*, IV, p. 105.

52 See G. Fohrer, *Introduction to the Old Testament* (1968), pp. 297-98.

53 H. Wildberger, 'מאס', *THAT*, I, pp. 879-92.

54 H. Wildberger, 'מאס', *THAT*, I, p. 880.

55 Cf. J.F.A. Sawyer, *Semantics in Biblical Research* (1972), p. 75-76.

56 H.J. Austel, 'שָׁלַך', *Theological Wordbook of the Old Testament* (ed. R.L. Harris, et al), II, p. 929.

57 M. Cogan, 'A Technical Term for Exposure', *JNES* 27 (1968), p. 133.

58 Cf. F. Stolz, 'שלך', *THAT*, II, pp. 916-17.

59 See BDB, p. 1021b, 2c. In those instances where השליך can be translated 'expose, abandon', F. Stolz notes: 'In each case *šlk* hi. or ho. means in these contexts a belittling, violent act against man' ('שלך', *THAT*, II, p. 917).

60 According to the count of V.P. Hamilton, 'שלך', *Theological Wordbook of the Old Testament* (ed. R.L. Harris, et al), II, p. 922.

61 C. Westermann, *Isaiah 40-66* (1969), pp. 218-19.

62 B.S. Childs, *Memory and Tradition in Israel* (1962), p. 34.

63 Childs, *Memory and Tradition in Israel*, p. 33.

64 S.E. Balentine, *The Hidden God: The Hiding of the Face of God in the Old Testment* (1983).

65 See especially Balentine, *The Hidden God*, pp. 50-56.

66 Balentine, *The Hidden God*, p. 77.

67 Balentine, *The Hidden God*, pp. 175-63. This contextual distinction must be maintained over against generalizations such as the one made by L. Perlitt regarding God's hiddenness with respect to the nation: The 'hiddenness' of God 'is different from that in the lament of the individual sick or innocent man—in the strictest sense

it is generally only a reaction to guilt' ('Die Verborgenheit Gottes', *Probleme biblischer Theologie* [1971], p. 375).

68 The expression of Yahweh scattering (זרה) his people among the nations was used particularly by Jeremiah and Ezekiel to speak of exile. The notion of Yahweh selling his people is used frequently in Judges (2.14; 3.8; 4.2; 10.7; cf. 1 Sam. 12.9).

69 If this is the proper interpretation, the Hiph. would then be most appropriate in this context (contra *BHS*).

70 J. Barr, 'Why? in Biblical Hebrew', *JTS* 36 (1985), p. 8. According to A. Jepsen, מַדּוּעַ introduces questions emerging from amazement (*Verwunderung*) and interest (*Teilnahme*), while לָמָּה introduces questions of reproach (*Vorwurf*) ('Warum?', *Das ferne und nahe Wort* [1967], p. 107). Barr in his study argues that 'Jepsen's ideas ... are almost entirely wrong' (p. 4). Regarding the difference between the two terms, he concludes that 'there is very little real distinction of meaning but that a multitude of syntactic and stylistic factors affect the choice of one term as against another' (p. 33).

71 Barr, 'Why?', p. 33.

72 The translation 'How long, Yahweh, will you be angry forever?' (Ps. 79.5; cf. 13.2; 74.10; 89.47) yields a contradiction. D.W. Thomas obviates this difficulty by securing a different meaning for לנצח) ('The Use of נצח as a Superlative in Hebrew', *JSS* 1 [1956], pp. 106-9; cf. 'Some Further Remarks on Unusual Ways of Expressing the Superlative in Hebrew', *VT* 18 [1968], p. 124). Drawing from a Syriac cognate he posits 'completely, utterly' as a meaning of נצח. As attractive as this suggestion is, it must not be overlooked that there are instances among these laments where לנצח) maintains its temporal sense (e.g. Ps. 77.9, // לדר ודר; Lam. 5.20, // לאָרך ימים). At best, one should say that the term conveys an intentional ambiguity between 'forever' and 'utterly' (so P.R. Ackroyd seems to argue with regard to the Septuagint's translation of Ps. 74.3, 'נצח-εἰς τέλος', *ExT* 80 [1968-69], p. 126).

73 Cf. Gunkel, *Einleitung*, Chapter 6, §§ 17-21.

Notes to Chapter 4

[1] For further description of these images in v. 7 as referring to the place of the dead, see O. Keel, *Symbolism of the Biblical World* (1978), pp. 69ff.

[2] Keel, *Symbolism of the Biblical World*, pp. 114, 115.

[3] C. Barth, *Die Errettung vom Tode* (1947), p. 93, also p. 111.

[4] Barth, *Die Errettung vom Tode*, p. 116.

[5] Barth, *Die Errettung vom Tode*, p. 118.

[6] Barth, *Die Errettung vom Tode*, p. 117.

[7] J.W. Rogerson, *Anthropology and the Old Testament* (1978), pp. 59ff.

[8] Rogerson, *Anthropology*, p. 60.

[9] See Westermann, *Praise and Lament*, pp. 155-61.

[10] Keel, *Symbolism of the Biblical World*, pp. 73-75.

[11] Keel, *Symbolism of the Biblical World*, pp. 67-69.

[12] One may think 31.13 should be included among those verses implying the psalmist is near death:

> I am forgotten as (כ) a dead man out of mind;
>
> I have become like (כ) a broken vessel.

The simile is given to illustrate the psalmist's alienation from people, not from God (see vv. 12, 14).

[13] See Keel, *Feinde und Gottesleugner*, pp. 199-200, and further S. Wagner, 'בקש', *TDOT*, II, pp. 233-34.

[14] The term בקש itself implies nothing more than the intent and perhaps the attempts of some to achieve something. Ps. 7.3 speaks of death as a possibility; 31.14 refers to it as the subject of a conspiracy. Ps. 55.5-6 emphasizes the psalmist's affective response to the social violence around him (vv. 10-12). In Pss. 56, 59 and 71 the enemies wait and watch.

[15] On the genre and an exilic dating of Ps. 106 see Allen, *Psalms 101-150*, pp. 49-52.

[16] For a confirmation of Ps. 126 as a 'communal complaint' and on its postexilic dating, see Allen, *Psalms 101-150*, pp. 171-73.

[17] Strictly speaking, the adjectival phrase of 140.3 ('... who stir up war every day') describes the general conduct of the wicked, not the specific distress of the psalmist.

[18] On יחילו cf. Job 20.21.

[19] On these two verses the textual work of D.W. Thomas (*JTS* 12 [1961], pp. 50-51) is accepted, except for his interpretation of יִדְעָתִי.

[20] Read כְּלֻמַּח.

Notes to Chapter 5

[1] See Westermann, *Praise and Lament*, pp. 102ff.

[2] See Westermann, *Praise and Lament*, pp. 155-61.

[3] C. Barth, *Errettung vom Tode*, pp. 71-75.

[4] See Otto Eissfeldt, '"My God" in the Old Testament', *EvQ* 19 (1947), pp. 7-20.

[5] Among the lament psalms, the references to calling to Yahweh are 3.8; 5.3; 7.2; 13.4; 25.2; 35.23, 24; 38.22; 40.18; 59.2; 71.4, 12; 83.14; 86.2; 102.25; 109.26; 140.7; 143.10. Among the praise psalms, the references to having called on Yahweh are 18.7; 30.3 (cf. 38.16). References to the psalmist's trusting are 25.2; 31.15; 38.16; 42.12; 43.5; 86.2; 91.2. References to the psalmist's praising are 18.3; 30.13; 42.12; 43.4-5; 71.22; 86.12; 118.28 (twice); 104.1, 33; 145.1; 146.2.

[6] References not included above are 7.4; 18.22, 29, 30; 40.6, 9; 42.7 (?); 63.2; 68.25; 69.4; 84.4, 11; 89.27; 94.22; 119.115.

[7] Gerstenberger, *Psalms* (FOTL), p. 84.

[8] This 'day' within which the psalmist both prays and expects an answer is not to be reckoned as a 24 hour period. 'In the day I call answer me quickly' is in parallel to 'in the day of my distress', a period of time which the next verse refers to as 'days': 'For my days have been consumed in smoke'. Kraus's interpretation (II, pp. 866) goes too far in trying to identify a literal referent for this 'day' when, as just noted, the next verse makes this supposition unsuitable.

[9] Ps. 94, the only plea psalm that contains 'How long?' addressed to God, may also presuppose ineffectual foregoing prayers. Note the absence of the frequent confession of trust, 'Yahweh will hear when I call'. The psalmist, however, is still able to restrain from direct complaint by drawing upon the teachings of the wise.

[10] Allen, *Psalms 101-150*, pp. 51-52.

[11] See Westermann, *Praise and Lament*, pp. 171-72, 202-203.

[12] See Allen, *Psalms 101-150*, pp. 238-39.

[13] See KRAUS, II, pp. 822.

[14] Keel, *Feinde und Gottesleugner*, pp. 107-108, 124-29.

[15] See Westermann, *Praise and Lament*, p. 193.

Notes to Chapter 6

[1] In addition to the commentaries, see also R. Gordis, 'Psalm 9-10—A Textual-Exegetical Study', *The Word and the Book* (1976), pp. 114-32.

[2] CRAIGIE, p. 117. J. Eaton dates it to the time of the monarchy (*Kingship and the Psalms* [1976], pp. 32-33).

[3] Keel, *Feinde und Gottesleugner*, pp. 127-29.

[4] See further KRAUS, I, p. 222.

[5] KRAUS, I, pp. 219-20.

[6] KRAUS, I, p. 220.

[7] W. Beyerlin, 'Die *toda* der Heilsvergegenwärtigung in den Klageliedern der Einzelnen', *ZAW* 79 (1967), pp. 221-24. WEISER also gives a similar interpretation (pp. 148-54).

[8] See CRAIGIE, p. 119.

[9] CRAIGIE, p. 124.

[10] זרה is frequently used by Jeremiah and Ezekiel to refer to the exile, but it is doubtful that one could infer from this an unequivocal clue to the historical origins of this psalm. פוץ, a synonym used as a parallel term with זרה in exile contexts (Ezek. 12.15; 20.23; 22.15; cf. 29.12-13; 30.23, 26), can also refer to an army 'scattered' in battle and not a to mass deportation (Num. 10.35 [cf. Ps. 68.2]; 1 Sam. 11.11; 2 Kings 25.5 = Jer. 52.8; cf. 1 Sam. 13.8). Cf. the use of פור Ps. 89.11. Since Ps. 44.12 is the sole instance where זרה appears in a specifically battlefield context, one cannot exclude the possibility that it may designate simply the capturing of prisoners of war.

[11] See further ANDERSON, I, pp. 336-37; KIRKPATRICK, pp. 234ff.

[12] KRAUS, I, p. 481.

[13] Though not named expressly, the motif uniting these two notions may be the ark. It symbolized the hope that Yahweh would go out with them into holy war (Num. 10.35; Josh. 6.6; 1 Sam. 4.3ff.; 2 Sam. 11.11) and also the place where Yahweh pronounced his judgment (see KRAUS, I, pp. 195ff., and G.H. Davies, 'The Ark in the Psalms', *Promise and Fulfillment* [1963], p. 60).

[14] On this see W. Beyerlin, 'Kontinuität beim "berichtenden" Lobpreis des Einzelnen', *Wort und Geschichte* (1973), pp. 17-24.

[15] As became evident in Chapter 2, most psalms express their distress in the form of an I/We- or foe-lament. The significance of the God-lament is therefore that it attributes the distress to God. The key to interpreting these verses in Ps. 44 is thus to be found in the grammatical subject.

[16] As with the third-person address to God in v. 9a, there is no reason to assume that the psalmist here turns to a soliloquy or turns to address the congregation. As the parallel line v. 9b implies that God is still addressed, so the more extended parallelism of vv. 18-23 mentioned above suggests that God is addressed in vv. 21-22. Moreover, the conjunctive כי that connects v. 23 with v. 22 (as it did with vv. 19-20) also implies that vv. 21 and 22 are directed to God.

[17] Cf. Pss. 7.10; 17.3; 26.2; 139.23-24, where in 'trial' contexts the penetrating knowledge of God plays such a crucial role.

[18] Two features of the psalm signal this altered conception. Verses 18ff. reflect a form of the 'assertions of innocence' (cf. Pss. 7.4-6; 17.3-5; 26.1ff.; 59.4-5), which presuppose God in the role of judge (7.7, 9, 12; 17.1-2; 26.1ff.; 59.6). Secondly, in the Psalms the provenance of imperatives such as עור, קיץ, and קום when directed to God appear to be judgment contexts. In all but two instances (3.8; 132.8), the imperatival forms of these verbs, when addressed to God, are tied to judgment contexts. See 7.7 (עור, קום); 17.13 (קום); 35.2 (קום), 23 (עור, קיץ); 59.5 (עור), 6 (קיץ); also 80.3 (עור, see Chapter 6). The following references employ קום: 9.20; 10.12; 74.22; 82.8. See also KRAUS, I, pp. 195ff.

[19] This 'motivation' is unique to the complaint psalms.

20 W. Beyerlin reads this petition as lacking specificity, and thus interprets this as the psalmist deliberately leaving the precise nature of deliverance to God's discretion ('Innerbiblische Aktualisierungsversuche: Schichten im 44. Psalm', *ZTK* 73 [1976], p. 458). In his view, the people are 'no longer fixed upon a specific horizon of expectation'. But here, as also in Ps. 89, where there is an extensive recitation of praise and pouring out of lament, the formal petitions play a minor role. The praise and lament evidently make the petition self-evident.

21 U. Kellermann, 'Erwägungen zum historischen Ort von Psalm LX', *VT* 28 (1978), p. 59.

22 Kellermann, 'Psalm LX', p. 64. For similar reservations against the view held by Kellermann, see KRAUS, II, p. 597.

23 On this cf. Mowinckel: 'Also, the defeat suffered need not to have been a great one; according to that which we have said above concerning Ps. 85, we understand that even smaller setbacks could have been sufficient cause for days of penance and stormy prayers; even the smallest misfortune sufficed as proof that Yahweh did not go out with the armies of Israel and thus must again be inclined favorably' (*Psalmenstudien*, III, p. 68).

24 GUNKEL, p. 257; KRAUS, II, pp. 588-89.

25 Cf. S. Mowinckel, *Psalmenstudien*, III, pp. 66-67.

26 KIRKPATRICK, pp. 338-39. B.S. Childs, while not arguing that Ps. 60 was actually composed in the situation described in the superscription, shows that both the psalm and its superscription can be harmonized with the narrative of David's life in Samuel-Kings ('Psalm Titles and Midrashic Exegesis', *JSS* 16 [1971], pp. 146-47).

27 *Psalmenstudien*, III, p. 67.

28 תשובב לנו should probably be understood either as a modal form, 'You should restore us', or as an imperative, with the ה appended because of dittography. See BDB, p. 998c, 1; GUNKEL, p. 259.

29 The picture of the cup of Yahweh's wrath is employed (later?) in the prophets to signify judgment (cf. Isa. 51.17, 21-22 where the cup is given to Israel). Although this image in Ps. 60 is certainly connected with God's wrath (v. 3), the psalm nowhere speaks of God's action as a moral judgment. Thus, the appearance

of this metaphor in this psalm need not presuppose prophetic usage (contra Kellermann, 'Psalm LX', p. 59).

[30] DAHOOD argues in favor of such a nuance of the perfect (*Psalms*, II, p. 79, see also I, pp. 20, 26), citing as well the work of M. BUTTENWIESER, pp. 18-25). Examination of the examples put forward, however, leads me to the conclusion of S.R. Driver: 'But the fact is that the evidence for this signification of the pf. is so precarious, the passages adduced in proof of it admitting of a ready explanation by other means, that it will be safer to reject it altogether' (*A Treatise on the Use of the Tenses in Hebrew* [1892], pp. 25-26). See also GKC, § 106n.

[31] Thus התנוסס would be derived from נוס ('to flee'), so LXX, Jerome, Vulgate and Symmachus (see BRIGGS, II, p. 63; KIRKPATRICK, p. 340). Even if this verb were a denominative form (נסס) derived from נס, hence 'to rally to the banner', the end result would be the same. Reading קשט as a (Aramaic?) form of קשת is supported by LXX, Syriac, Jerome and Symmachus.

[32] KIRKPATRICK, p. 341.

[33] התרעעי may be a hithpolel infinitive construct, or in keeping with the Syriac and the parallel Ps. 108.10 we may read אֶתְרוֹעָע. In any case עָלַי should read עֲלֵי.

[34] Cf. KRAUS, II, p. 590.

[35] Cf. WEISER, p. 438. Contrary to Mowinckel (*Psalmenstudien*, III, p. 66), one should not expect as a matter of course that citations of former prophecies would be introduced by an extended formula as in Ps. 89.20. Ironically, this oracle as it is found in Ps. 108, which Mowinckel does read as a citation, bears the same preface: אלהים דבר.

[36] J. Becker, *Israel deutet seine Psalmen* (1966), pp. 65-67; Kellermann, 'Psalm LX', pp. 64-65.

[37] Cf. KRAUS, II, p. 679, ANDERSON, II, pp. 538, 541.

[38] Cf. Ackroyd, *Exile and Restoration* (1968), pp. 45-46, 233, 225-26.

[39] F. Willesen, 'The Cultic Situation of Psalm LXXIV', *VT* 2 (1952), pp. 289-306.

[40] Within the lament category the image of the people as sheep is one peculiar to the complaint psalms. This figure of speech suggests dependence and helplessness.

[41] See J.J. Stamm, *Erlösen und Vergeben im AT* (1940), p. 36. קָנָה is not used elsewhere in connection with the Zion tradition. גּאל is used to refer to the liberation from Egypt in Exod. 6.6; Pss. 77.16; 78.35; 106.10.

[42] Although the psalmist's reference to the absence of 'one who knows how long' may suggest his question is simply a request for information, the hyperbole, 'Will the enemy spurn your name *forever?*', makes clear that the intent is persuasive.

[43] These verses may allude to both the ordering of creation and the deliverance at the Reed Sea. Both the 'deeds of salvation' (v. 12) that Yahweh performs in vv. 12-17 and his redemption of the people from Egypt (v. 2) are described as from 'of old' (vv. 2, 12). (Cf. Isa. 51.9-10 which blends the 'chaos myth' and the exodus.) But vv. 16-17 indicate that it is Yahweh's deed of ordering creation that is placed in the foreground. Note esp. vv. 16-17. See further A.H.W. Curtis, 'The "Subjugation of the Waters" Motif in the Psalms: Imagery or Polemic?', *JSS* 23 (1978), pp. 245-56; KRAUS, II, p. 681; J.A. Emerton, '"Spring and Torrent" in Psalm LXXIV 15', *Volume du Congres: Geneve 1965* (VTSup 15; 1966), pp. 122-33.

[44] This depiction of the enemies as 'beasts' may be an echo of the chaos monster imagery in vv. 13-14. Cf. v. 4 where the enemy 'roars'.

[45] Cf. KRAUS, II, p. 683.

[46] Cf. KRAUS, II, p. 694.

[47] On the textual problem in v. 5, see Chapter 3 n. 9.

[48] Read חַלּוֹתִי, a Qal infinitive construct of חלל, with Peshitta, the Targum, Symmachus, and Theodotian; and reading שְׁנוֹת as a Qal infinitive construct of שׁנה ('to change') with the LXX, Jerome, and all ancient versions (according to BRIGGS, II, p. 177).

[49] The *Kethib* reading of אֶזְכִּיר is therefore the more appropriate one. The interpretation, however, that the psalmist is here turning to praise, does not depend on one's pointing of this verb.

[50] B.S. Childs's analysis of this psalm in *Memory and Tradition in Israel* (pp. 61-63) is perceptive, but that vv. 12ff. necessarily reflect a change within the psalmist himself is not convincing.

[51] For further discussion see KRAUS, II, pp. 714-15.

248   *The Conflict of Faith and Experience in the Psalms*

52 עונת ראשנים could mean either 'our former iniquities' or 'the iniquities of our forebears.'. See ANDERSON, II, p. 579 and KRAUS, II, p. 716. Kraus suggests the latter may indicate a generation has passed since the overthrow of Jerusalem.

53 GUNKEL, p. 349.

54 Eissfeldt, 'Psalm 80', *Kleine Schriften* (1953, 1966), III, p. 224. For further discusion of the historical background see KRAUS, II, pp. 720ff.; Eissfeldt, 'Psalm 80 und Psalm 89', *Kleine Schriften* (1964-66, 1968), IV, pp. 132-36; H. Heinemann, 'The Date of Psalm 80', *JQR* 40 (1949-50), pp. 297-302. W. Beyerlin ('Schichten im 80. Psalm', *G. Friedrich Festschrift* [1973], pp. 9-24) considers the psalm to be a composite of several layers of redaction fitting various historical situations.

55 KRAUS notes that 'Joseph' signifies 'Israel in Egypt' (II, p. 722). Cf. Pss. 77.16; 81.6.

56 The notion of 'Yahweh of hosts' (vv. 5, 8, 15, 20) enthroned over the cherubim may well have been a Shiloh tradition (1 Sam. 4.4) later appropriated into the Zion tradition (Ps. 99.1-2). The imperative הופיע calls for a theophanic appearance (E. Jenni, 'יפע', *THAT*, I, pp. 753ff.; C. Barth, 'יָפַע', *TWAT*, III, pp. 794-95). The use of הופיע in a theophany of judgment in Ps. 50.2 (cf. 94.1) seems to locate this expression in Zion as well. It is, however, unlikely that these allusions in Ps. 80 should be limited to this locale (even aside from considerations of a northern provenance for the psalm). 1 Sam. 4.4 (cf. 2 Sam. 6.2) shows connections between the title 'Yahweh of hosts', ישב הכרבים, the ark and the tribes rallying to holy war. Verse 3 of Ps. 80 with its mention of Yahweh exhibiting his warrior strength (גבורה) before Ephraim, Benjamin and Manasseh suggests a similar alliance of tribes engaged in holy war. Since v. 2 refers to the exodus it seems likely that these allusions to the ark and holy war may well tie into the conquest-settlement period. (This would establish a parallel with the tradition employed in vv. 9ff.) The 'Song of the Ark' (Num. 10.35; 7.89 connects the cherubim and the ark), located in this time period, sings of the ark in connection with holy war. (It is very possible the psalmist had these particular traditions in mind, as the petitions for Yahweh to cause his face to shine also reflect on this material and the Aaronic blessing especially [Num. 6.24ff.].) The

preface to the 'Song of the Ark' (10.35a) along with v. 33 speak of the role the ark played in leading Israel. This may well imply that the 'leading' of Ps. 80.2 is also to be connected with the ark motif in its parallel line. The verb הופיע can also be tied in with this period (Deut. 33.2). (Barth believes this is the oldest use of the verb in a theophany context, from which all later instances derive.) Thus, instead of three separate allusions (as KRAUS seems to suggest [II, p. 722]) these verses in Ps. 80 appear to focus on the holy war tradition associated with the ark in the wilderness and conquest periods.

57 On this feature see J. Goldingay, 'Repetition and Variation in the Psalms', *JQR* 68 (1978), pp. 146-51.

58 GUNKEL, p. 352.

59 So GUNKEL, p. 352.

60 The phrase 'from heaven' may appear to suggest remoteness, but in other instances the implication is that of superiority with no hint of separation. On the contrary, when used in connection with verbs of seeing, it implies a superior vantage point (Pss. 14.2 = 53.3; 33.13; 102.20).

61 By analogy with Gen. 49.22, בן in v. 16b could mean the young growth of a plant. Though a dittograph would be expected only after its genuine occurrence (plus one would expect an exact reproduction), it does seem likely that v. 16b was an insertion of some kind. It is improbable that פקד should be used both transitively with 'this vine' and intransitively with 'upon (על) the son'. Moreover, פקד when followed by על normally implies a negative connotation (BDB, p. 823c, 3). The parallel line for v. 16 would then be v. 15b. הבט and ראה of v. 15a do appear in the explicit accusatives.

lem of this verse is not whether the verbal forms of be pointed as passive participles or as 3rd, masc., pl. l, fem., sing. suffixes, but whether יאבדו is a jussive ies as its subject or a finite verb with the people as the cedent. The former is more likely since the latter an awkward change not only from singular to plural metaphoric to literal language. This seems unlikely se immediately following turns to the figure of the king ect) while the people as a plural entity is not resumed until v. 19. If this is the case then the verbal forms of v. 17a are best pointed as 3rd, masc., pl. verbs.

[63] Mowinckel, *Psalmenstudien*, III, pp. 54-59; Dahood, II, p. 286.

[64] M. Goulder's comments regarding the nonspecific nature of the language in Ps. 85 are appropriate and thus echo the caution that must be exercised when trying to date any psalm (*The Psalms of the Sons of Korah* [1982], pp. 99-100). The parallels Goulder adduces, however, are much weaker than those proposed by the majority of commentators. The similarity that Pss. 44; 77; 80 exhibit (p. 101) is due more to the nature of appeal in complaint psalms than to any historical connection. Moreover, the parallels between Ps. 85 and Ex. 32-24 (pp. 106-107) are not surprising since both reflect a national crisis wherein God forgives the people's sin, and so makes known his merciful devotion. This is particularly true for a passage such as Exod. 32-34 where so many of Israel's paradigmatic traditions converge. (The interjection of Exod. 32-34 on the basis of his interpretation of Selah is not compelling.)

[65] There are no tangible signs that such may be the case, but vv. 2-4 may be a citation of a recent hymn, a common practice in such complaint psalms of the community.

[66] In general, scholarly opinion believes that שְׁבוּת was probably originally שְׁבוּת, which derived from שׁוב. In the postexilic period it became confused with שְׁבִית ('captivity', see Num. 21.29), which derived from שבה ('to take captive'). Job 42.10, though an untypical use of the phrase, strongly suggests that שְׁבוּת must originate from the former and not the latter. Although the phrase means 'to turn fortunes, to bring about a restoration', most instances are postexilic and therefore refer to the return from exile. Thus the distinction between שבות and שבית is not so crucial as might first appear (cf. ANDERSON, II, pp. 608, 610). See W.L. Holladay, *The Root šubh in the OT* (1958), pp. 110-14, esp. p. 113, and J.A. Soggin, 'שוב', *THAT*, II, pp. 886-87.

[67] This reading of v. 4b is supported by the LXX. G.R. Driver suggests the Hebrew originally read, עֶבְרָתְךָ שָׁבְתָ (*JTS* 44 [1943] 16). The LXX, Syr, Jer, V (also cf. Ps. 80.4, 8) suggest reading הֲשִׁיבֵנוּ in v. 5a. However, שׁובב may be retained if, as suggested by

Ugaritic constructions, the suffix is a dative form, thus 'Return to us.' Thus שׁוּב (Qal) retains its intransitive use (שְׁבוּת שׁוּב, as in v. 2, is virtually the only exception). This reading carries support from the Targums. See A.R. Johnson, *The Cultic Prophet and Israel's Psalmody* (1979) 200 n. 2, who cites Gordon's *Ugaritic Textbook*, p. 39, § 6.21. Cf. Isa. 63.17. וְהָפֵר is retained in v. 5b. If וְהָסֵר were the original one would expect מִן instead of עַם (see BDB, 694).

68 For further criticisms of this approach, see S. Mowinckel's review of G.W. Ahlström's *Psalm 89: Eine Liturgie aus dem Ritual des leidenden Königs in JSS* 5 (1960), pp. 291-98.

69 Further contrasts can be found in connection with the 'throne' (vv. 5, 30, 37 and v. 45), the 'enemy' (v. 23 and v. 43), the 'right hand' (v. 26 and v. 43), and the adverb 'forever' (vv. 2-3, 5, 29, 37-38 and v. 47).

70 See further R.J. Clifford, 'Psalm 89: A Lament Over the Davidic Ruler's Continued Failure', *HTR* 73 (1980), pp. 35-47; N.H. Sarna, 'Psalm 89: A Study in Inner Biblical Exegesis', *Biblical and Other Studies* (1963), pp. 29-46; J.M. Ward, 'The Literary Form and Liturgical Background of Psalm LXXXIX', *VT* 11 (1961), pp. 321-39.

71 Cf. GUNKEL, who notes that in the singing of the hymn the lament 'already resonates as an undertone' (p. 394).

72 See Ward, 'Psalm LXXXIX', pp. 324-25.

73 The exodus may be the archetype of such an event in Israel, but the indefiniteness of the verbs in v. 10 suggests the action should not be limited to a single historical referent. Moreover, the following verses refer to Yahweh's ownership of creation, and thus point toward a cosmic reference.

74 G. von Rad, *God at Work in Israel* (1980), p. 214.

75 So KRAUS, II, pp. 796-97, and W.J. Urbrock, 'Mortal and Miserable Man: A Form-Critical Investigation of Psalm 90', *SBL 1974 Seminar Papers* (1974), p. 8.

76 von Rad, *God at Work*, pp. 221-22.

77 KRAUS, II, p. 796; S. Schreiner, 'Erwägungen zur Struktur des 90. Psalms', *Bib* 59 (1978), p. 80.

78 B. Vawter, 'Postexilic Prayer and Hope', *CBQ* 37 (1975), p. 463.

79 Cf. Westermann, *The Psalms*, pp. 121-22.
80 Von Rad, *God at Work*, p. 217.

Notes to Chapter 7

1 See Seybold, *Gebet des Kranken*, pp. 66-67, 153-58.
2 CRAIGIE, p. 92.
3 On the occurrences of נבהל see BDB, p. 96b, 1. It is only the pronoun (ה)אתה which indicates this is a God-lament. For this reason it would be inappropriate to fill out the ellipsis with an impersonal subject: 'But you, Yahweh, how long [shall it continue]?' (contra Briggs, I, p. 47). The parallel line might suggest, 'How long [will you be dismayed]?', but Yahweh is nowhere made the subject of this verb in Niphal. The following imperative, 'Return, Yahweh!' and the repetition of 'soul' in these two verses, might at first reading suggest, 'How long [will you remain aloof from my soul]?' Although 'Return!' may imply spatial separation, and therefore absence, שוב, when addressed to God as an imperative and used absolutely, is found only in psalms of complaint where God is clearly not aloof but acting against the people in wrath (80.15; 90.13; cf. 85.5). The most plausible suggestion, therefore, would be to understand the predicate of וְאָתְּ to be the divine chastisement.
4 Contra Mowinckel, *Psalms in Israel's Worship*, II, pp. 6-7.
5 WEISER, p. 130. Weiser's comments regarding the psalm's use of traditional phrases cannot be disputed. See Culley, *Oral Formulaic Language in the Biblical Psalms* (1967), pp. 103, 105.
6 N.H. Ridderbos, *Psalmen* (1972), p. 131.
7 See BDB, p. 775b, 1a.
8 See further WEISER, pp. 131-32.
9 J. Begrich, 'Das priesterliche Heilsorakel', *ZAW* 52 (1934), pp. 81-92. A weakness in this essay is that it needs to be supplemented with further evidence that Deutero-Isaiah did not coin such 'salvation oracles' himself. One could envisage the prophet possibly picking up the language of lament, and then simply reversing it to convey his message of hope. Begrich does offer one such instance on p. 90. For further agruments that the salvation

oracle provides the most suitable explanation see Seybold, *Gebet des Kranken*, pp. 156-57.

[10] See Ridderbos, *Psalmen*, pp. 129, 131; CRAIGIE, pp. 91, 95.

[11] Seybold, *Gebet des Kranken*, p. 159.

[12] Gerstenberger, *Psalms* (FOTL), p. 85.

[13] This appears to an assumption of H. Vörlander in *Mein Gott: Die Vorstellungen vom persönlichen Gott im Alten Orient und im Alten Testament* (1975), p. 268.

[14] GUNKEL, p. 46.

[15] Cf. C. Westermann, *Praise and Lament*, pp. 70-75.

[16] Since v. 6b is the only verse of the psalm which addresses God in the third person, it is unlikely that אשירה functions as a petition.

[17] For an excellent discussion of this tension in the psalmist's faith, see J.L. Mays, 'Psalm 13', *Int* 34 (1980), pp. 281-82.

[18] S.B. Frost, 'Asseveration by Thanksgiving', *VT* 8 (1958), pp. 384-85; R. Kilian, 'Ps 22 und das priesterliche Heilsorakel', *BZ* 12 (1968), pp. 172-85; F. James, *Thirty Psalmists* (1938), p. 107; KIRKPATRICK, p. 120; Gerstenberger, *Psalms* (FOTL), p. 112.

[19] CRAIGIE, pp. 197-98; KRAUS, I, pp. 324, 329-30. The problematic עניתני ('you have answered me') could be emended to עֲנִיָּתִי ('my poor one', i.e. 'my poor soul'). This appears to have been the reading of the LXX.

[20] WEISER, pp. 219, 224-25; H. Gese, 'Psalm 22 und das Neue Testament', *ZTK* 65 (1968), pp. 11-13. A fourth possibility should be mentioned. A. Deissler considers this psalm to be a postexilic literary product. See '"Mein Gott, warum hast du mich verlassen ...!" (Ps 22.2) Das Reden zu Gott und von Gott in den Psalmen am Beispiel von Psalm 22', in *'Ich will euer Gott werden': Beispiele biblischen Redens von Gott*, (1981), pp. 105-106. The liturgical style (see esp. CRAIGIE, pp. 197-98) and the numerous cultic allusions (esp. in vv. 23ff.), however, argue against this.

[21] See GUNKEL, p. 93.

[22] Read מִשְׁעַתִּי for the sake of parallelism.

23 See J.S. Kselman, '"Why have you abandoned me?" A Rhetorical Study of Psalm 22', in *Art and Meaning* (1982), pp. 172-98, esp. pp. 172, 188-93; Ridderbos, *Psalmen*, pp. 190, 192.

24 See Gese, 'Psalm 22 und das Neue Testament', pp. 11-12.

25 See Keel, *Symbolism*, pp. 86-88.

26 On v. 19 see ANDERSON, I, p. 191; cf. KRAUS, I, p. 329.

27 According to Ridderbos, vv. 28-32 are the hymnic praise announced in vv. 23-27. More particularly, according to the invitation in v. 27a, vv. 28-32 appear to have been the praise sung during the *todah*. See p. 190 for further connections between vv. 23-27 and 28-32. This implies not only that vv. 28-32 form an integral unit with vv. 23-27, but also that the latter is incomplete without the former. It therefore seems unnecessary to consider vv. 28ff. as a later addition reflecting a belief in the return from exile as an eschatological event. See esp. J. Becker, *Israel deutet seine Psalmen* (1966), pp. 49-53. It seems strange that Becker should note six references for כי עשה referring to Yahweh's deliverance of the individual (p. 50 n. 74) and one for it referring to Yahweh's deliverance of the people (Isa. 44.23), but still he considers this last reference as the key to interpreting Ps. 22.28-32.

28 Cf. GUNKEL, p. 93.

29 The opening כי of v. 17 may also provide a clue. If one thus understands v. 17 as an explanation of v. 16b, then the sense of v. 16b is that Yahweh by abandoning (עזב) the psalmist to this pack of 'dogs' has in effect placed him at death's door.

30 Ridderbos, *Psalmen*, p. 187.

31 Read לִּי with LXX, Syriac and Jerome. Cf. Matt. 27.43.

32 For another view of the placement of vv. 11, 12 in the structure of the psalm, see Gese, 'Psalm 22 und das Neue Testament', p. 8.

33 That v. 16b reaches a climax in this part of the poem see also Ridderbos, *Psalmen*, p. 191, and Gese, 'Psalm 22 und das Neue Testament', p. 9.

34 Kselman, 'Psalm 22', p. 187.

35 J. Eaton, *Kingship and the Psalms* (1976), pp. 41-42; CRAIGIE, p. 285-86.

36 Cf. GUNKEL, p. 146.

37 GUNKEL, p. 146.

[38] ANDERSON, I, p. 275.

[39] KRAUS, I, p. 427.

[40] KRAUS, I, p. 429; ANDERSON, I, p. 280; GUNKEL, p. 148.

[41] Seybold, *Gebet des Kranken*, p. 67. He also notes that צלע in Job 18.12 is used in a context referring to illness but in Jer. 20.10 this is less clear. Hence this term by itself cannot be taken as a clear reference to illness (p. 27).

[42] Cf. Ridderbos, *Psalmen*, p. 252; ANDERSON, I, p. 275.

[43] Cf. Ridderbos, *Psalmen*, pp. 258-59.

[44] See DAHOOD, I, p. 214.

[45] Cf. Ridderbos, *Psalmen*, p. 258.

[46] The suffix of אספם demands an accusative for יצבר. Moreover, the other verbs of this verse adjoined to the same grammatical subject are all singular. Cf. 37.16. Whether this conjecture is accepted or not, the verbs יצבר and אספם still imply the notion of 'possessions'.

[47] Seybold, *Gebet des Kranken*, pp. 25-26.

[48] In addition, cf. Ps. 90, which also contains themes similar to Ps. 39. It refers to God's hostile opposition (vv. 7-9, 11, 15) but does not relate this to sickness. In fact, it speaks of a full 70-80 years of life (v. 10).

[49] Cf. KRAUS, I, p. 452.

[50] Ridderbos, *Psalmen*, pp. 283-85.

[51] Even WEISER who believed the psalmist was 'disloyal to his own resolution' argues that vv. 4ff. do not sound like the rebellious speech intimated in vv. 2-3. Weiser therefore supposes that vv. 4ff. are subsequent to the initial violation of his vow and thus represent 'the earnest attempt of a sensitive man to recover once more ... his right mind ...' (pp. 328-29).

[52] Ridderbos, *Psalmen*, p. 285.

[53] Ridderbos, *Psalmen*, p. 285.

[54] Gerstenberger, *Psalms* (FOTL), p. 168.

[55] CRAIGIE suggests that it may have been sickness which made travel to the temple impossible (p. 325). GUNKEL with reference to the imagery of death in v. 8 believes the psalmist has suffered a mortal illness (p. 178).

[56] According to BRIGGS זנח is 'stronger than forget' (I, p. 371).

[57] Pss. 18.17; 32.6; 69.3; 130.1 also use the image of 'deep waters' to depict distress. 42.8 is identical to Jon. 2.4b. In Jonah's 'prayer' this line refers to God's casting of Jonah into a literal sea, which in the poet's mind also signifies the place of the dead (vv. 3b, 7b). For a similar reference to God 'oppressing' the psalmist with *his* waves, see 88.8.

[58] CRAIGIE, p. 326.

[59] KRAUS, I, p. 475.

[60] Cf. J. Goldingay, *Songs from a Strange Land* (1978), pp. 38-39. On this 'remembering' of God when separated from God see B.S. Childs, *Memory and Tradition* (1962), pp. 64-65.

[61] See WEISER, p. 352.

[62] L. Alonso Schökel, 'The Poetic Structure of Psalm 42-43', *JSOT* 1 (1976), p. 7.

[63] See further Goldingay, *Songs from a Strange Land*, p. 40; ANDERSON, I, p. 335.

[64] See Keel, *Symbolism*, pp. 62ff.

[65] Seybold, *Gebet des Kranken*, pp. 70, 113-17.

[66] On the syntax of בלילה ... יום see DAHOOD, II, p. 302.

[67] The wider parallelism inherent in the psalm's structure thus becomes apparent. Strophes 1 and 3 thus contain the same order of motifs: the psalmist's persistent prayers (vv. 2, 14), his nearness to death (vv. 3-7a, 16), the image of drowning (vv. 7b-8, 17-18), and his alienation (vv. 9, 19). Strophes 2 and 3 also have corresponding motifs: the psalmist's persistent prayers (vv. 10-14) and rhetorical questions (11-13, 14).

[68] Cf. O. Eissfeldt, '"My God" in the Old Testament', *EvQ* 19 (1947), pp. 7-20, esp. p. 12. As ANDERSON notes, 'The most striking fact is that the afflicted man prays at all ...' (II, p. 623).

[69] See Keel, *Symbolism*, pp. 70-71.

[70] Keel, *Symbolism*, pp. 63ff.

[71] Keel, *Symbolism*, pp. 67-68.

[72] Also, KRAUS notes that in the Babylonian laments the healing of a sick person may be described as 'loosening one who is bound' (II, p. 775).

[73] That the rhetorical question in v. 15 corresponds to those in vv. 11-13 see note 4 above. Further see T. Boys, *A Key to the Book of Psalms* (1825), p. 91.

[74] Cf. Seybold, *Gebet des Kranken*, p. 117.

[75] Seybold, *Gebet des Kranken*, pp. 138-42, esp. p. 71.

[76] See ANDERSON, II, pp. 706-7.

[77] Seybold, *Gebet des Kranken*, pp. 139-41.

[78] Verses 13, 26-28 are hymnic; vv. 14-23 are prophetic. See GUNKEL, p. 437, and KRAUS, II, p. 864. The former believes vv. 14-23, 29 are dependent on the classical prophets, esp. Isaiah 40-55 (p. 438). Kraus reads them as confessions of trust in Yahweh's unchanging rule and in his certain intervention, which in effect become prophetic (II, pp. 868-69).

[79] KRAUS, II, p. 866; KIRKPATRICK, pp. 593, 599.

[80] On this interpretation, cf. ROGERSON and MCKAY, III, pp. 18, 22.

Notes to Chapter 8

[1] R.P. Carroll, *When Prophecy Failed: Reactions and Responses to Failure in the Old Testament Prophetic Traditions* (1979), pp. 86-110.

BIBLIOGRAPHY

Achtemeier, E.R. 'Overcoming the World: an Exposition of Psalm 6', *Int* 28 (1974), pp. 75-88.

Ackroyd, P.R. 'Continuity and Discontinuity: Rehabilitation and Authentication', *Tradition and Theology in the Old Testament*, pp. 215-34. Edited by D.A. Knight. London: SPCK, 1977.

—*Exile and Restoration.* Old Testament Library. London: SCM, 1968.

—'נצח-*els τέλος*', *ExpTim* 80 (1968-69), p. 126.

Ahlström, G.W. *Psalm 89: Eine Liturgie aus dem Ritual des leidenden Königs.* Lund: G.W.K. Gleerups, 1959.

Albertz, R. *Persönliche Frömmigkeit und offizielle Religion.* Calwer Theologische Monographien 9. Stuttgart: Calwer, 1978.

ALLEN, L.C. *Psalms 101-150.* Word Biblical Commentary 21. Waco, TX: Word Books, 1983.

Alonso Schökel, L. 'Hermeneutical Problems of a Literary Study of the Bible', *Congress Volume: Edinburgh 1974*, pp. 1-15. VTSup 28. Leiden: Brill, 1975.

—'Hermeneutics in the Light of Language and Literature', *CBQ* 25 (1963), pp. 371-86.

—'The Poetic Structure of Psalm 42-43', *JSOT* 1 (1976), pp. 4-11. Responses by M. Kessler, pp. 12-15, and by N.H. Ridderbos, pp. 16-21.

—'Psalm 42-43. A Response to Ridderbos and Kessler', *JSOT* 3 (1977), pp. 61-65.

ANDERSON, A.A. *The Book of Psalms.* 2 vols. New Century Bible. London: Oliphants, 1972.

Anderson, B.W. *Out of the Depths: The Psalms Speak for Us Today.* Philadelphia: Westminster, 1974.

Anderson, G.W. 'Enemies and Evildoers in the Book of Psalms', *BJRL* 48 (1965-66), pp. 18-29.

—'Israel's Creed: Sung, Not Signed', *SJT* 16 (1963), pp. 277-85.

—'"Sicut cervus": Evidence in the Psalter of Private Devotion in Ancient Israel', *VT* 30 (1980), pp. 388-97.

Anders-Richards, D. *The Drama of the Psalms.* London: Darton, Longman & Todd, 1968.

Ap-Thomas, D.R. 'Appreciation of Sigmund Mowinckel's Contribution to Biblical Studies', *JBL* 85 (1966), pp. 315-25.

—'Notes on Some Terms Relating to Prayer', *VT* 6 (1956), pp. 225-41.

Balentine, S.E. *The Hidden God: The Hiding of the Face of God in the Old Testament*. Oxford Theological Monograph. Oxford: Oxford UP, 1979.

Barr, J. *The Bible in the Modern World*. London: SCM, 1973.

—'Reading the Bible as Literature', *BJRL* 56 (1973-74), pp. 10-33.

—*The Semantics of Biblical Language*. Oxford: Oxford UP, 1961.

—'Why? in Biblical Hebrew', *JTS* 36 (1985), pp. 1-33.

Barth, C. *Die Errettung vom Tode in den individuellen Klage- und Dankliedern des Alten Testaments*. Basel: Zollikon, 1947.

—*Introduction to the Psalms*. New York: Chas. Scribner's Sons, 1966.

Becker, J. *Israel deutet seine Psalmen: Urform und Neuinterpretation in den Psalmen*. Stuttgarter Bibelstudien 18. Stuttgart: Katholisches Bibelwerk, 1966.

—*Wege der Psalmenexegese*. Stuttgarter Bibelstudien 78. Stuttgart: Katholisches Bibelwerk, 1975.

Begrich, J. 'Das Priesterliche Heilsorakel', *ZAW* 52 (1934), pp. 81-92. Also in *Gesammelte Studien zum Alten Testament*. Theologische Bücherei 21. Munich: Chr. Kaiser, 1964.

Bentzen, A. 'Der Tod des Beters in den Psalmen', *Festschrift Otto Eissfeldt*, pp. 57-60. Edited by J. Flück. Halle an der Saale: Max Niemeyer, 1947.

Berger, P.R. 'Zu den Strophen des 10. Psalms', *UF* 2 (1970), pp. 7-17.

Beyerlin, W. 'Innerbiblische Aktualisierungsversuche: Schichten im 44. Psalm', *ZTK* 73 (1976), pp. 446-60.

—'Kontinuität beim "berichtenden" Lobpreis des Einzelnen', *Wort und Geschichte (FS* K. Elliger), pp. 17-24. Edited by H. Gese and H.P. Rüger. Alter Orient und Altes Testament 18. Neukirchen-Vluyn: Neukirchener Verlag, 1973.

—*Die Rettung der Bedrängten in den Feindpsalmen der Einzelnen auf institutionelle Zusammenhänge untersucht*. Forschungen zur Religion und Literatur des Alten und Neuen Testaments 99. Göttingen: Vandenhoeck & Ruprecht, 1970.

—'Schichten im 80. Psalm', *Das Wort und die Wörter (FS* G. Friedrich), pp. 9-24. Edited by H. Balz and S. Schulz. Stuttgart: Kohlhammer, 1973.

—'Die tôdā der Heilsvergegenwärtigung in den Klageliedern der Einzelnen', *ZAW* 79 (1967), pp. 208-24.

Birkeland, H. *The Evildoers in the Book of Psalms*. Oslo: J. Dybwad, 1955.

Blackmann, A.M. 'The Psalms in the Light of Egyptian Reserach', *The Psalmists*, pp. 177-97. Edited by D.C. Simpson. London: Oxford UP, 1926.

Blank, S.H. 'Men Against God—The Promethean Element in Biblical Prayer', *JBL* 72 (1953), pp. 1-14.

Blenkinsopp, J. 'Stylistics of Old Testament Poetry', *Bib* 44 (1963), pp. 352-58.

Bonhoeffer, D. *Psalms: The Prayer Book of the Bible*. Minneapolis: Augsburg, 1970.

Botterweck, G.J., and Ringgren, H., eds. *Theological Dictionary of the Old Testament*. Vols. 1-4. Grand Rapids: Eerdmans, 1974-80.

Boys, T. *A Key to the Book of Psalms*. London: L.B. Seeley and Son, 1825.

BRIGGS, C.A., and Briggs, E.G. *A Critical and Exegetical Commentary on the Book of Psalms*. 2 vols. International Critical Commentary. Edinburgh: T. & T. Clark, 1906-1907.

Brown, F., Driver, S.R., and, Briggs, C.A. *A Hebrew and English Lexicon of the Old Testament*. Oxford: Clarendon, 1907.

Brueggemann, W. 'Formfulness of Grief', *Int* 31 (1977), pp. 263-275.

—'From Hurt to Joy, From Death to Life', *Int* 28 (1974), pp. 3-19.

—*The Message of the Psalms*. Augsburg Old Testament Studies. Minneapolis: Augsburg, 1984.

—'Psalms and the Life of Faith: A Suggested Typology of Function', *JSOT* 17 (1980), pp. 3-32.

Buss, M.J. 'Idea of *Sitz im Leben*: History and Critique', *ZAW* 90 (1978), pp. 157-70.

—'Meaning of "Cult" and the Interpretation of the Old Testament', *JBR* 32 (1964), pp. 317-25.

—'Psalms of Asaph and Korah', *JBL* 82 (1963), pp. 382-92.

—'The Study of Forms', *Old Testament Form Criticism*, pp. 1-56. Edited by J.H. Hayes. San Antonio, TX: Trinity UP, 1974.

—'Understanding Communication', *Encounter with the Text: Form and History in the Hebrew Bible*, pp. 3-44. Edited by M.J. Buss. Philadelphia: Fortress; Missoula, MT: Scholars Press, 1979.

Butler, T.C. 'Piety in the Psalms', *RevExp* 81 (1984), pp. 385-94.

BUTTENWIESER, M. *The Psalms*. Prolegomenon by N.M. Sarna. New York: Ktav, 1938, reprinted with new matter, 1969.

Buttrick, G.A., and Crim, K., eds. *Interpreter's Dictionary of the Bible*. 4 vols. with Supplementary Volume. Nashville: Abingdon, 1962-76.

Caird, G.B. *The Language and Imagery of the Bible*. London: Duckworth, 1980.

Calvin, J. *Commentary on the Book of Psalms*. 5 vols. Edinburgh: Calvin Translation Society, 1845-1849.

Carroll, R.P. *When Prophecy Failed*. London: SCM, 1979.

Childs, B.S. *Introduction to the Old Testament as Scripture*. Philadelphia: Fortress, 1979.

—*Memory and Tradition in Israel*. Studies in Biblical Theology 23. London: SCM, 1962.

—'Psalm Titles and Midrashic Exegesis', *JSS* 16 (1971), pp. 137-50.

—'Reflections on the Modern Study of the Psalms', *Magnalia Dei: The Mighty Acts of God (FS* G.E. Wright), pp. 377-88. Edited by F.M. Cross, et al. Garden City, NY: Doubleday, 1976.

—'The Sensus Literalis of Scripture: An Ancient and Modern Problem', *Beiträge zur alttestamentlichen Theologie (FS* W. Zimmerli), pp. 80-93. Edited by H. Donner, et al. Göttingen: Vandenhoeck & Ruprecht, 1977.

Clements, R. *A Century of Old Testament Study*. London: Lutterworth, 1976.

—*God and Temple*. Oxford: Blackwell, 1965.

—*Old Testament Theology: A Fresh Approach*. Marshalls Theological Library. London: Marshall, Morgan & Scott, 1978.

Clifford, R.J. 'Psalm 89: A Lament Over the Davidic Ruler's Continued Failure', *HTR* 73 (1980), pp. 35-47.

—'Rhetorical Criticism in the Exegesis of Hebrew Poetry', *SBL 1980 Seminar Papers*, pp. 17-28. Edited by P.J. Achtemeier. Chico, CA: Scholars Press, 1980.

Clines, D.J.A. 'The Psalms and the King', *Themelios* 71 (1975), pp. 1-6.

—'Psalms Research Since 1955: I. The Psalms and the Cult', *TB* 18 (1967), pp. 103-26.

—'Psalms Research Since 1955: II. The Literary Genres', *TB* 20 (1969), pp. 105-25.

—'Story and Poem: The Old Testament as Literature and as Scripture', *Int* 34 (1980), pp. 115-27.

—*The Theme of the Pentateuch*. JSOTSup 10. Sheffield: JSOT, 1978.

Cogan, M. 'A Technical Term for Exposure', *JNES* 27 (1968), pp. 133-35.

CRAIGIE, P.C. *Psalms 1-50*. Word Biblical Commentary 19. Waco, TX: Word Books, 1983.

Crenshaw, J.L. 'The Human Dilemma and Literature of Dissent', *Tradition and Theology in the Old Testament*, pp. 235-58. Edited by D.A. Knight. London: SPCK, 1977.

Crüsemann, F. *Studien zur Formgeschichte von Hymnus und Danklied in Israel*. Wissenschaftliche Monographien zum Alten und Neuen Testament 32. Neukirchen-Vluyn: Neukircher Verlag, 1969.

Culley, R.C. 'An Approach to the Problem of Oral Tradition', *VT* 13 (1963), pp. 113-25.

—*Oral Formulaic Language in the Biblical Psalms*. Toronto: University of Toronto, 1967.

—'Oral Tradition and the Old Testament: Some Recent Discussion', *Semeia* 5 (1976), pp. 1-33.

Curtis, A.H.W. 'Subjugation of the Waters Motif in the Psalms: Imagery or Polemic?', *JSS* 23 (1978), pp. 245-56.

DAHOOD, M. *Psalms I-III*. 3 vols. Anchor Bible. Garden City, NY: Doubleday, 1966-70.

Davidson, R. *The Courage to Doubt: Exploring an Old Testament Theme*. London: SCM, 1983.

—'Some Aspects of the Theological Significance of Doubt in the Old Testament', *ASTI* 7 (1968-69), pp. 41-52.

Davidson, R., and Leaney, A.R.C. *Biblical Criticism*. The Pelican Guide to Modern Theology 3. Harmondsworth: Penguin, 1970.

Davies, G.H. 'The Ark in the Psalms', *Promise and Fulfillment: Essays Presented to Professor S.H. Hooke*, pp. 51-61. Edited by F.F. Bruce. Edinburgh: T. & T. Clark, 1963.

De Catanzaro, C.J. 'Fear, Knowledge, and Love: a Study in Old Testament Piety', *CJT* 9 (1963), pp. 166-73.

Deissler, A. '"Mein Gott, warum hast du mich verlassen ...!" (Ps 22:2) Das Reden zu Gott und von Gott in den Psalmen am Beispiel von Psalm 22', *'Ich will euer Gott werden'*, pp. 97-121. Stuttgarter Bibelstudien 100. Edited by H. Merklein and E. Zenger. Stuttgart: Katholisches Bibelwerk, 1981.

Delitzsch, F. *Biblical Commentary on the Psalms*. 3 vols. London: Hodder & Stoughton, 1889-1902.

De Pinto, B. 'The Torah and the Psalms', *JBL* 86 (1967), pp. 154-74.

Donner, H. 'Argumente zur Datierung des 74. Psalms', *Wort, Lied und Gottesspruch (FS* J. Ziegler), II, pp. 41-50. 2 vols. Edited by J. Schreiner. Wurzburg: Echter, 1972.

Doty, W.G. 'The Concept of Genre in Literary Analysis', *SBL Seminar Papers 1972*, II, pp. 413-48. Edited by S.C. McGaughy. n.p., 1972.

Drijvers, P. *The Psalms: Their Structure and Meaning*. New York: Herder & Herder, 1964.

Driver, G.R. 'Notes on the Psalms. I. 1-72', *JTS* 43 (1942), pp. 149-60.

—'Notes on the Psalms. II. 73-150', *JTS* 44 (1943), pp. 12-23.

—'Problems in the Hebrew Text of Proverbs', *Bib* 32 (1951), pp. 173-97.

—'The Psalms in the Light of Babylonian Research', *The Psalmists*, pp. 109-75. Edited by D.C. Simpson. London: Oxford UP, 1926.

—'Textual and Linguistic Problems of the Book of Psalms', *HTR* 29 (1936), pp. 171-95.

Driver, S.R. *Deuteronomy*. 3rd ed. International Critical Commentary. Edinburgh: T. & T. Clark, 1902.

—*A Treatise on the Use of the Tenses in Hebrew*. 3rd ed. Oxford: Clarendon, 1892.

DUHM, B. *Die Psalmen*. Kurzer Hand-commentar zum Alten Testament 14. Freiburg: J.C.B. Mohr, 1899.

Eaton, J.H. *Kingship and the Psalms*. Studies in Biblical Theology 2/32. London: SCM, 1976.

EATON, J.H. *Psalms*. Torch Bible Paperbacks. London: SCM, 1967.

—'The Psalms and Israelite Worship', *Tradition and Interpretation*, pp. 238-73. Edited by G.W. Anderson. Oxford: Clarendon, 1979.

Eichrodt, W. *Theology of the Old Testament*. 2 vols. The Old Testament Library. London: SCM, 1961-67.

Eissfeldt, O. '"My God" in the Old Testament', *EvQ* 19 (1947), pp. 7-20.

—'Psalm 80', *Kleine Schriften*, III, pp. 221-32. Edited by R. Sellheim and F. Maass. Tübingen: J.C.B. Mohr, 1966.

—'Psalm 80 und Psalm 89', *Kleine Schriften*, IV, pp. 132-36. Edited by R. Sellheim and F. Maass. Tübingen: J.C.B. Mohr, 1968.

Emerton, J.A. 'Notes on Three Passages in Psalms Book III', *JTS* 14 (1963), pp. 374-81.

—'Notes on Jeremiah 12.9', *ZAW* 81 (1969), pp. 182-88.

—'"Spring and Torrent" in Psalm LXXIV 15', *Volume du Congres: Geneve 1965*, pp. 122-33. VTSup 15. Leiden: Brill, 1966.

Engnell, I. *Critical Essays on the Old Testament*. London: SPCK, 1969.

Feininger, B. 'A Decade of German Psalm-Criticism', *JSOT* 20 (1981), pp. 91-103.

Fohrer, G. *Introduction to the Old Testament*. Nashville: Abingdon, 1968.

Franken, H.J. *The Mystical Communion with JHWH in the Book of Psalms*. Leiden: Brill, 1954.

Frost, S. 'Asseveration by Thanksgiving', *VT* 8 (1958), pp. 380-90.

Frye, R.M. 'A Literary Perspective for the Criticism of the Gospels', *Jesus and Man's Hope II*, pp. 193-221. Edited by D.G. Miller and D.Y. Hadidian. Pittsburgh: Pittsburgh Theological Seminary, 1971.

Gardner, H. *The Business of Criticism*. Oxford: Clarendon, 1959.

Gelin, A. *The Psalms are Our Prayers*. Collegeville, MN: Liturgical Press, 1964.

Gerstenberger, E. *Der bittende Mensch: Bittritual und Klagelied des Einzelnen im Alten Testament*. Wissenschaftliche Monographien zum Alten und Neuen Testament 51. Neukirchen-Vluyn: Neukirchener Verlag, 1980.

—'Enemies and Evildoers in the Psalms: A Challenge to Christian Preaching', *HBT* 4/5 (1982-83), pp. 61-77.

—'Der klagende Mensch', *Probleme biblischer Theologie (FS G. von Rad)*, pp. 64-72. Edited by H.W. Wolff. Munich: Chr. Kaiser, 1971.

—'Literatur zu den Psalmen', *Verkündigung und Forschung* 17 (1972), pp. 82-99.

—'Psalms', *Old Testament Form Criticism*, pp. 179-223. Edited by J.H. Hayes. San Antonio, TX: Trinity UP, 1974.

—*Psalms: Part I*. Forms of Old Testament Literature 14. Grand Rapids: Eerdmans, 1988.

—'Zur Interpretation der Psalmen', *Verkündigung und Forschung* 19 (1974), pp. 22-45.

Gerstenberger, E.S., and Schrage, W. *Suffering*. Nashville: Abingdon, 1980.

Gese, H. *Essays on Biblical Theology*. Minneapolis: Augsburg, 1981.

—'Psalm 22 und das Neue Testament', *ZTK* 65 (1968), pp. 1-22.

Goldingay, J. 'Repetition and Variation in the Psalms', *JQR* 68 (1978), pp. 146-51.

—*Songs from a Strange Land*. The Bible Speaks Today. Leicester: Inter-Varsity, 1978.

Gordis, R. 'Psalm 9-10—A Textual-exegetical Study', *The Word and the Book*, pp. 114-32. New York: Ktav, 1976. Also in *JQR* 48 (1957), pp. 104-22.

—'A Rhetorical Use of Interrogative Sentences in Biblical Hebrew', *The Word and the Book*, pp. 152-57. New York: Ktav, 1976.

Gordon, A.R. *The Poets of the Old Testament*. London: Hodder & Stoughton, 1912.

Goulder, M.D. *The Psalms of the Sons of Korah*. JSOTSup 20. Sheffield: JSOT, 1982.

Graham, P. 'Psalm 77: A Study in Faith and History', *ResQ* 18 (1975), pp. 151-58.

Gray, J. *The Biblical Doctrine of the Reign of God*. Edinburgh: T. & T. Clark, 1979.

Greenwood, D. 'Rhetorical Criticism and Formgeschichte: Some Methodological Considerations', *JBL* 89 (1970), pp. 418-26.

Gunkel, H. *Einleitung in die Psalmen*. Completed by J. Begrich. Göttingen: Vandenhoeck & Ruprecht, 1933.

GUNKEL, H. *Die Psalmen*. Handkommentar zum Alten Testament. Göttingen: Vandenhoeck & Ruprecht, 1926.

—*The Psalms: A Form-Critical Introduction*. Introduction by J. Muilenburg. Facet Books, Biblical Series 19. Philadelphia: Fortress, 1967.

—'The Religion of the Psalms', *What Remains of the Old Testament. And Other Essays*, pp. 69-114. London: George Allen & Unwin, 1928.

Gunn, G.S. *God in the Psalms*. Edinburgh: St. Andrew Press, 1956.

Guthrie, H.H. *Israel's Sacred Songs: A Study of Dominant Themes*. New York: Seabury, 1966.

Haag, E. 'Die Sehnsucht nach dem lebendigen Gott im Zeugnis des Psalms 42/43', *Geist und Leben* 49 (1976), pp. 167-77.

Habel, N.C. *Yahweh versus Baal*. New York: Bookman, 1964.

Hallo, W.W. 'Individual Prayer in Sumerian. The Continuity of a Tradition', *Essays in Memory of E.A. Speiser*, pp. 71-89. New Haven: American Oriental Society, 1968.

Hanson, A.T. *The Wrath of the Lamb*. London: SPCK, 1957.

Haran, M. 'Divine Presence in the Israelite Cult and the Cultic Institutions', *Bib* 50 (1969), pp. 251-67.

Harrelson, W. 'A Meditation on the Wrath of God: Psalm 90', *Scripture and Theology* (*FS* J.C. Rylaarsdam), pp. 181-91. Edited by A.L. Merrill and T. W. Overholt. Pittsburgh Theological Monograph Series 17. Pittsburgh: Pickwick, 1977.

Harris, R.L., Archer, G.L., and Waltke, B.K., eds. *Theological Wordbook of the Old Testament*. 2 vols. Chicago: Moody, 1980.

Hayes, J.H. *An Introduction to Old Testament Study*. Nashville: Abingdon, 1979.

Heinemann, H. 'The Date of Psalm 80', *JQR* 40 (1949-50), pp. 297-302.

Heinen, K. "'Jahwe, heile mich!" Klage und Bitte eines Kranken: Psalm 6',
    Erbe und Auftrag 48 (1972), pp. 461-66.
Henshaw, T. The Writings: The Third Division of the Old Testament Canon.
    London: Allen & Unwin, 1963.
Hermisson, H.-J., and Lohse, E. Faith. Nashville: Abingdon, 1981.
Hill, D. 'Son of Man in Psalm 80:17', NovT 15 (1973), pp. 261-69.
Hohenstein, H.E. 'Oh Blessed Rage', CurTM 10 (1983), pp. 162-68.
Holladay, W.L. A Concise Hebrew and Aramaic Lexicon of the Old Testament.
    Grand Rapids: Eerdmans, 1971.
—The Root šubh in the Old Testament. Leiden: Brill, 1958.
James, F. Thirty Psalmists. New York: G.P. Putnam's Sons, 1938.
Jänicke, H. 'Futurum exactum. Eine Bibelarbeit über Psalm 13', EvT 11
    (1951-52), pp. 471-78.
Jefferson, H.G. 'Psalm LXXVII', VT 13 (1963), pp. 87-91.
Jenni, E., and Westermann, C., eds. Theologisches Handwörterbuch zum Alten
    Testament. 2 vols. Munich: Chr. Kaiser, 1971-76.
Jepsen, A. 'Warum? Eine lexikalische und theologische Studie', Das ferne und
    nahe Wort (FS L. Rost), pp. 106-13. Edited by F. Maass. Beihefte zur
    Zeitschrift für die Alttestamentliche Wissenschaft 105. Berlin:
    Töpelmann, 1967.
Johnson, A.R. The Cultic Prophet and Israel's Psalmody. Cardiff: University
    of Wales, 1979.
—'The Psalms', The Old Testament and Modern Study, pp. 162-209. Edited by
    H.H. Rowley. Oxford: Clarendon, 1951.
—The Vitality of the Individual in the Thought of Ancient Israel. Cardiff:
    Wales, 1949.
Jones, E. 'Suffering in the Psalter', Congregational Quarterly 34 (1956), pp.
    53-63.
Kapelrud, A.S. 'The Role of the Cult in Old Israel', The Bible in Modern
    Scholarship, pp. 44-56. Edited by J.P. Hyatt. Nashville: Abingdon, 1965.
—'Scandanavian Research in the Psalms After Mowinckel', ASTI 4 (1965),
    pp. 74-90.
—'Tradition and Worship: The Role of the Cult in Tradition Formation and
    Transmission', Tradition and Theology in the Old Testament, pp. 101-24.
    Edited by D.A. Knight. London: SPCK, 1977.
Kautzsch, E., ed. Gesenius' Hebrew Grammar. 2nd ed. Oxford: Clarendon,
    1910.
Keel, O. Feinde und Gottesleugner: Studium zum Image der Widersacher in den
    Individualpsalmen. Stuttgarter Biblische Monographien 7. Stuttgart:
    Katholisches Bibelwerk, 1969.
—The Symbolism of the Biblical World. London: SPCK, 1978.
Kellermann, U. 'Erwägungen zum historischen Ort von Psalm 60', VT 28
    (1978), pp. 56-65.
Kelley, P.H. 'Prayers of Troubled Saints', RevExp 81 (1984), pp. 377-83.

Kessler, M. 'An Introduction to Rhetorical Criticism of the Bible: Prolegomena', *Semitics* 7 (1980), pp. 1-27.

—'A Methodological Setting for Rhetorical Criticism', *Semitics* 4 (1974), pp. 22-36.

—'New Directions in Biblical Exegesis', *SJT* 24 (1971), pp. 317-25.

KIDNER, D. *Psalms 1-72, 73-150*. 2 vols. Tyndale Old Testament Commentaries. Leicester: Inter-Varsity, 1973-75.

Kikawada, I.M. 'Some Proposals for the Definition of Rhetorical Criticism', *Semitics* 5 (1977), pp. 67-91.

Kilian, R. 'Psalm 22 und das priesterliche Heilsorakel', *BZ* 12 (1968), pp. 172-85.

KIRKPATRICK, A.F. *The Book of Psalms*. The Cambridge Bible for Schools and Colleges. Cambridge: Cambridge UP, 1902.

Kittel, G., and Friedrich, G., eds. *Theological Dictionary of the New Testament*. 10 vols. Grand Rapids, Eerdmans, 1964-76.

Knierim, R. 'Old Testament Form Criticism Reconsidered', *Int* 27 (1973), pp. 435-68.

Knight, D.A. *Rediscovering the Traditions of Israel*. SBL Dissertations 9. Missoula, MT: Scholars Press, 1973.

—'The Understanding of "Sitz im Leben" in Form Criticism', *SBL 1974 Seminar Papers*, I, pp. 105-25. Edited by G. MacRae. n.p., 1974.

Koch, K. *The Growth of the Biblical Tradition: The Form Critical Method*. London: Adam & Charles Black, 1969.

KRAUS, H.-J. *Psalmen*. 2 vols. 5th ed. Biblischer Kommentar Altes Testament XV/1-2. Neukirchen-Vluyn: Neukirchener Verlag, 1978.

—*Theologie der Psalmen*. Biblischer Kommentar Altes Testament XV/3. Neukirchen-Vluyn: Neukirchener Verlag, 1979.

—*Worship in Israel: A Cultic History of the Old Testament*. Oxford: Blackwell, 1966.

Kselman, J.S. '"Why have you abandoned me?" A Rhetorical Study of Psalm 22', *Art and Meaning: Rhetoric in Biblical Literature*, pp. 172-98. JSOTSup 19. Edited by D.J.A. Clines, et al. Sheffield: JSOT, 1982.

Kunz, L. 'Psalm 85 als westorientalischer Nomos', *TGl* 67 (1977), pp. 373-80.

Labuschagne, C.J. *The Incomparability of Yahweh in the Old Testament*. Pretoria Oriental Series 5. Leiden: Brill, 1966.

Lauha, A. '"Dominus benefecit". Die Wortwurzel GML und die Psalmenfrömmigkeit', *ASTI* 11 (1977-78), pp. 57-62.

Lentzen-Deis, F. 'Methodische Überlegungen zur Bestimmung literarischer Gattungen im Neuen Testament', *Bib* 62 (1981), pp. 1-20.

LESLIE, E.A. *The Psalms*. Nashville: Abingdon-Cokesbury, 1949.

Lewis, C.S. *Reflections on the Psalms*. London: Geoffrey Bles, 1958.

Lohfink, N. *Great Themes from the Old Testament*. Edinburgh: T. & T. Clark, 1982.

Long, B.O. 'Recent Field Studies in Oral Literature and the Question of Sitz im Leben', *Semeia* 5 (1976), pp. 35-49.

—'Recent Field Studies in Oral Literature and Their Bearing on Old Testament Criticism', *VT* 26 (1976), pp. 187-98.

May, H.G. 'Some Cosmic Connotations of *Mayim Rabbim*, "Many Waters"', *JBL* 74 (1955), pp. 9-21.

Mays, J.L. 'Psalm 13', *Int* 34 (1980), pp. 279-83.

Miller, P.D., Jr. *Interpreting the Psalms*. Philadelphia: Fortress, 1986.

—'Trouble and Woe: Interpreting the Biblical Laments', *Int* 37 (1983), pp. 32-45.

Miskotte, K.H. *When the Gods are Silent*. London: Collins, 1967.

Montefiore, C.G. 'Mystic Passages in the Psalms', *JQR* (1889), pp. 143-61.

Moulton, R.G. *The Literary Study of the Bible*. London: Isbister, 1896.

Mowinckel, S. 'Notes on the Psalms', *ST* 13 (1959), pp. 134-65.

—'Psalm Criticism Between 1900 and 1935', *VT* 5 (1955), pp. 13-33.

—*Psalmenstudien I-VI*. 2 vols. Amsterdam: P. Schippers, 1921-24.

—*The Psalms in Israel's Worship*. 2 vols. Oxford: Blackwell, 1962.

Muilenburg, J. 'Form Criticism and Beyond', *JBL* 88 (1969), pp. 1-18.

—'The Gains of Form Criticism in Old Testament Studies', *ExpTim* 71 (1959-60), pp. 229-33.

—'A Study in Hebrew Rhetoric: Repetition and Style', *Congress Volume: Copenhagen 1953*, pp. 97-111. VTSup 1. Leiden: Brill, 1953.

Murphy, R.E. 'The Faith of the Psalmist', *Int* 34 (1980), pp. 229-39.

—'A New Classification of Literary Forms in the Psalms', *CBQ* 21 (1959), pp. 83-87.

—*The Psalms, Job*. Proclamation Commentaries. Philadelphia: Fortress, 1977.

Nötscher, F. *'Das Angesicht Gottes schauen'*, Würzburg: C.J. Becker, 1924.

Nowottny, W. *The Language Poets Use*. London: Athlone, 1965.

Oesterley, W.O.E. *A Fresh Approach to the Psalms*. New York: Charles Scribner's Sons, 1937.

Osswald, E. 'Glaubenszuversicht und Glaubensanfechtung im Alten Testament unter besonderer Berücksichtigung der Psalmen', *TLZ* 104 (1979), pp. 705-12.

Oswalt, J.N. 'The Myth of the Dragon and Old Testament Faith', *EvQ* 49 (1977), pp. 163-72.

Otzen, B., Gottlieb, H., and Jeppesen, K. *Myths in the Old Testament*. London: SCM, 1980.

Pedersen, J. *Israel: Its Life and Culture, I-II, III-IV*. 2 vols. London: Geoffrey Cumberlege, 1926-59.

Perlitt, L. 'Anklage und Freispruch Gottes', *ZTK* 69 (1972), pp. 290-303.

—'Die Verborgenheit Gottes', *Probleme biblischer Theologie (FS* G. von Rad), pp. 367-82. Edited by H.W. Wolff. Munich: Chr. Kaiser, 1971.

Ploeg, J.P.M. van der. 'Psalm 74 and Its Structure', *Travels in the World of the Old Testament (FS* M.A. Beek), pp. 204-10. Edited by M.S.H.G. Heerma van Voss, et al. Assen: Van Gorcum, 1974.

Preuss, H.D. 'Psalm 88 als Beispiel alttestamentlichen Redens vom Tod', *Der Tod—ungelöstes Rätsel oder überwunderer Feind?*, pp. 63-79. A. Strobel. Stuttgart: Calwer, 1974.

Pritchard, J.B., ed. *Ancient Near Eastern Texts Relating to the Old Testament and Supplement*. Princeton: Princeton UP, 1950-68.

Rad, G. von. *Old Testament Theology*. 2 vols. London: SCM, 1962-65.

—*God at Work in Israel*. Nashville: Abingdon, 1980.

—'"Righteousness" and "Life" in the Cultic Language of the Psalms', *The Problem of the Hexateuch and Other Essays*, pp. 243-66. Edinburgh: Oliver & Boyd, 1965.

—'Some Aspects of the Old Testament World-view', *The Problem of the Hexateuch and Other Essays*, pp. 144-65. Edinburgh: Oliver & Boyd, 1965.

Rast, W.E. 'Disappointed Expectation in the Old Testament', *Perspective* 12 (1971), pp. 135-52.

Reindl, J. *Das Angesicht Gottes im Sprachgebrauch des Alten Testaments*. Erfurter Theologische Studien 25. Leipzig: St. Benno, 1970.

Reumann, J.H. 'Psalm 22 at the Cross', *Int* 28 (1974), pp. 39-58.

Richards, I.A. *Principles of Literary Criticism*. London: Routledge and Kegan Paul, 1926.

Richter, W. *Exegese als Literaturwissenschaft: Entwurf einer alttestamentlichen Literatur Theorie und Methodologie*. Göttingen: Vandenhoeck & Ruprecht, 1971.

Ridderbos, N.H. *Die Psalmen: Stilistische Verfahren und Aufbau mit besonderer Berücksichtigung von Ps 1-41*. Beiheft zur Zeitschrift für die alttestamentliche Wissenschaft 117. Berlin/New York: de Gruyter, 1972.

Ringgren, H. *The Faith of the Psalmists*. Philadelphia: Fortress, 1963.

Roberts, J.J.M. 'Of Signs, Prophets, and Time Limits: A Note on Psalm 74:9', *CBQ* 39 (1977), pp. 474-81.

Robertson, D. *The Old Testament and the Literary Critic*. Guides to Biblical Scholarship. Philadelphia: Fortress, 1977.

Robinson, H.W. 'The Inner Life of the Psalmists', *The Psalmists*, pp. 45-65. Edited by D.C. Simpson. Oxford: Oxford UP, 1926.

—'The Social Life of the Psalmists', *The Psalmists*, pp. 67-86. Edited by D.C. Simpson. Oxford: Oxford UP, 1926.

Robinson, T.H. 'The God of the Psalmists', *The Psalmists*, pp. 23-44. Edited by D.C. Simpson. Oxford: Oxford UP, 1926.

Rogerson, J.W. *Anthropology and the Old Testament*. Growing Points in Theology. Oxford: Blackwell, 1978.

ROGERSON, J.W., and MCKAY, J.W. *Psalms 1-50, 51-100, 101-50*. 3 vols. The Cambridge Bible Commentary. Cambridge: Cambridge UP, 1977.

Ross, J.F. 'Job 33:14-30: The Phenomenology of Lament', *JBL* 94 (1975), pp. 38-46.

Rowley, H.H. 'The Structure of Psalm XLII-XLIII', *Bib* 21 (1940), pp. 45-50.

—*Worship in Ancient Israel*. London: SPCK, 1967.

Ryken, L. *The Literature of the Bible*. Grand Rapids: Zondervan, 1974.

Sabourin, L. *The Psalms: Their Origin and Meaning*. New York: Alba House, 1974.

Sanders, J.A. *Suffering as Divine Discipline in the Old Testament and Post-Biblical Judaism*. Colgate Rochester Divinity School Bulletin, Special Issue 28. Rochester: Colgate Rochester Divinity School, 1955.

Sarna, N.H. 'Psalm 89: A Study in Inner Biblical Exegesis', *Biblical and Other Studies*, pp. 29-46. Edited by A. Altmann. Cambridge, MA: Harvard UP, 1963.

Sawyer, J.F.A. *Semantics in Biblical Research*. Studies in Biblical Theology 2/24. London: SCM, 1972.

Schreiner, S. 'Erwägungen zur Struktur des 90. Psalms', *Bib* 59 (1978), pp. 80-90.

Seybold, K. *Das Gebet des Kranken im Alten Testament*. Beiträge zur Wissenschaft vom Alten und Neuen Testament 99. Stuttgart: Kohlhammer, 1973.

Skehan, P.W. 'A Broken Acrostic and Psalm 9', *CBQ* 27 (1965), pp. 1-5.

Soggin, J.A. 'Notes for Christian Exegesis of the First Part of Psalm 22', *Old Testament and Oriental Studies*, pp. 152-65. Biblica et Orientalia 19. Rome: Biblical Institute, 1975.

—'Philological and Exegetical Notes on Psalm 6', *Old Testament and Oriental Studies*, pp. 133-42. Biblica et Orientalia 19. Rome: Biblical Institute, 1975.

Springer, S. *Neuinterpretation im Alten Testament*. Stuttgarter Biblische Beiträge. Stuttgart: Katholisches Bibelwerk, 1979.

Stamm, J.J. *Erlösen und Vergeben im Alten Testament*. Bern: A. Franke, 1940.

—'Ein Vierteljahrhundert Psalmenforschung', *TRu* 23 (1955), pp. 1-68.

Stek, J.H. 'The Stylistics of Hebrew Poetry', *CTJ* 9 (1974), pp. 115-30.

Taylor, I. *The Spirit of Hebrew Poetry*. London: Bell & Daldy, 1861.

Terrien, S.L. 'Creation, Cultus, and Faith in the Psalter', *Theological Education* 2 (1966), pp. 116-28.

—*The Elusive Presence: Toward a New Biblical Theology*. Religious Perspectives 26. New York: Harper & Row, 1978.

—*The Psalms and Their Meaning for Today*. Indianapolis, IN: Bobbs-Merrill, 1952.

Thomas, D.W. 'Some Further Remarks on Unusual Ways of Expressing the Superlative in Hebrew', *VT* 18 (1968), pp. 120-24.

—*The Text of the Revised Psalter*. London: SPCK, 1963.

—'צַלְמָוֶת in the Old Testament', *JSS* 7 (1962), pp. 191-200.

—'The Use of נצח as a Superlative in Hebrew', *JSS* 1 (1956), pp. 106-109.

—'Psalm 35:15 f.', *JTS* 12 (1961), pp. 50-51.

Tucker, G.M. *Form Criticism of the Old Testament*. Guides to Biblical Scholarship. Philadelphia: Fortress, 1971.

Tur-Sinai, N.H. 'The Literary Character of the Book of Psalms', *OTS* 8 (1950), pp. 263-81.

Ullmann, S. *Semantics: An Introduction to the Science of Meaning*. Oxford: Blackwell, 1962.

Urbrock, W.J. 'Mortal and Miserable Man: A Form-Critical Investigation of Psalm 90', *SBL Seminar Papers 1974*, I, pp. 1-33. Edited by MacRae. n.p., 1974.

Vaux, R. de. *Ancient Israel*. London: Darton, Longman & Todd, 1961.

Vawter, B. 'Postexilic Prayer and Hope', *CBQ* 37 (1975), pp. 460-70.

Vorländer, H. *Mein Gott: Die Vorstellungen vom persönlichen Gott im Alten Orient und im Alten Testament*. Alter Orient und Altes Testament 23. Neukirchen-Vluyn: Neukirchener Verlag, 1975.

Vosberg, L. *Studien zum Reden vom Schöpfer in den Psalmen*. Beiträge zur evangelischen Theologie 69. Munich: Chr. Kaiser, 1975.

Waldow, H.E. von. 'Some Thoughts on Old Testament Form Criticism', *SBL Seminar Papers 1971*, II, pp. 587-600. 2 vols. n.p., 1971.

Ward, J.M. 'The Literary Form and Liturgical Background of Psalm LXXXIX', *VT* 11 (1961), pp. 321-39.

Watson, W.G.E. 'Chiastic Patterns in Biblical Hebrew Poetry', *Chiasmus in Antiquity*, pp. 118-68. Edited by J.W. Welch. Hildesheim: Gerstenberg, 1981.

Weiser, A. 'Psalm 77: Ein Beitrag zur Frage nach dem Verhältnis von Kult und Heilsgeschichte', *TLZ* 72 (1947), pp. 133-40.

WEISER, A. *The Psalms*. Old Testament Library. London: SCM, 1962.

Weiss, M. 'Die Methode der "Total-Interpretation"', *Uppsala Congress Volume 1971*, pp. 88-112. VTSup 22. Leiden: Brill, 1972.

—'Wege der neuen Dichtungswissenschaft in Ihrer Anwendung auf die Psalmenforschung', *Bib* 42 (1961), pp. 255-302.

Welch, A.C. *The Psalter in Life, Worship, and History*. Oxford: Clarendon, 1926.

Wellek, R., and Warren, A. *Theory of Literature*. Harmondsworth: Penguin, 1956.

Westermann, C. 'Anthropologische und theologische Aspekte des Gebets in den Psalmen', *Zur neueren Psalmenforschung*, pp. 452-68. Wege der Forschung 192. Edited by P.H.A. Neumann. Darmstadt: Wissenschaftliche Buchgesellschaft, 1976.

—*Elements of Old Testament Theology*. Atlanta: John Knox, 1982.

—*Gewendete Klage: Eine Auslegung des 22. Psalms*. Bibelstudien 8. Neukirchen-Vluyn: Neukirchener Verlag, 1955.

—*Isaiah 40-66*. Old Testament Library. London: SCM, 1969.

—*Praise and Lament in the Psalms*. Edinburgh: T. & T. Clark, 1965, 1981.

—'Der 90. Psalm', *Forschung am Alten Testament*, pp. 344-50. Theologische Bücherei 24. Munich: Chr. Kaiser, 1964.

—*The Psalms: Structure, Content and Message*. Minneapolis: Augsburg, 1980 (German original, 1967).

—'The Role of Lament in the Theology of the Old Testament', *Int* 28 (1974), pp. 20-39.

Wevers, J.W. 'Study in the Form Criticism of Individual Complaint Psalms', *VT* 6 (1956), pp. 80-96.

Widengren, G. *The Accadian and Hebrew Psalms of Lamentation as Religious Documents*. Stockholm: Bokförlags Aktiebolaget Thule, 1937.

Willesen, F. 'The Cultic Situation of Psalm LXXIV', *VT* 2 (1952), pp. 289-306.

Williams, R.J. *Hebrew Syntax: An Outline*. 2nd ed. Toronto: University of Toronto, 1976.

Wimsatt, W.K. *The Verbal Icon: Studies in the Meaning of Poetry*. London: Methuen, 1954.

Wolverton, W.I. 'Psalmists' Belief in God's Presence', *CJT* 9 (1963), pp. 82-94.

Yaron, R. 'The Meaning of ZANAḤ', *VT* 13 (1963), pp. 237-39.

Zimmerli, W. *Old Testament Theology in Outline*. Edinburgh: T. & T. Clark, 1978.